Philosophy
A Beginner's Guide

Philosophy
A Beginner's Guide

Third Edition

Jenny Teichman
&
Katherine C. Evans

BLACKWELL
Publishers

First published 1991
Reprinted 1991, 1992, 1994

Second edition published 1995
Reprinted 1996 (three times), 1997 (twice), 1998

Third edition published 1999

2 4 6 8 10 9 7 5 3 1

Blackwell Publishers Ltd
108 Cowley Road
Oxford OX4 1JF
UK

Blackwell Publishers Inc.
350 Main Street
Malden, Massachusetts 02148
USA

British Library Cataloguing in Publication Data

A CIP catalogue record for this book is available from the British Library.

Library of Congress Cataloging-in-Publication Data

Teichman, Jenny.
Philosophy: a beginner's guide / Jenny Teichman & Katherine C.
Evans. — 3rd ed.
p.   cm.
Includes bibliographical references (p.   ) and index.
ISBN 0-631-21320-1 (hc. : alk. paper). — ISBN 0-631-21321-X (pbk.
: alk. paper)
1. Philosophy—Introductions.   I. Evans, Katherine C.   II. Title.
BD21.T35   1999
100—dc21   99-19756
CIP

Typeset in 11 on 13 pt Bembo
by Best-set Typesetter Ltd, Hong Kong
Printed in Great Britain by T.J. International, Padstow, Cornwall

This book is printed on acid-free paper.

Contents

Contents

Preface to the Second Edition

This book was written both for the general reader and for university and college freshers. It is the brain-child of Katherine Evans, a Cambridge graduate, who saw a need for a work which would introduce readers to most or many of the topics in philosophy studied in mainstream colleges and universities; which would present those topics succinctly in self-contained sections and chapters; and which would be free of technical jargon.

Few if any of the existing introductions satisfied all these conditions. Traditional introductory texts tend to concentrate on two or three areas, usually metaphysics and ethics, and not all such books manage to avoid jargon. The *Beginner's Guide* begins with sections devoted to metaphysics and ethics but contains in addition material on the philosophy of science, political theory, feminism, logic and the meaning of life. Some of the topics have been adapted from Cambridge syllabuses but treated in such a way as to make the ideas accessible to people who have had no previous contact whatever with philosophy. The history of philosophy is not discussed as such but the problems, and their proposed solutions, are for the most part directly or indirectly located in an historical context. Moreover, the appendices describing great or famous philosophers do give an overview of the history of the subject.

The text for the second edition has been corrected and brought up to date, and two extra chapters have been added, making twenty-five in all. One new chapter, 'Life and Death', deals with issues in practical ethics, and the other, 'Marx and Marxism', gives a readable account of Marx's political theory.

Because of its comparatively wide range, and its freedom from jargon, the book will be useful not only for philosophy students but also for people interested in politics, social theory, science and theology.

Preface to the Third Edition

The first and second editions of *Philosophy: A Beginner's Guide* have already been translated into Spanish, Polish and Russian, and a translation into the language of Georgia (formerly a Republic incorporated in the USSR) is proposed for 1999.

This third edition of the original English language version corrects minor errors, brings examples and bibliography up to date, and includes a new chapter entitled 'Scepticism Old and New'.

Jenny Teichman
Katherine C. Evans

Introduction
What is Philosophy?

Philosophy is a study of problems which are ultimate, abstract and very general. These problems are concerned with the nature of existence, knowledge, morality, reason and human purpose.

The Branches of Philosophy

Academic philosophy divides the subject as a whole into different branches. The major traditional branches are metaphysics, ethics, political philosophy, philosophy of science and logic, and in this book we will discuss all these. Here to begin with are some preliminary explanations.

Metaphysics – the study of being and knowing

The word 'metaphysics' is the name that an early editor, Andronicus★, gave to some treatises written by Aristotle★. Aristotle himself had called these treatises 'first philosophy'. By 'first' he meant fundamental, or basic, or most important. The topics of this 'first philosophy' are the nature of being, the nature of causation (or coming to be) and the nature of knowledge.

The title *Metaphysics* was attached to 'first philosophy' more or less by accident. When Andronicus edited Aristotle's works he put the treatises on 'first philosophy' and a treatise called *physics* together

1

into the same book, placing the *Physics* at the beginning. Now, the Greek word *meta* means 'after', and Andronicus called the second part of the book *Metaphysics*, meaning 'the bit which comes after the *Physics*'.

'First philosophy', or metaphysics, can be defined as made up of *ontology*, which is the study of the nature of existence and of coming to be, together with *epistemology*, which is the theory of knowledge. But it also asks questions about the mind and the soul and God and time and space and free will. This is because an enquiry into the general nature of being and knowing inevitably leads on to many other related questions. For instance, asking 'What is existence?' leads to asking 'What is substance? What is matter? What is space? What can be said about non-existence?' Asking 'What is a cause?' leads to asking 'Did the world have a beginning in time? Did it have a cause? What is time? Is there a God?' Asking 'What is knowledge?' leads to questions like 'Is knowledge possible? Is it a type of belief? Is it a mental state? Is there unconscious knowledge?'

Ethics – the study of value

The word 'ethics' comes from a Greek word meaning manners, but ever since the seventeenth century it has meant, in English, the study or science of morals, or, more widely, the science of human duties of all kinds including moral, legal and political duties.

In modern times 'ethics' has two different meanings. First, it can mean the study of theories about the intellectual origins and justification of moral codes and of morality in general. Second, it can mean the particular codes of conduct adopted by individuals or professions. The word is used in the second sense when people speak about the work ethic, medical ethics, business ethics, and so on. We shall be chiefly concerned with ethics in the first sense.

Ethics, which is also called moral philosophy, discusses, among other topics, its own status as an objective enquiry. It is also importantly concerned with motivation, especially with altruism and selfishness. Ethics asks questions about moral principles, and about happiness, justice, courage, and in a general way about any human states and traits which are regarded as valuable and desirable or valueless and undesirable.

Political philosophy – the study of citizen and state

Political philosophy has to do with questions about government, the citizen and the state. But it is not much concerned with the details, the nuts and bolts, of particular governments or modes of governing. Rather it tries to answer more general questions, including the following: Why should one obey the government of the state one lives in, is there any reason for obedience apart from fear? Do we need states, or would we be better off without them? What is liberty? How much liberty can citizens have, and how much ought they to have? What is equality, and is it desirable?

During the first half of this century professional philosophers seemed to lose interest in questions about the state and the citizen. So it is perhaps worth noting that until then the subject had always been an important part of philosophy. Ever since Plato's day nearly all those who have a claim to be remembered as significant philosophical thinkers have written about political questions. Plato himself wrote two long political works, *The Republic* and *The Laws*, Aristotle wrote a book called *Politics*, Augustine wrote *The City of God*, Thomas Aquinas discussed the rights and duties of rulers and their subjects, Thomas Hobbes' most important work is about the state (which he called the Leviathan), John Locke's large output includes his immensely influential *Treatises on Civil Government*, David Hume wrote on history and politics, and from more recent times we can mention Hegel, Bentham, John Stuart Mill and of course Karl Marx.

After an interregnum of three or four decades political topics returned to the philosophical agenda with two big works from America, John Rawls' *A Theory of Justice* (1979) and Robert Nozick's *Anarchy, State and Utopia* (1974).

The philosophy of science

The idea that there are philosophical problems which are peculiar to the systematic sciences is fairly recent. Until the nineteenth century what is now called philosophy of science formed part of the general theory of knowledge. Some nineteenth-century authors, including, for example, John Stuart Mill, treated it as a branch of logic – 'inductive logic'.

Nowadays philosophy of science is regarded as a distinct branch of philosophical endeavour and is taught as such in many universities, sometimes to science students, sometimes to philosophy students and sometimes to both. It is often studied alongside the history of science. A significant number of those who teach the philosophy of science began their academic lives as science students and then turned to philosophy later on.

Philosophical problems associated with science include ontological questions, that is, questions about the reality of theoretical entities such as gravity, magnetic force, electrons and anti-matter. It also examines the relationships between the various special sciences and theorizes about the possibility of reducing all the sciences to one master study, usually taken to be physics. Philosophy of science concerns itself too with methodological questions connected with inductive reasoning, reasoning from effects to causes and vice versa, and scientific reasoning generally.

Logic – the philosophy of inference and argument

The word 'logic' comes from the Greek *logos*, which means 'thought' or 'reason' or 'word', and it is possibly because of this that logic has sometimes been defined as *the study of the laws of thought*.

But Aristotle, who may be said to have invented the subject, described logic as the study of proof.

Now, not all reasoning aims to prove things strictly. Much reasoning aims merely to show that something is probable or possible. The reliability or otherwise of reasoning that is intended to support probabilities is not part of formal logic, which studies only strict proof, sometimes called deductive proof. Since strict proofs are found in mathematics many people, whether they realize it or not, are in a sense quite familiar with examples of such proofs, because many people have studied some mathematics.

Logic can best be defined as: *the study of that aspect of strict or deductive proof which is concerned with its soundness (or unsoundness).*

Some philosophers have held that logic ought to study truth as well as soundness. But truth is a much wider topic than soundness. It

4

is possible to devise general rules for testing soundness, but there are no *general* rules for finding out what is true, because different kinds of enquiry have different ways of finding out what is true. For instance, the various different sciences have different techniques of observation and experimentation. So it is possible, and useful, to study soundness and unsoundness without considering questions of truth and falsity.

How exactly does logic study this mater? Basically, it sets out general rules for testing soundness. We explain this in more detail in Part V.

The Other Branches of Philosophy

This book aims to be as comprehensive as possible but there are some branches of philosophy which it excludes. Thus we do not discuss philosophy of mathematics, philosophy of language, philosophy of law (jurisprudence) or philosophy of art (aesthetics). The reason is that these 'philosophy-of' subjects are not suitable for an introductory text. They are relatively difficult, because they presuppose that the reader already has some knowledge of mathematics, or law, or linguistics and grammar, and so on.

Different Approaches to Philosophy

Broadly speaking, philosophy can be studied in one or other of two ways. Either the philosopher attempts to define and analyse abstract concepts and to investigate many possible interpretations of questions involving such concepts, or else he or she attempts to construct a very general, and, if possible, completely self-consistent theory which will somehow explain the abstract ideas (like the ideas of existence and knowledge) which are the main concern of philosophy.

The contemporary labels for these two ways of doing philosophy are 'analytic' and 'continental'; but it has to be said that the labels are not especially precise.

One or other of these two kinds of approach to philosophy can be found in most universities of the modern world.

The 'analytic' approach is found mainly in the universities of the English-speaking countries and Scandinavia.

Analytic philosophy is so called first, because it involves analysing, defining and as it were separating out the various elements or parts of complex questions; and second, because it generally proceeds by considering all the different possible interpretations of abstract concepts and the complex questions which can be asked about them. The 'analytic' approach is not new: it comes down to us from Socrates, Aristotle and Thomas Aquinas. Socrates, for example, usually began his discourses by asking for definitions (analyses) of the ideas he wanted to talk about; Aristotle very often proceeded by listing and discussing many possible alternative theories and interpretations; Aquinas' method was to distinguish the different 'parts' of a question before answering it. More recently analytic philosophy has been associated with the names of such twentieth-century British philosophers as Gilbert Ryle, J. L. Austin and G. E. M. Anscombe, and with such Americans as Donald Davidson, Hilary Putnam and Saul Kripke.

The 'continental' approach is found in the universities of continental Europe, South America and in some parts of the United States. It is associated with the names of the great system-builders of philosophy, particularly Hegel, Schopenhauer, Marx and Heidegger, and more recently with such individuals as Sartre, Habermas and Derrida.

In this book we shall be adopting the analytic approach.

---

* Most of the philosophers and philosophical books mentioned in the text are described either in the Appendices, or in the Bibliography, or in both.

Part I
Metaphysics: The Philosophy of Being and Knowing

1

Some Puzzles about Existence

One of the most important questions of metaphysics is: What things exist? What is 'the furniture of the world'?

The Furniture of the World: Parts and Wholes

There are some ancient puzzles about the existence of parts and wholes.

Common sense tells us that trees and mountains, and stars and grains of sand, and people, and other animals such as cats and dogs and horses, all really do exist. However, according to the science of physics, trees and mountains, and dogs and cats (etc.) are fundamentally nothing but a lot of molecules – molecules of course being made up of atoms, and atoms being made up of sub-atomic particles.

The science of physics teaches that sub-atomic particles are a true reality. Are they therefore the only reality? In other words, if we agree that atoms and sub-atomic particles really do exist, are we then forced to say that chairs and mountains etc. do not exist? After all, it would surely be unreasonable to believe that chairs and tables exist *as well* as atoms and molecules. That would be like insisting that armies exist as well as generals and officers and NCOs and private soldiers. The world would contain too much furniture if that were true.

Let us consider piles of sand. Material objects are in a way somewhat similar to piles of sand. Piles of sand are nothing more than primitive uncomplicated collections of easy-to-separate grains of sand, and material objects are extremely complicated collections of difficult-to-separate atomic particles.

Do heaps of sand exist, or only grains of sand? Surely we can say that a heap of sand exists precisely because the grains that make it up exist. The existence of the heap is the very same thing as the existence of the grains at certain places (i.e. near to one another) at the same time.

By analogy we can say that trees and mountains, and men and women, and cats and dogs, and so on and so forth, exist precisely *because* the particles which make them up exist. The existence of a diamond, say, is the very same thing as the existence of certain sub-atomic particles linked in complex ways and existing at the same time and in (roughly) the same place. Without the particles there would be no diamond, but since there are the particles it follows that there is a diamond. The existence of a living thing, such as a tree or a pig, is somewhat different, because it consists in the existence of streams of particles which change constantly as the tree or pig grows and takes in nutrition. But still, without the particles there would be no pig, and on the other hand, given the right kind of particles in the right kind of arrangement the pig will exist.

Thus armies exist because soldiers exist, cities exist because houses and roads exist, landscape exists because mountains and trees and rivers exist. In short the existence of the world needs the existence of its parts. But the parts have to be arranged in certain patterns.

Generally speaking the parts of a whole have to be together in space and time for the whole to exist *as* a whole. Napoleon's army would be no army at all if its soldiers existed in different centuries, or were scattered across the galaxy. So it seems that a whole is not merely the same thing as its parts. It is, in a sense, something 'over and above' its parts, it is a spatial and temporal *arrangement*, a disposition of parts of elements in time and space.

This raises new metaphysical questions, namely: Do spatial and temporal arrangements exist? Do places exist? Do times exist?

The Furniture of the World: Places, Times, Qualities, Events

Suppose that on a certain occasion an astronomer called Linda Sparke, dressed in a yellow dress, is observing an eclipse of the sun through a telescope from an observatory near the equator.

Linda herself, and everyone else, will agree that Linda exists, and the dress exists, and the sun exists, and the telescope exists. That is only common sense. But what, if anything, does common sense tell us about the existence of the yellowness (of the dress), the existence of the eclipse, the existence of the equator and the existence of Linda's mental states associated with her observation of the eclipse?

Some philosophers have held that such items as qualities like yellowness, and events like eclipses, are special things or objects which exist somewhat in the way that ordinary things like tables exist. But this is not a very commonsensical theory, nor does it really help us to understand the puzzles of existence.

A different kind of answer can be found in the work of Aristotle, who was an eminently commonsensical philosopher.

Aristotle held that reality is made up of ten categories of 'things'. These categories are:

1 Substances: by which Aristotle meant such items as houses and horses and men and mountains and trees and statues.
2 Qualities (attributes): for example, green, massive, brave, wise.
3 Quantities: for instance, a metre, a ton.
4 Relations: such as half of, bigger than.
5 Places: such as in the market.
6 Times: such as last year, yesterday.
7 Positions (postures): sitting, standing.
8 States: being shod, wearing a coat.
9 Actions: hitting, cutting, hurling.
10 Affections (things that happen to substances): for example, being burnt, being strangled.

Aristotle reasoned that things in different categories exist in different ways, dependently or independently.

Qualities, quantities and relations certainly exist, but they exist only in so far as substances are yellow or green, or tall or short or heavy, or side by side, or older or younger than one another, and so on. Qualities, quantities and relations are dependent on substances.

Actions, like watching an eclipse, for instance, exist whenever substances act. Actions too are dependent on substances.

Happenings, such as falling over, exist whenever something happens to a substance, in this case, whenever a thing falls over.

Reproduction exists; it is the coming-to-be of substances.

Decay exists; it is the ceasing-to-be of substances.

Positions and states exist when a substance is in a position, or in a state, as the case may be.

In short, being, or reality, is manifold, but the ultimate or most important form of existence, upon which the other kinds depend, is the being or existence of substances.

What did Aristotle mean by substance? Basically, Aristotelian substances are just ordinary objects, like trees, chairs, dogs, and so on.

The theory of the categories could be taken to imply that the word *is* has ten different meanings. If you say 'Pavarotti is tall' you use the *is* of quantity. If you say 'Pavarotti is in Fiji' you use the *is* of place. If you say 'Pavarotti is slouching' you use the *is* of position (posture). And if you say 'Pavarotti is a man' you use the most important *is* of all, the *is* of substance. Readers can no doubt think up their own examples of the other six kinds of *is*.

Aristotle's list of categories is useful but not one hundred per cent satisfactory.

First, some of the categories seem redundant. Thus the category of position/posture looks to be redundant because it can easily be reduced to the categories of place and relation. The position or posture of a body is nothing more than the spatial relationships between its parts.

Similarly it could be argued that we do not really need the category of being-acted-on (affections) because an affection is only an action looked at from the other end (as it were).

These problems, however, are mere matters of detail. There is a more difficult question which has to do with places and times. It is this: Can places and times exist independently of substances, or not? If they can, are they then somehow fundamental, like substances themselves? Physicists as well as philosophers have puzzled over this question, and like philosophers they have held differing theories about the matter. We will not attempt to answer this question here, but will leave our readers to think about it for themselves.

Another difficult question is this: What category do fictitious creatures like unicorns belong to? Are unicorns substances? If not, what are they?

Finally, the doctrine of categories fails to make some quite important distinctions, which we discuss in the following section. Meanwhile, it should be noted that the absence from the doctrine of categories of certain important distinctions does not mean that Aristotle himself did not discuss those distinctions elsewhere.

The Furniture of the World: Predication and Existence

The theory of the categories lists ten different kinds of 'thing' and thereby can be interpreted as distinguishing ten different senses of the word 'is'. Yet while the list of categories lists types of things that exist it does not give us a way of *saying* that they exist.

Take an example:

1   Using Aristotle's categories we could say (at least) ten kinds of thing about Katherine Evans:

Katherine Evans is a woman (substance).
KE is thin (quality).
KE weighs 9 stone (quantity).
KE is in England (place).
KE writes letters (action).
(And so on.)

All these statements presuppose that there really is something in the world called Katherine Evans, that Katherine Evans, whatever she or it may be, really does exist. The different 'is's' are used to predicate various things of this individual who is assumed to exist.

2   Consider now a question and an answer:
   Is there such a person as Katherine Evans at all? Yes, there is.

In the question Ms Evans is not *assumed* to exist; rather, it is asked *whether* she exists. In the answer it is not *assumed* that she exists, rather it is *asserted* that she exists.

These examples illustrate a difference which cannot be contained within the list of categories, the difference between the 'is' of predication and the 'is' of existence. The list of categories is a list of different kinds of predication: the 'is' of existence transcends the list.

The distinction is of some importance in the history of philosophy, one reason being that a famous proof of God's existence, the so-called ontological argument, is thought to rest on a confusion between the two fundamentally different kinds of 'is'.

The ontological argument will be discussed in the next chapter. First we will take a look at non-existence.

The Furniture of the World: The Non-existent King of France

Common sense tells us that unicorns, and elves, and Father Xmas and the present King of France do not exist. For one thing we know that France at present is a Republic, so by definition it cannot have a present King. As to unicorns and elves, we are unable to find these things however hard we search for them, and we cannot even find any unicorn bones or elf fossils.

Yet ever since ancient times some philosophers have believed that, if you can think about some thing, then that thing must exist *in some sense*. They argue that if a thing did not exist at all you could not think about it. You cannot think about nothing, only about something; and if a thing is a something then it must *somehow exist*. Thus the present King of France, and elves, and unicorns, must all exist *in some sense*, otherwise you could not think about them.

But surely the idea that non-existent things exist is very paradoxical.

One common way of trying to avoid paradox is to say that non-existent things exist only in the mind. This proposed solution is a bit vague as it stands. What kind of existence is existence-in-the-mind?

Bertrand Russell, when discussing the question of 'non-existent entities', advises his readers to keep a good grasp on a 'robust sense of reality'.

The modern approach to the problem, exemplified in the work of Russell himself, is to treat it as one which can be resolved by a proper understanding of logic and language.

Let us begin with the non-existent present King of France.

Russell held that every meaningful statement must be either true or false. A meaningful and unambiguous statement cannot be *both* true *and* false, and it cannot be *neither* true *nor* false.

Russell considered the possible statement 'the present King of France is bald', and asked: Is this true or false? If it is true then the King really is bald, not hairy. If it is false then the King is hairy, not bald. But how to decide the matter? It is impossible to examine the scalp of the present King of France.

Russell's solution is part of his Theory of Descriptions. It consists in analysing statements into what he took to be their hidden constituents.

According to Russell, the statement 'the present King of France is bald', though it looks quite simple, is really complex. It contains not just one 'is' but four, and, most importantly, three of the four are 'is's of existence.

'The present King of France is bald' is three statements rolled into one:

1   There IS at least one King of France.
2   There IS at most one King of France.
3   There IS nothing which IS both King of France and not bald.

When the original statement has been analysed in this way it can be seen to be false because its first constituent (1) is false. The constituent (1) is false because the King does not exist. The whole statement is false, not because the King is not bald, but because he does not exist at all.

What about 'the present King of France is not bald'? Is that statement true? No. It too is false, since its analysis will be:

1   There is at least one King of France.
2   There is at most one King of France.
3   There is nothing which is both King of France and bald.

Again the first constituent is false, so the whole original statement is false.

The upshot, of course, is that 'The King of France is bald' and 'The King of France is not bald' are both of them false.

Russell's explanation about how best to understand statements about things that do not exist is not accepted by everyone. For instance, Peter Strawson has argued that statements about non-existent things such as the present King of France are not false, but neither true nor false.

Philosophers are still divided on the question as to whether Russell or Strawson has the best answer.

This completes our discussion of existence in general. In the next chapter we examine some of the problems surrounding the traditional proofs of the existence of God.

2
The Existence of God

Judaism and Christianity conceive God as an eternal, infinite, uncreated Being, who has made the universe and everything in it. This Being stands to the human race not only as its creator but also in some sense as a person, and indeed as a father, who rewards and punishes his human children, either in this life, or in a later existence, or both. Islam, the third major monotheism, shares part of this conception of God with the older religions, though it does not (officially) regard God as a Father but rather as a non-personal Being. Despite that, Allah, the God of Islam, refers to himself in the Koran as 'he', and he punishes and rewards, just like the God of the Hebrews and the Christians.

The idea of gods is of course older than any of these faiths. It seems to have been an essential concept in virtually every human community known to history. Our own time is exceptional in this regard.

As to philosophers, they have been thinking about God for centuries. Their interest has often centred on the idea of proof. Can God's existence be proven? Or can it only be accepted as a matter of faith?

The most important proofs or attempted proofs of the existence of God are, respectively, arguments from revelation, the argument from miracles, the first cause argument, the ontological argument and the argument from design.

The Arguments from Revelation

The three major monotheistic religions all claim that God sometimes reveals himself to particular men and women. Thus all three teach that

God revealed himself to Moses on Mount Sinai, giving him the ten commandments, the Tablets of the Law. Furthermore, Christians believe that the New Testament is an account of how God revealed a new law to humankind through Jesus Christ, while Islam teaches that Allah spoke to Mahomet, giving that prophet various instructions and promises for the faithful.

From time to time, too, ordinary believers have claimed to have had personal revelations of God's existence, sometimes in the form of dreams or visions or inner voices, and sometimes in the form of extraordinary and miraculous experiences.

Non-believers, however, argue that personal experiences which seem to signal the existence of a divinity might have other more humdrum explanations. Dreams and visions tell us all kinds of things which we know perfectly well to be false; for instance, we might dream about elves or unicorns, but that does not prove such creatures really exist. Dreams and visions are not reliable witnesses, and personal experiences which would not be regarded as proofs of the existence of elves and goblins cannot by themselves count as satisfactory proofs of the existence of God, even if they are very convincing for the person who has them.

The Argument from Miracles

What are miracles? The commonest idea suggests that a miracle is an extraordinary event in human affairs, usually beneficial to some good or unfortunate person, and brought about either by the direct intervention of God, or by prophets and saints with God's help. Miracles often or always go against the laws of nature; for example, ordinarily when people die they stay dead, but if God so wishes he, or his saints, can raise the dead to life again.

However, this account of miracles *presupposes* that God exists, and hence it cannot be used as a premise in a *proof* of his existence. A neutral definition of miracles is needed, that is, one which does not presuppose anything about the existence of God. Here is one such possible definition:

Miracles are extraordinary events which cannot be explained by science, and which benefit individual human beings, and which have a similarity to helpful interventions carried out by benevolent people.

To scientifically-minded materialist philosophers, however, even the most extraordinary events are not so extraordinary as to lack a material cause. The ordinary material world looks fairly coherent to the scientifically-minded philosopher. Fire always burns, ice is always cold, all physical objects obey the law of gravity, summer always follows spring, and all animals come to death. It is obvious that the world is governed by the laws of cause and effect, and apparent exceptions can in principle be explained in terms of such laws. If we fail today to explain exceptions and aberrations we may yet be confident that the scientists of the future will succeed.

David Hume (1711–76), who is responsible for many anti-religious arguments, including most of those current today in ordinary unbelieving circles, claims that there must always be a presumption against the occurrence of a miracle. The evidence for a miracle, says Hume, will always be weaker than the evidence for some other hypothesis. This is because there is a lot of evidence in support of the laws of nature – the law of gravity for instance – and much less evidence for the miracle that violates those laws. What is more, Hume argues, it is well known that people tell lies and make mistakes. It is always more likely that someone has lied or made a mistake than that the laws of nature were overturned.

There are four different questions here which need to be disentangled from one another.

The first is: Do extraordinary, seemingly inexplicable events ever happen in human life? In spite of Hume the answer to this must surely be: yes.

The second question is: Can we be sure that science will eventually explain all such extraordinary events in ordinary scientific terms? The answer to this must be: no, we cannot be sure. After all, no human beings, not even scientists, not even the scientists of the future, are omniscient. It is not impossible that some questions might remain dark to us forever.

The third question is: Does the existence of unanswered questions, questions, perhaps, which no human being can answer, prove that there is a God? The answer to this must be: no. The existence of humanly unanswerable questions might only prove that the human race is not as clever as it thinks it is, that we are not omniscient – which we know already. It does not prove that there is someone else who *is* omniscient, i.e. God.

The fourth question is: Does the fact that some seemingly inexplicable events appear to help particular individuals at crucial moments in their lives prove that there is a benevolent personal God who watches over us? The answer to this must be: it does not *prove* it. Yet, on the other hand, if it is indeed the case that some inexplicable events have a markedly beneficial character, if it is indeed the case that some of the strange events that occasionally happen actually help good or unfortunate individuals at crucial points in their lives, then that perhaps is the most important aspect of the argument from miracles. The seemingly beneficial character of some miracles surely constitutes a psychologically stronger reason for belief than the much less astonishing fact that some things are just inexplicable, and a stronger reason, too, than the claims to special knowledge made by human institutions.

The First Cause Argument

The most important version of the first cause argument comes to us from medieval theology.

The argument runs like this: everything that happens has a cause, and that cause itself has a cause, and that cause too has a cause, and so on and so on, back into the past, in a series that must either be finite or infinite. Now if the series is finite it must have had a starting point, which we may call the first cause. This first cause is God.

What if the series is infinite? Aquinas after some consideration eventually rejects the possibility that the world is infinitely old and had no beginning in time. Certainly the idea of time stretching backwards into the past forever is one which the human mind finds hard to grasp. An infinity which stretches forward into the future is a little easier for us mortals to conceive. Still, we might note here that Aristotle found no difficulty in the former idea. He held that the world has existed forever. Aristotle's opinion, if correct, invalidates the first cause argument.

Another difficulty lies in the fact that the argument depends on our human conception of causality. Can we be sure that our reasonings about cause and effect are foolproof? And is it not possible, even, that the cause–effect nexus is nothing in itself, but only an idea invented by the human mind?

There are other problems which concern the nature of the cause itself. Suppose there is a first cause, can we know that this cause is a personal god? Suppose that the first cause is a personal god, must we conclude that he has existed forever? Or did he have a beginning in time?

If Aquinas is correct in deciding that it is impossible to conceive of the world having existed forever, we have to ask whether, and why, it is any easier to conceive of the creator of the world having existed forever.

There is a dilemma:

If God has existed eternally, then there is no difficulty in the idea of eternal existence as such. Aristotle might be right: the universe itself might have existed forever.

Contrariwise, if God has not existed eternally then it seems that he too must have a cause, and then that cause will need a cause, and so on and so on.

Some philosophers describe God as a self-caused cause. But the notion of a self-caused cause seems even more difficult than the idea of eternity. How can a being which does not exist bring itself into existence?

The Ontological Argument

The ontological argument was formulated by Anselm (1033–1109), who was Archbishop of Canterbury during the reigns of William Rufus and Henry I. Centuries later René Descartes (1596–1650) produced a rather simpler version of the argument.

Anselm begins by quoting Scripture: 'The fool hath said in his heart: there is no God.' He argues that even atheists must have an idea of God, otherwise they would not be able to understand their own words, the words 'there is no God'. Now, what precisely is this idea which even the fool has in his heart? The idea of God, says Anselm, is the idea of 'a being greater than which cannot be conceived'. By this he means that we cannot conceive of or imagine anything greater than God because the very idea of God is the idea of an omniscient, all-powerful, eternal and completely perfect being. It is impossible to think of a being which is more eternal than eternal, more infallible than infallible, or more perfect than completely perfect.

This then is the idea of God. So far it is only an idea, and it has not been shown that there is anything existing in reality which matches the idea.

Anselm next states that there are two different kinds of existence, existence in the mind and existence in reality. We know that God exists in human minds, as an idea; does God also exist in reality?

Anselm claims that existing in the mind is a less perfect kind of existence than existing in reality. (It has to be admitted that this point has a certain plausibility.) He then reasons as follows: if God existed only in the mind he would be less perfect, less great, than if he existed in reality. If God existed only in the mind then we would be able to conceive a being greater than God, namely, a being which as well as existing in the mind also existed in reality. This greater being, existing both in the mind and in reality, would be the real God, because the first God we thought of, the one that existed only in the mind, would not after all be a being greater than which cannot be conceived.

Anselm concludes that the greatest being we can conceive of must exist in reality as well as in the mind: therefore God exists in reality.

Anselm also combines the idea of God with the idea of necessity.

If God existed accidentally he would be less great than if his existence was necessary. Since God is a being greater than which cannot be conceived he must exist necessarily and not accidentally. Therefore it is certain that God exists, and it is certain that he always has existed and always will exist, for that is what necessary existence means.

Descartes' version of the ontological argument is somewhat simpler. It runs as follows.

Our idea of God is an idea of a perfect being.
A perfect being must have every perfection.
It is better to exist than not to exist.
It is better to exist in reality than merely to exist in someone's mind.
So existence, i.e. existence in reality, is a perfection.
Therefore our idea of a perfect being is an idea of a being which exists in reality.
Therefore the Perfect Being (God) exists in reality.

The ontological argument has had many critics. One of Anselm's contemporaries, the monk Gaunilo, wrote a reply which he called 'In behalf of the fool' (that is, the fool who 'said in his heart: there is no God').

Gaunilo claims that Anselm's argument if applied in other fields would lead to ridiculous conclusions. You could use the argument to 'prove' the existence of a perfect island, for instance, by claiming that the perfect island is 'an island a better than which cannot be conceived'.

Anselm bases his reply on his claim that God's existence is not only certain, but necessary. A perfect island, even if it existed in reality, would not have necessary existence in eternity, only accidental existence in time.

Is Existence a Property?

More recently philosophers have objected to the ontological argument on the grounds that existence is not a perfection. A perfection is a special kind of property (for instance, complete goodness), but existence is not a property at all.

The objection can be summed up in the slogan 'existence is not a property'. The truth of the slogan can be supported by examining language, by comparing the word 'exists' with other words.

The word 'exists' does not behave like an action word, nor like a quality word, nor like words which name times and places and relations.

Take an action word, say the word 'growls', and consider the following examples:

1a   No tigers growl. – This is doubtless false but it is not nonsense.
2a   All tigers growl. – Also not nonsense.
3a   Most tigers growl but a few do not. – Also not nonsense, and probably true.

Now compare the word 'exists':

1b   No tigers exist.
2b   All tigers exist.
3b   Most tigers exist but a few do not.

'No tigers exist' does make sense, though it happens to be false. It is somewhat similar to 'no dodos exist now', which also makes sense and happens to be true.

But 'all tigers exist' is empty, it gives no information; and 'most tigers exist but a few do not' makes no sense at all.

By parity of reasoning it can be shown that 'exists' is different from quality words and hence different from words such as 'sublime', 'perfectly wise', 'infinite and eternal', which refer to perfections.

Consider:

1c   No professors are perfectly wise.
2c   All professors are perfectly wise.
3c   Most professors are perfectly wise but a few are not.

Whether true or false all these sentences make sense. But again compare 'exists':

1d   No professors exist.
2d   All professors exist.
3d   Most professors exist but a few do not.

Again, the first sentence (no professors exist), though false, makes sense. But the second sentence (all professors exist) is empty of meaning. The third (some professors exist but a few do not) is surely nonsense. The word 'exists' does not work like the expression 'perfectly wise'.

We can conclude then that existence is not an action, it is not like growling, and it is not a perfection, it is not like perfect wisdom.

The Argument from Design

This is possibly the most telling of the philosophical arguments in favour of the existence of a god. Briefly, it states that the universe and everything in it is wonderfully organized, just as if it were the work of a superb designer. Everything we look at seems to show this, from the motion of the planets to the extraordinary construction of the brain. Nothing is random, everything appears to follow a plan or design.

Such a universe could not have come into existence by chance and without thought. In some respects our world is like a marvellous artefact. William Paley (1743–1805) compared it to a watch. If we found a watch in a sandy waste we would never suppose that its existence and structure were the result of chance, even if we had never seen a watch before. Instead we would at once infer that it had been deliberately made by some intelligent being. God is thus compared with a watchmaker.

David Hume is the chief critic of the argument from design.

He remarks that even if we could prove that the universe has an intelligent designer, that would not show that the designer is a person, or wise, or good. It would not tell us which of all the warring religions is the true one.

He also says the universe is not really much like a human artefact, in spite of claims that it is. In his view it is just as much like a vast animal or a huge vegetable as like a clock. Animals and vegetables, unlike clocks and watches, do not come about by intelligent design but by natural reproduction.

Finally, Hume claims that the universe is bound to have the appearance of being designed. Our universe is comparatively stable, and the parts of a stable universe have to be adapted to one another. For instance, the various animals in the world have to be adapted for survival, otherwise there would be no animals. However this raises the question: Could there be a universe at all, without a designer? To this Hume answers that stability by definition lasts longer than instability or chaos. If the universe began as an undesigned chaos and reached stability by accident or chance the state of stability would remain, at least for a time.

This completes our account of some of the main philosophical arguments for and against the existence of God. We will end with a brief reference to the work of Immanuel Kant (1724–1804).

Kant held that it is impossible to prove the existence of God, yet he argues all the same that we need to believe in God. The idea of God and the idea of freedom (free will), which Kant calls Ideas of Reason, are necessary presuppositions in human life. The necessity is not psychological or social, but goes much deeper. The life of reason, the life of human beings as creatures endowed with reason, would be impossible without these two ideas. According to Kant, our scientific and philosophical theories would make no sense without the idea of God, and the ordinary co-operative practical life of humanity would fall into chaos without the idea of free will.

3
The Existence and Identity of Persons

Philosophers have long felt that there is some mystery about the nature of persons, a mystery connected with consciousness, memory and mental life.

Let us begin by looking at three related questions.

First, how can we tell when one (or two) persons are the same or different? For instance, how do we know that person A, whom we met on Monday, is identical with, or different from, person B, whom we met on Friday?

Next, how do you know that you are the same person as you were yesterday or last year?

These two questions are concerned with the conditions for identity (identity conditions). We probably won't be able to answer them unless we also answer the third question:

What is a person, exactly, anyway?

John Locke on Identity

Current philosophical discussion about personal identity is still influenced very much by the work of John Locke (1632–1704).

Locke begins his treatment of identity by distinguishing different kinds of things and then suggesting identity conditions for each type.

First, he considers inanimate objects, taking as his example a diamond. There is just one identity condition for a diamond, he says, and that is that it should have the same atoms, or 'minute particles'. In other words, the diamond you see on Monday is exactly the same diamond as the one you see on Wednesday if, and only if, it has the same atoms. If the atoms have changed you have a new and different diamond.

But even things made from very hard material lose a few atoms over time. Nowadays, too, we know about radioactive materials, which lose, expel or give off 'minute particles' continually. Locke of course knew nothing of radioactivity, but he accepted that all material substances may undergo a gradual loss of particles, and for that reason he suggests that even a diamond might not have absolutely perfect identity over time.

Still, a diamond seems to be more stable than things that grow and decay. Locke took a fairly common-sense view of the differences between minerals and living things. He says that although pure and absolute identity requires unchanging matter, in practice we must perforce think of the identity of a living thing in a different way.

What then are the identity conditions of an oak tree, for example? Certainly not always having the same atoms. For a tree grows, sheds its leaves, has branches fall off in storms and so on, and yet it remains the same tree.

Locke concludes that the identity condition for a living tree is *a continuous life* which follows the normal cycle for that type of tree.

That the life of a tree has to be continuous is shown by the fact that when the tree is chopped down and burnt as firewood (say) then no new tree can be the very same tree as the old one. In other words, trees do not undergo reincarnation.

We could make quibbles here about grafted branches, and trees that grow from cuttings, and so on. Does a tree grown from a cutting of an old tree now dead and burnt have the same continuous life as the old one? Or is it a new tree? Perhaps it is not so different from a new tree grown from a seed: cuttings, in the lives of trees, function much as seeds. The new tree, then, could be said to be the child of the old one.

There is a special problem about the olive tree, for the olive tree, in a sense, never dies. It regenerates itself over and over again from the original roots. So it looks as if there is a relatively small number of olive trees in the universe which have all lived more or less forever.

Locke's account, if interpreted sensibly, can cover the tricky-looking cases, which are tricky mainly because trees surprise us by not behaving like animals. They have their own laws of life and death, though, and Locke is able to build his definition of identity conditions for vegetables on those laws. Each type of tree has its own kind of life-cycle, and reproduction by grafting and from cuttings, and the regeneration of the olive, are normal facts of life, for trees. The olive is a vegetable version of a parrot – they are both very long-lived.

Locke next considers the identity conditions for animals. The basic identity condition for an animal, a cat let us say, turns out not to be different from the identity condition of a tree, namely, the same continuous life. The kitten grows continuously until it reaches adulthood and during that time its constituent cells, the atoms that make it up, change several times, though gradually. But provided its life is not interrupted by death it remains the same cat. Cats, on this view, cannot be reincarnated, because the death of an animal ends its identity condition. No cat born after the death of Tibbles will be the same Tibbles.

Finally, Locke considers the identity conditions of persons. And he begins this part of his discussion by remarking that human beings have a twofold nature. Human beings are animals and they are also persons. According to Locke a person is not a special kind of animal but something different altogether.

Human Beings and Persons

Locke's view that persons are not simply human animals has been accepted in some form or other by almost every twentieth-century philosopher writing on the subject, including many who do not share any of his other theories. But we will beg to differ from him, and from them.

Locke's account of personal identity, then, differentiates it from human, that is, animal identity. It is based solely on mental life and specifically on memory. If you should happen to remember doing all the things Socrates did in Athens 2,500 years ago, then according to Locke, you are the very same *person* as Socrates – though a different *human being*. This makes perfect sense in the Lockean theory, even though it sounds weird to us. For the Lockean theory does not accept that persons are just human animals; human beings can be persons, but personhood is not the same thing as animalhood and has nothing to do with physical features. Human beings are persons only in so far as they have consciousness and memory.

We might find the theory a little less weird if we consider an analogy.

Bertie Wooster can be both a graduate and an heir. Being a graduate is not the same thing as being an heir. Bertie could be an heir in virtue of his aunt's Will, but he is a graduate in virtue of having studied at Oxford and obtained a 4th Class Honours degree. In virtue of the fact that he has graduated Bertie goes on being a graduate all his life, and he is always the same graduate. However he could easily stop being an heir if his aunt decided to disinherit him.

In this analogy, being some one particular graduate is to be taken as the analogue of being some specific person, and being someone's heir is to be taken as the analogue of being a specific human being, a specific human animal.

When Socrates died he ceased to exist as a man. But the possibility of his continuing to exist as a person remained open. If (as in Locke's little story) 'the present Mayor of Queensborough' had all Socrates' memories he, the Mayor, would be Socrates – the person Socrates, that is, not the man.

Memory and False Memory

Locke's theory seems at first sight to be a good one for answering the second of our three original questions, namely: How does anyone know, from day to day, that he or she is the same person as yesterday? For it gives the answer: from your own point of view it is your memories which make you the same person, or a different person. You only know that you are the same person as yesterday because your memories today are much the same as those of yesterday.

The answer, though, raises the spectre of false memory, a spectre destined to shatter Locke's theory altogether.

I cannot, after all, rely on my memory to tell me if I am the same (Lockean) person, because there is always a possibility that my memories could be false memories. So I need a way to make sure my memories are true ones. But that would mean relying on a second memory to tell me whether my first memories are true ones. And then I will need a third memory to tell me if the second memory is a true one – and so on, and so on, forever.

As Wittgenstein remarked in another context, you cannot check the accuracy of today's newspaper by buying a second copy of it (or a third copy or a fourth . . .).

Is there any way of checking up on your own or other people's memories to see if they are true memories? Yes there is, but the method itself presupposes that personal identity conditions are the same as human (animal) identity conditions – which shatters Locke's theory.

What is a false memory? Essentially it is a memory that tells you that your body was in some particular place at some particular time when it can be proved that your body was in fact elsewhere.

Suppose for instance you think you remember being Winston Churchill. You remember being made Prime Minister of Great Britain, you also remember making many speeches in the House of Commons and to the nation. You remember being married to Clementine Churchill.

How will you, and other people, discover whether your claims are true or false? What identity conditions will be used to establish your real identity?

Your real identity will be discovered, and can only be discovered, by finding out where your body has been during Churchill's lifetime. It will be discovered only after the following questions have been answered: Is this individual body the same body as Churchill's body? Does this individual body share the same continuous life with Churchill's body? Was this individual body in all the same places at all the same times as Churchill's body?

Unless the answer to these questions is affirmative in each case the memory claims will be false. For a false memory, as we have already stated, is essentially a memory that tells you that your body was in some particular place at some particular time, when in fact it was elsewhere.

Suppose that it has been shown by all the evidence available that your body and Churchill's body are not coterminous. Might you not still feel convinced that you are Churchill? Might your memories not still seem to you to be his memories? Yes, that could happen. But they would be false memories all the same. One's own convictions about one's identity are not invariably correct. It is possible to suffer amnesia, and even possible to lose all sense of identity. Yet even then you still go on being the same original human animal that you were before you lost your memory, and it will therefore always remain possible for other people to identify you – as a particular human being.

Locke's Theory in Modern Times

Locke's theory of personal identity lingers on, and modern philosophers continue to insist that human beings are not the same things as persons. In modern times the theory has developed unfortunate parallels with the 'theories' of racism, sexism and ageism.

It is an interesting point that philosophy students use the terms 'person' and 'human being' interchangeably – until they are taught not to by philosophy teachers. Does that mean the philosophy teachers know a lot of recondite physiological facts about persons and human beings that the students do not? Of course not. Philosophers are not physiologists, and anyway the *relevant* facts are known to everyone. Then do the philosophy teachers know better than the students what the words 'person' and 'human being' mean? No, they do not. As far as language goes, ordinary usage, and the dictionary, support the student not the teacher.

Usually the teacher never gives reasons for his distinction, but simply stipulates. Thus Professor Michael Tooley, in a paper defending infanticide, writes, '*I shall treat* the concept of a person as a purely moral concept . . . free from all descriptive content . . . synonymous with "has a serious moral right to life" ' (our italics).

Well, stipulation is free, so Tooley could just as well have said: 'I shall treat the concept of a person as a purely entomological concept, synonymous with "beetle" . . . .'

The main long-term result of Locke's distinction between human beings and persons (and for which of course he is not to blame) has been that philosophers have divided the human race into two kinds of being, those that have a right to life and those that do not. It is this distinction, drawn up by Tooley and others, which constitutes the parallel, mentioned above, with racism, sexism and ageism. Racist, sexist and ageist 'theories' also divide the human race into two types, those who have or deserve moral rights and those who (allegedly) do not.

Human Persons

What then is a person? And what makes one person the same person as the person he or she was yesterday? We would like to suggest that persons, on this planet, are nothing more nor less than human animals — white or black, male or female, child or adult, as the case may be. It follows that the identity conditions for a person are simply the identity conditions for a human being.

That does not mean the human animal is not a very special kind of animal. Human beings are capable of consciousness, and of thought, and can remember things. Peter Strawson writes: 'persons are individuals of a certain unique type such that to every individual of that type there must be ascribed or ascribable *both* states of consciousness *and* corporeal characteristics.' This seems to be roughly right, though one would need to add that a sleeping or otherwise unconscious person is still a person. The states of consciousness referred to in Strawson's definition need not be perpetually present, they can be potential as well as actual. The concept of potentiality gives a non-stipulative reason for holding (*contra* Tooley et al.) that infant human beings, as well as adults, are persons. Society too recognizes the importance of potentiality, for example by recognizing infants as persons in the legal system.

We need not jump to the conclusion that human beings are the only special animals in the universe. Somewhere out there in the vast regions of space there might be species of non-human animals which like us can think and remember and which have complex states of consciousness. If they were special animals in the way in which human beings are special then they too would be persons.

Finally, we need not leap to the conclusion that there could not be purely spiritual persons, gods and angels and so on. That is perhaps a logical possibility. Still, we know for sure that we human beings are not purely spiritual. We know for sure that we are human animals, and that on this planet a person is nothing but that.

4

The Problem of Free Will

The problem of free will is related to questions about cause and effect, and to issues in the philosophy of religion and moral philosophy.

Roughly speaking, freedom of the will means freedom to make choices. The denial of free will is determinism, the theory that no individual has any control over his or her own actions.

According to determinists everything people do is caused by factors over which they have no control. Human actions do not arise out of free choices, but out of the individual's genetic blueprint, or instincts, or early childhood experiences, or from social conditioning. The iron law of causation means that in some sense the future is already written and cannot be altered.

It is a matter of common experience that we feel that we can make choices. On the other hand, we see the dominion of cause and effect in the whole of nature, and we know that we ourselves are part of nature.

Because the issue touches on questions about moral responsibility many people have been forced to think about it at one time or another, for example, when they ask: 'Can criminals help doing what they do?' For it seems that there can only be any genuine morality if we can act freely. If we are not free we cannot be held responsible for our actions and should not be either blamed or praised for them.

Some philosophers have insisted on the existence of free will partly because they think that to deny it would have 'mischievous effects' on morality.

Cause versus Chance

Suppose for the sake of argument that human actions are an exception to the rule of causation. Wouldn't that mean that they occur randomly? For surely the absence of causation is just the same thing as chance or randomness. Now, is a person whose actions are random any more free than one whose actions are determined? It would seem not.

To defend the doctrine that the human will is free it is not enough simply to reject determinism, for freedom of the will is not the same thing as mere absence of causation, not the same thing as chance or randomness.

There is a dilemma here which will have to be resolved. It is this:

If human actions are uncaused, the result of chance, then the individual is not free. A person who behaves randomly is not free but insane. In any case, actions that are chosen are not random. If I *choose* to visit Bognor I can hardly say that I got there by pure chance.

On the other hand, if all human actions are caused then again the individual is not free. For if all one's actions are caused then one's choosing must be caused too. Choosing cannot escape the dominion of causation. Most likely one's choices are determined by instinct or by social conditioning.

So either way there is no such thing as freedom of the will.

We may suspect that something might have gone wrong with our reasoning if two contrary or opposite theses both lead to the same conclusion, in this case, that there is no free will.

Are Free Will and Determinism Compatible?

Hume attempted to resolve the dilemma by arguing that free will and causation are not strictly speaking opposites. Free will, he says, is compatible with causation, and more than that, it is dependent on causation. We can only make free choices in a world governed by causation. If the world was not governed by causation we could not know what would happen after we made our choices, and so our choices would be pointless. Choices themselves are causes: in a world without causation, choices would have no effects.

Take as an analogy the movement of the bone of the arm in its socket at the shoulder. Assuming that you do not suffer from rheumatism or such then your arm bone will be able to 'move freely in the socket' (as we say).

Now suppose that someone complains 'It isn't moving freely at all, because it is restrained by the shape of the socket.' Would that be a sensible comment? No, for it suggests that only if your arm were separated from the shoulder socket could its movements be completely free. But that is not the case. An arm floating by itself in space has no power of movement at all.

Should we decide that free will is made possible by causation? We might well agree that choice is made possible by causation. The trouble is that once causation is introduced into the picture we will have to say that choices themselves are caused. So we end up with choice, but not with free choice.

Part of the problem might be due to the fact that the terms free will, liberty and determinism can be understood in different ways.

Wanting and Choosing

It looks as if free will cannot mean randomness. Perhaps then free will only means that one has the power to get what one wants – food, or cigarettes, or revenge or whatever. Such freedom would be compatible with determinism. You want bread; you have the power to go out and buy some bread, so that is what you do. It does not matter, on this account, that you were caused to want the bread in the first place by hunger, or a neurotic craving, or an addiction, or something nasty in your social conditioning.

One consequence of accepting this account of the matter is that we have to say, if we want to be consistent, that the heroin addict may well be acting freely when taking heroin.

In an effort to rebut this kind of objection some philosophers have formulated a theory of second-order desires. Freedom of the will is to be defined in such a way that one acts freely only when one *desires to have the desires* one in fact has. Thus heroin addicts would not necessarily be acting freely if they desired heroin and so took some, because presumably they do not *desire to have the desire* for heroin. They are different from people who desire something harmless, like bread. They are unfree.

But do ordinary people really have the desire to desire bread? That seems rather artificial. The desire for bread is well known, but the supposed desire to desire bread looks like a figment of the imagination.

Second, it is not too fantastic to imagine an addict who *wants to want* the drug to which he or she is addicted. This is at least a logical possibility. In the face of such an example we who are not addicted might not be in a position to disagree with the addict's description of desire.

Nevertheless perhaps even addicts who *want to want* to take heroin are not acting freely. After all they are addicted, which means that they could not stop even if they wanted to. If their wanting to want to changed, so that they wanted not to want heroin, they would still be stuck with the craving.

The example shows that there is more to having free will than the mere power to satisfy one's desires, even one's second-order desires.

Positive and Negative Determinism

Determinism can be understood as either negative or positive, and as either rigid or not rigid.

Even the most hardline supporters of free will have to agree that many of our choices and actions are determined in a weak or negative sense. For example, some theoretically possible choices are negatively determined, i.e. ruled out, by the fact that we are not fish but human beings. Not being fish naturally imposes certain restrictions on us; thus since we have no gills we cannot choose to live (without special apparatus) under the water. But negative determination is not usually felt as a constraint, or as a reduction of freedom. The fact that you cannot jump over the moon does not mean that you have no freedom of choice. You cannot choose the impossible, so the question of choice, free or unfree, does not arise.

Human beings are also more positively determined, though often in a very general way. We act in a generally human fashion simply by virtue of being human beings. But many possibilities of action lie within that human framework.

Hume speaks about the 'uniformity in the actions of all men in all nations and ages' and says that 'human nature remains the same in all its principles and operations'. To put the point in a more modern style: like effects are produced by like causes, and human beings are determined in a general way by a common biological programme.

Having a common human biological programme is quite compatible with being free to act in a number of different ways. Ordinary observation suggests that the common biological programme does not prevent people from having very different ways of developing (or neglecting) their human capacities and tendencies. That is how it comes about that there are and have been different kinds of people in the world: Stalin and Florence Nightingale, Ivan the Terrible and Francis of Assisi.

Rigid and Non-rigid Determinism

Broadly speaking there are two varieties of rigid determinism, the religious and the scientific.

Strict Calvinism teaches that God's omniscience is not compatible with human free will. Since God knows everything he must know about every human action which ever has and ever will take place. Calvinists infer from this that human actions are all fixed in advance, and cannot be altered or avoided by any human means whatsoever. Since God also knows, of course, which actions are good and which are bad, he knows in advance which people are destined for Heaven and which for Hell.

However, other versions of Christianity argue that it is evident from Scripture and from experience that God gave humanity free will; what is more, God's punishments and rewards, his Heaven and Hell, would make no sense unless we mortals were free to choose between good and evil.

Scientific determinism is well exemplified by the work of the eighteenth-century mathematician Pierre Simon LaPlace (1749–1827). LaPlace is commonly supposed to have believed that everything in the physical world can be explained by the science of mechanics.

Great faith in deterministic science has persisted into this century, though the sciences appealed to today are not mathematics and mechanics. Nowadays some of those of a deterministic persuasion believe our actions in later life are determined by a genetic blueprint given in embryo. Others hold that our actions and our characters are determined by events in our childhood. Not only our neuroses are so determined but even our ability to overcome those neuroses. And some thinkers combine these two views. Thus the American psychologist B. F. Skinner argues that every human action is the result either of the genetic blueprint or of reinforcing experiences. Like many determinists Skinner insists that belief in free will is not based on reason but is a primitive superstition.

Modern defenders of free will reject the religious determinism of Calvinistic predestination, either because they are agnostics, or because they have some different non-Calvinist religious belief. It would be generally agreed too that here the burden of proof lies on the Calvinist.

Where does the burden of proof lie when it comes to scientific determinism? Might it not lie on the determinists? It is not good enough to follow Skinner and accuse the opposite party of superstition. Rigid determinists need to produce evidence; they need to show how, and whether, all actions are rigidly determined. A general appeal to the value of science is not good enough. For one thing, the characteristics of scientific explanation have undergone considerable changes during this century. Determinism based on the methodology of the older physical sciences, such as astronomy, now looks less plausible than it did to LaPlace. Not all scientists now believe that science will discover strict and eternal laws which dictate how all things necessarily are in the universe. Those who are seeking to understand human beings focus on the explanatory concepts of biological science rather than on the concepts of physics, mechanics or chemistry. And it is often said that we may have to settle for loose explanations arrived at by reference to whole biological complexes and interactive systems. We cannot hope to discover straightforwardly mechanistic laws which would explain every individual human action because most likely there are no such laws.

It looks as if causation itself is not very 'rigid'. Not everything that is caused is rigidly determined. Much that is caused is rendered probable, not certain. So we need not accept the assumption that 'not rigidly determined' means the same thing as 'random'. Nor, conversely, need we say that if an event is not random it must be fully determined.

Explanations

The theories of free will and determinism are concerned with the explanation of human behaviour. Hence in trying to decide which is correct it is a good idea to ask which has the greater explanatory power. Which concept, the concept of free will or the concept of determinism, best fits the facts of our experience?

If people were not free they would not be responsible for their actions. But if no one was responsible there would be no place in the world for emotions such as gratitude or resentment. It is foolish to feel resentment towards beings which have no power of choice – bacteria for instance. What is more, there would be no sense in forgiveness either. If a human being who chose to injure me was caused to choose by things outside his or her control, if he or she was a mere instrument in a rigidly deterministic universe, how could I forgive? I might as well forgive the force of gravity for causing me to fall downstairs.

Our human reactions of resentment, gratitude, forgiveness, praise, blame, and so on, only make sense on the assumption that we ourselves and other human beings are responsible for our actions, or if not for all our actions, then at least for many of them. (This might be part of what Kant means when he describes the idea of freedom as an Idea of Reason – see chapter 2.)

The supposition that one's own actions are all completely determined is counter-intuitive for human beings. In ordinary life we possess a complex system of explanation which contains ideas like resentment, gratitude, forgiveness, praise, blame, love, hate, etc., not to mention the idea of choice itself. These ideas are too important to us in explaining ourselves and others for us to be able to give them up in favour of a wholly deterministic system of explanation.

Consider this example. The philosopher Mary Midgeley described (in a television broadcast) the diaries of the multiple killer Denis Nilsen. Nilsen's emotionally deprived childhood was very much in keeping with the psychologist's Identikit picture of a type of background that produces a certain kind of criminal. Yet Mary Midgeley's understanding of the diaries is that Nilsen did not think of himself as having had no freedom of choice. He appears to have had a conscience like the rest of us. He states in his diaries that he saw himself as having a good and an evil side. He 'wrestled with himself' when thinking whether or not to commit murder. The evil side eventually won, but it seems that the other side could have triumphed, and might have triumphed.

Mary Midgeley admits that certain types of background make it easier for someone to give in to the evil side, but her main point is that the evidence indicates that evil doers are not mere automata with no free will. Nilsen did not feel like an automaton, he did not feel he had no choice. He believed that, after swaying first one way and then the other, he chose freely to commit murder.

Some might think that Mary Midgeley saw what she wanted to see in those diaries. Yet her account of human agency has the stamp of psychological veracity. The rigid determinist's account does not. We have all experienced the battle of conscience that she talks about. Each individual believes of himself or herself that he/she is not rigidly determined. However inclined one might be to blame one's fate for the bad things that happen, one still silently believes that in some things at least it is one's own choices that make the difference. All our ordinary conversation, and most of our behaviour, shows that we cannot help believing that we are able to act freely. Nilsen too believed he was free to choose, in spite of the way he was affected by the childhood that he had experienced.

The idea that we can make an uncaused choice is not necessarily incoherent. It is not incoherent if we interpret it to mean, not that our choices are random, but rather that they are not fully and rigidly determined by factors outside our control. We ourselves are the causes of our choices. Our choices are caused by us.

The exercise of free will consists in making genuine choices between genuine alternative courses of action. The alternatives have to be genuine, thus for instance we cannot freely choose to breathe through non-existent gills. A genuine alternative is one that is at least minimally possible for human beings. And here we need to remember that human beings are amazingly inventive.

What makes a choice genuine? A genuine choice flows from, is caused by, the person who makes it. Here we have to remember that human beings are not inanimate but dynamic. This is a condition of their causal powers.

Of course a genuine choice has to be made within a framework of more general causation – otherwise it would have no effects.

A genuine choice is also one which is accepted by the person as his or her own choice and responsibility.

We believe that this is a satisfactory explanation of free will. Our kind of free will does not presuppose a random universe, but neither does it allow the possibility that all choices are themselves forced by outside circumstances. We have set up a third way of understanding freedom, a way which asserts that, when complex dynamic livings things (such as human beings) have genuine alternatives, they act, when choosing, as the initiating causes of the effects they bring about. It is from this fact, the sheer fact of complex dynamism, the sheer fact of initiating causes, that the indispensable explanatory ideas of responsibility, blameworthiness, praiseworthiness, gratitude, resentment and forgiveness all flow.

5

The Existence of Evil

The existence of evil is a problem mainly for monotheistic theological traditions in which God is held to be all-loving and all-powerful. There are other religions which worship gods who are neither specially powerful nor specially benevolent. There are also religions which hold that the natures of the gods are unknowable; hence their adherents say that they worship 'unknown gods'.

Polytheism, unlike Christianity, Judaism and Islam, can blame the existence of evil on quarrels between gods who are neither omnipotent nor benevolent.

David Hume states the problem of evil as follows:

> If evil in the world is from the intention of the Deity, then He is not benevolent. If evil in the world is contrary to His intention, then He is not omnipotent. But it is either in accordance with His intention or contrary to it. Therefore, either the Deity is not benevolent or He is not omnipotent.

There is a third possible conclusion, and that is that God does not exist. Hume is never explicit about this third alternative but there are hints in his writings which suggest that he may have seen the problem of evil as evidence that there is no such being as God. For the moment however we will ignore this third alternative.

The Reality of Evil

One possible solution to the problem is to deny that evil is real. But this attempt at an answer is not very convincing. Its

43

weakness becomes apparent as soon as we define what is meant by evil.

It is usual to draw a distinction between the evil perpetrated by mankind and the evil over which human beings have no control. Acts committed by human beings, usually against other human beings, which involve for example cruelty such as torture, may be called morally evil. Such things as famines, diseases and earthquakes in inhabited places are said to be cases of natural evil.

Can it be maintained that cruelty, torture, famines and diseases do not really exist? The suffering associated with human cruelty and natural disasters certainly seems very real.

Some theologians argue that evil might be a purely subjective notion. Perhaps terms like 'bad' and 'evil' are nothing more than adjectives of disapproval, perhaps the statement 'torture is evil' means nothing more than 'I personally am against torturing people'.

But there is a difference between likes and dislikes on the one hand, and good and evil on the other. Likes and dislikes vary from one person to another. Some people like milk in their tea. Others dislike milk and take rum instead. When we consider evil and badness we enter an altogether different conceptual arena. Generally speaking we do indeed dislike that which we consider evil, but not in the trivial sense in which we might have an aversion to strawberries. Furthermore people do not always dislike things which they believe to be evil; some are attracted to that which they consider evil. In any case dislike is not the primary motive for holding that something or other is evil in the first place. Much more fundamental considerations are involved. People apply the term 'evil' to disease, or famine or gratuitous killing for a variety of serious reasons. They may say, for instance, that such things upset the balance of the world, and are not items which a benevolent designer would have included in creation. It is not just that they dislike the idea of mopping up the blood after a murder has been committed.

Is Evil Positive or Negative?

Some philosophers have believed that evil is not a positive thing, but a privation of good. Thus Maimonides writes: 'dying is an ill for man, but it consists in non-being. And likewise disease, poverty, and ignorance are ills that concern him; however they all consist in the non-presence of certain qualities.' He adds: 'one cannot say that God creates an ill. That is simply inconceivable . . . for he creates only Being, and all Being is good. The ills are all privations to which creation does not refer.'

We might agree that the evil of blindness (say) is merely the privation of sight. Yet not all privation is necessarily evil. It would seem trivial to call baldness an evil *qua* privation of hair. On the other hand, malaria sufferers are not merely undergoing a privation of health, or any kind of privation. Malaria consists in an excess not a privation, it consists of an excess of the micro-organism *plasmodium* in the bloodstream.

Another objection to the privation theory concerns evil considered as a causal force. It can be argued that the absence or the privation of something cannot cause anything. Now, even if we congratulate ourselves on being too sophisticated to believe in evil spirits, we do believe that certain persons such as Hitler and Stalin caused tremendous evils, and these evils in turn caused further evils. Since both the men and the states of affairs they brought about were causes (of evils, and of more evils respectively) it seems that neither the men nor their wickedness nor the effects of that wickedness can have been mere negations or privations of anything.

It is not, however, absolutely self-evident that absences cannot cause anything. If absences and privations can indeed be causes, then a hardline defender of the theory that evil is mere privation of good might still hold that the evils of the Third Reich, and the wickedness of the individuals who ruled in the Reich, were nothing but absences and privations. This is perhaps implausible in itself, but that is another matter.

Ultimately, though, the privation theory does not solve the problem of evil. The reason is that the theory merely leads to a new form of the problem. If evil were indeed mere privation of good we still need to ask why it is that these terrible privations of good occur. Why does the Deity allow terrible privations if he is all-benevolent and all-powerful?

Benevolence and Power

Is God's benevolence of a different kind from human benevolence? Should it be judged by human standards?

Suppose it is agreed that human benevolence and God's benevolence are different in kind. Is this a solution to the problem of evil?

The proposed solution invites the question as to whether a God who is not benevolent in the ordinary meaning of that word deserves to be worshipped. On an ordinary notion of benevolence it seems impossible that a benevolent god could command or allow the dreadful pain and evil which exists in the world. If a person herded a group of children into a compound and starved them to death, we would commit this person to a mental hospital, we would lock him up and throw away the key. Yet it seems that an omnipotent god allows children to die from famine every day.

There is also a question as to whether the claim is compatible with Genesis 1:26, where it is said that God made man in his own image. Theologians (and the majority of ordinary lay believers) hold that the likeness between God and mankind does not consist in bodily similarity but rather in a spiritual similarity, a similarity of consciousness.

Should we then deny the generally accepted interpretation of Genesis? David Hume for one seems to think that the idea that God could be anything like human beings is quite wrong-headed:

> And is it possible . . . that . . . you can still persevere in your anthropomorphism, and assert the moral attributes of the Deity, His justice, benevolence, mercy and rectitude to be of the same nature with those in human creatures? His power, we allow, is infinite; whatever He wills is executed; but neither man nor any other animal is happy; therefore He does not will their happiness.

Let us now consider what C. S. Lewis says about evil in his book *The Problem of Pain*. Lewis argues that to reconcile the apparent paradox of an omnipotent and benevolent God with the existence of evil in the world it is necessary to give up one kind of Christian idea about God's love, an idea that he maintains is too dependent on the notion of kindness:

> You asked for a loving God: you have one – not a senile benevolence that drowsily wishes you to be happy in your own way, not the cold philanthropy of a conscientious magistrate . . . but the consuming fire Himself, the love that made the world, persistent as the artist's love for his work . . . jealous, inexorable, exacting as a love between the sexes.

This is a very radical line. Love may well not be properly equated with mere kindness, but Lewis's 'consuming fire' is even less like love as we ordinarily understand it.

Should we then conclude that God is benevolent but not all-powerful? The ironical Hume suggests that the god who designed the universe must have been a failure at the job and should have tried his hand at something else. The creator of our universe, says Hume, might have been a god in his dotage. Or perhaps he was 'an infant deity' still practising his craft.

Leibniz and Voltaire

Leibniz (1646–1716) turned the problem inside out and upside down. He argued that since God must be benevolent and all-powerful, it follows that any world he makes must be the best possible one that can be made. Hence the universe we live in must be 'the best of all possible worlds'.

Voltaire (1694–1778) satirized Leibniz as the character Dr Pangloss in his novel *Candide*. In this work the hero, Candide, imbibes the Panglossian doctrine, or rather the Leibnizian one, and then goes out into the great world to seek his fortune. He experiences an unending series of disasters, but always tries to comfort himself by reciting the teachings of Pangloss. These teachings are made to look more and more ridiculous as diasaster is heaped on disaster.

Good and Evil and Free Will

Perhaps the most satisfactory kind of solution or attempted solution has to do with human free will.

According to this proposed solution, evil is a consequence of the existence of human free will. It is argued that a universe in which there are beings who possess free will is richer and more varied and in some important sense better than one containing only kindly automata. If human beings were always good, that could only be because God had created them as one hundred per cent obedient to his laws, and in that case they would be like mere machines, doing good automatically.

The existence of human free will, then, explains moral evil, and the value of freedom justifies God's decision to create free human beings, who are creatures able to choose both good and evil.

However, even if free will thus offers both an explanation and a justification of the existence of moral evil, it does not seem to explain the sheer quantity of evil. Could we not have had less evil and still had freedom? Intuition suggests that the quantity of evil in the world is greatly in excess of the amount needed to guarantee free will.

Second, the proposed answer does not explain natural evils like floods, famines and disease. If we human beings are free, then of course we must be able to choose evil as well as good, but generally speaking the evils of famine, disease, drought, floods, hurricanes and earthquakes do not result from human choices, even indirectly.

Hume's conclusion is that God's nature is not known to us and cannot be known to us. We cannot know God's attributes, nor the relationships between those attributes.

Atheism and Evil

For those who are already atheists there is of course no *problem* of evil. The universe happens to contain evils, that is just how things happen to be, and there is nothing more to be said. On the other hand, there are some converts to atheism who say that the existence of evil is exactly what convinced them that atheism is correct.

But the problem of evil, so-called, is not a completely sound basis for atheism. The problem is indeed sometimes taken as knock-down proof of God's non-existence, but in fact it is not a knock-down proof of any one particular thesis.

The original problem can be stated as follows.

The three propositions:

Evil exists.
God is all-loving.
God is all-powerful.

are mutually inconsistent – any two of them can be true, but not all three.

There are many possible answers. If experience leads us to reject the first answer (below) we are still left with alternatives, so that atheism (the second answer, below) is not forced upon us; though the other alternatives might not seem any better.

The main possible answers are:

1 Evil does not exist.
2 God does not exist.
3 Evil exists and God exists: he is all-loving but not all-powerful.
4 Evil exists and God exists: he is all-powerful but not all-loving.
5 Evil exists and God exists: he is neither all-loving nor all-powerful.
6 God exists but his nature cannot be known or understood by us.
7 No problem; God's known benevolence, his known power and the known existence of evil are mutually compatible, but their compatibility is a mystery beyond human understanding.

6

The Problem of Knowledge

What do we mean when we claim to know something? How is knowledge related to truth and falsehood, to belief and to evidence?

Knowledge, Truth and Falsehood

Can one know something which is not true? For instance, once upon a time people thought there were only seven planets. Then they thought there were eight. In fact there are nine planets (as far as we know). Did the people in the past who thought there were only seven planets know the numbers of planets? It seems rather that they only thought they knew.

The people of the past believed there are seven planets, but they did not know it, because it is not true. Beliefs can be either true or false but knowledge cannot be false. False beliefs do not count as knowledge.

One ancient view was that knowledge cannot be false because knowing is an infallible faculty or an infallible state of mind. The modern view is that knowledge cannot be false because the definition of the word 'knowledge' is such as to make the idea of false knowledge a contradiction in terms. The two views are not actually incompatible, for it could be the case both that knowledge is true by definition and that it is an infallible state of mind.

We will assume that knowledge is true by definition. We will not discuss infallibility.

Knowledge, Truth and Reasons

Human knowledge must have some connection with mental powers. Knowledge must be a state of mind, or a mental disposition of some kind. It is rather like belief, though belief, as we have seen, can be either true or false whereas knowledge must be true.

According to an old theory, which goes back to Plato, knowledge is the same thing as true belief.

Plato, however, decided that this theory is not quite good enough. The reason is that it is possible to come to believe a truth by accident. Plato's own example, from his dialogue *Meno*, is as follows. Suppose you want to travel to Larissa. You meet a man at a fork in the road and you ask him which road goes to Larissa, the one on the left or the one on the right. This individual has no idea which road goes to Larissa, but like the proverbial Irishman he wants to be helpful so he makes a guess, and tells you in a confident voice 'It's the road on the right.' Off you go, and soon you actually reach Larissa because the man guessed right. Consequently:

1 It was true that the right fork led to Larissa, and
2 You believed that it did.

So you had a true belief.

Plato thinks, though, that this particular true belief is not a case of knowledge. You did not really know how to get to Larissa, you got there because of a happy accident. He therefore added a third element to his description of knowledge. Knowledge, he suggested, is true belief with a reason. If some person X knows something (call it *p*) then:

1 *p* must be true, and
2 X must believe *p*, and
3 X must have a good reason to believe *p*.

In the case of the road to Larissa there was a reason, but it was a poor reason. You believed the word of a kindly but simple-minded stranger who did not know the way himself.

This three-part analysis of knowledge is perhaps the best available, yet it has been widely criticized because it leads to troublesome difficulties.

Knowing-That and Knowing-How

Let us consider some questions about belief.

Does one really have to believe something in order to know it? Do you believe everything you know? The answer must be no, unless an arbitrarily narrow view of knowledge is accepted.

Real knowledge includes practical skills. Examples of practical skills include knowing how to use a sewing machine, how to ride a bicycle, how to mend a broken window, how to forge a cheque. Practical knowledge is knowing-how. Some practical knowledge is instinctive. A baby knows how to cry, for example, and fish know how to swim. Knowing-how is largely a matter of can-do.

Knowing-how is different from knowing-that. Knowing-how is possessing an ability, knowing-that is possessing a bit of information. Possessing information, if you are human, usually means that you believe the information. But having a skill does not mean you believe the skill, because it makes no sense to believe a skill. You can believe that you have a skill, or don't have it, but you can't believe *it*.

If it is conceded that practical skills are a type of knowledge it follows that not all knowledge involves belief.

Three Types of Unconscious Knowledge

Some 'knowing-that' seems to be unconscious, or non-conscious, or buried. It is not clear that unconscious or buried knowledge has to involve belief.

We need not go into the intricacies of Freud's theory of the Unconscious, because there are simpler examples of non-conscious knowledge.

1   Much ordinary humdrum knowledge lies 'at the back of the mind' for much of the time. Often there is no special reason to think about some of the things we know for years on end. Yet there will be no difficulty in recollecting them as soon as we are prompted. This ordinary kind of unconscious knowing appears to be unconnected with any consciously held beliefs, because while the knowledge lies dormant

so too do the corresponding beliefs. Does that matter? If we can accept the idea of unconscious knowledge we can surely also accept the idea of unconscious belief. So the mere fact that some knowledge appears to be unconscious does not necessarily settle the question about whether or not knowledge, i.e. knowing-that, involves belief.

2 Now consider temporary loss of memory of the kind that is not easily removed by prompting. In such a case there is no conscious knowledge and also no conscious belief. Yet often enough when something has been forgotten, the name of an acquaintance for instance, one has the feeling that one 'really' knows the forgotten fact. The English expression used to describe this state of affairs is 'it's on the tip of my tongue'. One can feel absolutely confident that the memory loss is not permanent.

Yet what if the loss of memory turned out to be permanent after all? What if you never did manage to recollect the forgotten name?

Permanent loss of memory is surely nothing more nor less than loss of knowledge. A fact that has been permanently forgotten is a fact no longer known. Although there is indeed a kind of feeling which may occur when one has forgotten something temporarily (i.e. temporarily as it turns out), there is no guarantee that that feeling might not itself be a mistake. Since the feeling of something being 'on the tip of the tongue' does not positively guarantee that you will ever remember the information, then it cannot be known for sure that the memory loss is not permanent. So it follows that you cannot know for sure that you 'really' know the forgotten name.

This kind of unconscious knowledge, then, is such that you cannot know for sure that you have got it: only future events can settle the matter. But perhaps that is what unconscious knowledge ought to be like. And anyway it does not prove that belief (unconscious) is or is not part of unconscious knowledge.

3 Here is a different kind of example. Everyone knows things that they have never thought about. If you have never so much as thought about a possibility surely you cannot have any beliefs about it. The case of never having thought about something is different from the case of having thought about it and then forgotten it.

People know many silly things which they have never given any thought to at all. For instance, you know that you are not descended from a marriage between an oak tree and a tortoise. Yesterday, before you read this ridiculous suggestion on this page, did you consciously hold the belief 'I am not descended from the marriage of an oak tree with a tortoise'? Surely not. You knew it, in a subterranean way, but there was no corresponding conscious belief. Was there a corresponding unconscious belief? That too seems incredible. Where did the unconscious belief come from? Was it once a conscious belief? How can you have a belief about some idea which has never crossed your mind?

This sort of unconscious knowledge concerns facts, often negative in character, which logically follow from other, consciously known, facts. In the example above the fact that you are not descended from a marriage between a tortoise and an oak tree follows from the fact that human beings are generated only from human genetic material. You consciously know and believe that fact about the generation of human beings. You may be said also to know, unconsciously, the negative facts that follow from it. But since you have never even considered the idea of being descended from a tortoise, you do not either believe or disbelieve, consciously or unconsciously, the proposition that you are not so descended. That is, you have no beliefs about this until the idea is presented to you. Then the unconscious knowledge at once becomes conscious, and you simultaneously acquire the relevant belief.

We can conclude that not all knowledge involves belief, first, because some knowing is knowing-how, and second, because one kind of unconscious knowing-that does not presuppose previous thinking about, and therefore does not presuppose conscious or unconscious beliefs.

Nevertheless the original three-part analysis of knowledge has not been completely overturned. Even though it does not fit knowing-how, and does not fit certain recherché examples of unconscious knowledge, it does fit ordinary conscious knowing-that quite well. But the three-part definition has another more serious difficulty.

The Regress of Reasons

The most serious difficulty for the three-part definition of knowledge has to do with evidence and reasons.

What is a good reason? What is good evidence? For instance, what would be good evidence that the road on the right is the road to Larissa? Well, perhaps you have a map, and the map shows the road on the right goes to Larissa. Is this good enough? Plainly not, for maps can be inaccurate; for instance they can be out of date, not showing new roads. Well, suppose we change the example and say that you have actually been to Larissa before and can remember taking the road to the right. Is this good enough? Not really. The road might now be blocked, or a new road might have been built. Or possibly you don't know the difference between left and right.

What does this show? It shows that you need to know the map is up to date and accurate, you need to know that there have been no road-building works, you need to know the difference between left and right. In other words, in order to know which is the road to Larissa you first have to know other things. But then, in order for you to know those other things you will, by the same reasoning, have to know yet other things: and so on *ad infinitum*. Thus:

1   X knows the road on the right goes to Larissa =
    i   It is true that the right-hand road goes to Larissa, plus
    ii X believes that the right-hand road goes to Larissa, plus
    iii X has good reason for this belief.
        Now, *iii* above, viz. X has good reason for the belief that the road on the right goes to Larissa, means:

2   X *knows* the map is accurate and *knows* the difference between left and right (etc.)
        Since this mentions knowing it must be analysed as:
    iv It is true that map is accurate (etc.), plus
    v   X believes that the map is accurate (etc.), plus
    vi X has good reason for the belief that the map is accurate (etc.).
        But *vi* above, viz. X has good reason for his belief that the map is accurate (etc.) means:

3   X *knows* the map is up to date and *knows* there have been no road works. Since this also mentions *knowing* it must be analysed as:
    vii It is true that the map is up to date (etc.), plus
    viii X believes that the map is up to date (etc.), plus

ix X has good reason to believe that the map is up to date.

And *ix*, viz. X has good reason to believe that the map is up to date (etc.) means:

4 X knows the map is labelled '1999' – which must be analysed as:

   x It is true that the map is labelled '1999', and

   xi X believes . . .

   xii X has good reason . . . .

And so on, and so on, forever.

In short, if the three-part analysis of knowledge is correct, then in order to know one small thing one would have to know an infinite number of things. But since the human mind is finite this is impossible. Therefore knowledge is impossible for human beings.

This troublesome conclusion goes against common sense. Even if the answer to the Riddle of the Universe remains unknown, we human beings do know some other more simple things. We know what we had for breakfast, for instance, and many of us know how many yards there are in a mile, and what is the capital city of France, and things like that.

Sceptics hold that knowledge is impossible. But non-sceptics look for possible answers; and of these there are several.

'Knowledge is Practical, not Theoretical'

The pragmatist, or practical person, argues that although there is an infinite regress of reasons in theory, in practice the regresss comes to a halt quite soon. We ought to grasp the nettle and agree that human knowledge is finite. Well, what is this finite human knowledge? The pragmatist answers: human knowledge is what works in practice. If our methods of obtaining information work in practice, then that is good enough. In practice, of course, it is fairly easy to get to Larissa, provided one uses up-to-date maps, or relies on sensible testimony from responsible people.

'The Regress is Harmless: Human Reasoning is Unending'

Another possible solution begins by asking rhetorically: What is so bad about an infinite regress? Maybe there is indeed an infinite regress involved in the analysis of knowledge, but what's the problem? No one human mind is infinite of course, but the total mental power of the human race is unending. The human race keeps on finding out more and more things. Knowledge is not a static state of the individual, it is a sort of process of discovery, engaged in by the whole species, and that process may well go on forever – it just depends on how long the human race lasts.

The drawback of this answer is that while it allows that the total human race, past, present and future, has genuine knowledge, it does not allow that individuals can genuinely know things. But common sense tells us that individuals in fact know plenty of things.

'The Regress is not Infinite but a Circle'

According to this proposed solution the regress of reasons is not infinite but goes around in a big circle and comes back to its starting point. Knowing *a* means first knowing *b* which means first knowing *c* (and so on), but the process is not infinite, because when we get to knowing *z* (for instance) we find that knowing *z* means knowing *a* – and so we start all over again.

The trouble with this is that a vicious circle is just as bad as an infinite regress. For if knowing *a* means you have to know *b*, *c*, *d* . . . *z*, and if knowing *z* means you have to know *a*, why start on the progress in the first place? You end up saying that in order to know *a* you must know *a*, which is a pretty feeble statement to say the least.

'The Regress is not Infinite but Finite'

According to this solution, if we follow the regress of reasons it will always end with a reason which needs no reason. Such a reason would be either a self-evident axiom or some piece of 'irresistible' information presented to the mind by the senses, for instance, the perception of pain.

The idea that knowledge has a foundation in truths which are absolutely or relatively certain is called epistemological foundationalism. Perhaps the most famous foundationalist is Descartes, who says that human knowledge is founded on the proposition 'I think therefore I exist'. Other foundationalists claim that knowledge starts with the self-evident axioms of mathematics or of logic, for example '1 + 1 = 2' or 'a thing is itself and not another thing'. Others again say knowledge starts with primitive sensory experience.

One drawback of foundationalism is that no one has ever proved that every piece of human knowledge rests on self-evident truths, and no one has ever proved that human knowledge always rests on sensory experience. So these proposed solutions are only hypotheses. Still, they seem to be useful hypotheses which might perhaps combine well with the pragmatist's answer to the infinite regress problem.

Ramsey's Answer

Frank Ramsey (1903–30) suggests that having good reasons for a belief means that you obtained the belief by 'a reliable process'.

He asks: Is memory a reliable process? Is telepathy a reliable process? Is intuition a reliable process? And he decides that all these processes *could* be reliable, provided that in each case there is a chain of causes and effects linking the information which is remembered (or telepathized, or intuited, or whatever) with the memory (or the intuition, or the telepathic communication, or whatever).

A chain of causes and effects of the right kind, which connects one's experiences with one's beliefs, ensures that the beliefs are true and therefore cases of genuine knowledge.

The drawback with Ramsey's theory seems to be that knowledge remains impossible because the infinite regress remains with us, in another form. It rears its ugly head as soon as we try to decide what processes are reliable. It looks as if that question can only be answered if we have a reliable process for getting to the answer. And that seems to lead to an infinite regress of reliable processes. For in order to have real knowledge one would need to *know* that the reliable process really was a reliable process; one would need a reliable process for testing reliable processes.

Ramsey himself, in his very short paper, does not say whether he thinks his idea will solve the problem of the infinite regress.

The definitions of knowledge produced by philosophers relate to a sort of ideal, a static, unchanging state of mind or state of affairs. But perhaps real knowledge is more ambiguous. In real life it is not only matters that have been finally proven beyond all shadow of doubt that are said to be known. Often in science current theories are said to be *known*; yet at the same time it is accepted as a fundamental principle that old theories continually give way to new ones. The expression 'our present state of knowledge' suggests that knowledge itself can be as it were temporary in character. If 'the present state of knowledge' turns out to be rather short-lived there is the escape route available of saying 'we didn't know after all'.

Knowledge is also related to what works in practice. This, the prag-matist's conception of knowledge, turns up in many areas of life. Now, the difference between what works in practice and what does not is not a difference in kind but a difference in degree. Some ideas work better than others, and then give way to new ideas which work better still. Often we say we *know* when we have good reason to think we are operating with the best available ideas. Sensible people never claim infallibility. They claim that they know – as far as they know.

7

Scepticism Old and New

Varieties of Scepticism

There are different kinds of scepticism. Sceptics can be people who like to suspend judgement till the last possible moment before making up their minds; or people who distrust conventional views on religion, or politics, or morality; or people who distrust authority of any sort.

Philosophical scepticism, however, goes beyond ordinary distrust and ordinary cynicism. It can take two forms: either it casts doubt on beliefs and theories that seem to most people to constitute genuine knowledge, or else it positively denies propositions that most people take for granted. Bishop Berkeley (1685–1753), who positively denied the existence of material objects, was a sceptic of the second kind. In fact he said he wasn't a sceptic at all because sceptics ought to feel doubt whereas he claimed to have no doubts whatsoever about the reality, or rather, the unreality, of matter. However, Berkeley's definition of scepticism was too narrow.

Philosophical scepticism can affect different branches of enquiry, or all branches of enquiry. It also has a variety of motivations. Thus the principle behind *methodological scepticism* is that knowledge cannot be achieved except by temporarily rejecting as false every proposition that can possibly be doubted. By doing this one will eventually reach knowledge in the form of propositions which it is impossible to doubt. This is a method usually attributed to René Descartes, who claimed to have discovered an absolutely doubt-free principle, namely, 'I think therefore I exist'. Methodological scepticism is merely temporary or pretended scepticism, so we will not be further concerned with it in this chapter.

Limited scepticism involves either doubting, or rejecting, the possibility of genuine truth and knowledge in some one particular field. For example, there can be scepticism about morality (which we discuss in chapter 8) or scepticism about scientific induction (which we discuss in chapter 19), and in the eighteenth and nineteenth centuries philosophers worried about whether the five senses can be relied on to give knowledge about the material world. Limited forms of scepticism have a tendency to expand. Thus doubts about the existence of the material world lead into doubts about the reality of time and space and causation, while doubts about the existence of other minds lead into doubts about personal identity as such.

Total ('global') scepticism rejects the possibility of objective truth and knowledge in every field of enquiry. It involves the idea that there is no such thing as knowledge, no such thing as truth and no such thing as reason. According to this view 'truth', 'knowledge' and 'reason' are meaningless words, mere empty noises.

A Brief History of Philosophical Scepticism

Scepticism has a long history. It can be said to begin with the Greek philosophers Pyrrho and Protagoras.

Pyrrho (4th–3rd century BC) was a priest of Elis who argued that one should seek tranquillity by following custom rather than by trying to abide by positive beliefs. His philosophical method consisted in confronting every possible belief with a plausible opposite belief, and he personally refused to commit himself to any positive belief whatsoever. Unlike modern sceptics he seems to have made serious efforts to live according to sceptical principles, one result being that – according to legend – he had to be repeatedly protected from danger by his friends. For he held that one cannot *know* that anything is dangerous. Pyrrho thus illustrates a fact mentioned by Hume, namely, that a reasoned belief in sceptical principles does not make it safe to live by those principles.

Protagoras (490–420 BC) was famous in his time for sceptical agnosticism regarding the existence of the gods. Today his best-known doctrine is: 'man is the measure of all things'. This saying means that all perceptions and all beliefs are true – *but only for the persons whose perceptions and beliefs they are*. He is therefore understood to have denied the very possibility of objective truth, all 'truth' being subjective and personal.

Plato attacked Protagoras's theory, arguing that it is self-refuting. For if all subjective beliefs are equally true, then the belief 'some subjective beliefs are not true' is just as true as any other. Plato's attack on scepticism has retained its original force and is often cited, or adapted, in modern philosophy.

During the sixteenth and seventeenth centuries scepticism frequently took the form of questioning standard religious beliefs. Thomas Hobbes (1588–1679), for example, and Baruch Spinoza (1632–77) both questioned the then orthodox view of the Old Testament according to which the first five books of that document, the Pentateuch, were written by Moses. They noted that Moses' death is recorded in the Pentateuch and wondered how he could have recorded his own demise.

In the seventeenth and eighteenth centuries scepticism began to involve doubts about the reality of matter (or substance) and about the reliability of the five senses. This was in part a result of the work of three famous British philosophers, the Englishman John Locke, the Irishman George Berkeley and the Scotsman David Hume.

Locke drew a distinction between the primary and secondary qualities of material things. The primary qualities, he said, are shape, size, solidity, number and movement and rest. These really belong to objects and are more or less as we perceive them with the senses. The secondary qualities, which include colours, sounds, smells and tastes, do not really belong to objects but are created, as it were, by the reaction of the eyes and ears and taste buds to light, and to movements of 'minute particles' on the surfaces of objects and in the air. Secondary qualities thus turn out to be merely the effects of primary qualities, for movement is a primary quality. Sounds, for instance, are really only vibrations in the air which affect the ears, while colours are only light rays which affect the eyes – and so on.

Locke was not a sceptic strictly speaking, but his discussions about the existence of a substance underlying the primary and secondary qualities of material things, and his conclusion that substance is 'I know not what', make him seem like one.

Bishop Berkeley argued that primary qualities are no more real than secondary qualities and concluded that the only realities are ideas in the mind, and minds themselves. Thus he was led to deny the existence of matter altogether. What we see and hear and touch are ideas in the mind. And about the reality of our ideas we need feel no sceptical doubts because that reality is guaranteed by God.

Locke probably believed in substance, even though he described it as 'I know not what'; Berkeley's denial of matter, partly on the grounds that if it existed it would be inert and useless, astonished the multitude, as his commemorative window in the chapel of Trinity College, Dublin so aptly states.

David Hume's work on the topic appeared first in his *A Treatise of Human Nature*, and especially in the two chapters 'Of scepticism with regard to reason' and 'Of scepticism with regard to the senses'. As can be seen from these chapter titles, his scepticism is more wide-ranging than Berkeley's. On the other hand Hume is also the author of a rather telling practical argument against scepticism. We discuss that argument later in this chapter.

Locke, Berkeley and Hume are jointly labelled 'the British Empiricists' for the reason that their arguments, sceptical or otherwise, are based on empirical considerations; Locke in particular based his reasonings on the science of his day.

The Refutation of Scepticism

In this section we will discuss some ways of refuting scepticism, particularly the wider forms. The widest possible form is what we have called global scepticism, which nowadays is embraced by many influential British and American professors in English Literature and Modern Languages. There are even some fashionable global sceptics who claim to be teaching philosophy.

Note that modern scepticism has acquired a lot of new names, including *post-modernism*, *total relativism*, *constructivism* and *neo-pragmatism*.

Contemporary relativistic doctrines deny the existence and even the possibility of objective truth and objective reason. Truth, knowledge and reason, it is said, are creations of human minds and differ from mind to mind. Differences of opinion, it is said, should never be seen in terms of a true/false dichotomy but always as products of a local culture or a personal history.

Modern sceptics overlook the fact that an opinion's having an origin is compatible with its having a truth value. Moreover, they tend to rely on all-purpose comments about reason in general and reply to criticism by simply repeating those comments.

Plato, as we have seen, rejected the doctrines of Protagoras on the grounds that they are self-refuting. In our opinion this objection to scepticism retains its force in so far as the claims of global scepticists tend to rely on the concepts they pretend to abolish. Thus if global sceptics believe 'It is true that there is no such thing as truth', it is clear that they have refuted themselves. Some sceptics feel worried by the accusation of self-refutation and try to rebut it; others do not.

The worried ones try to rebut the accusation by arguing that the sceptical claim 'there is no such thing as truth' escapes criticism if it is itself relativized. But that is a mistake. The reason is that the relativization of relativism generates a paradox. In other words, the common claim (that the sceptic can rebut criticism by saying 'I believe, but you might not, that scepticism is true') is simply wrong. The relativized sentence just quoted is not, indeed, self-refuting; instead, it is paradoxical. It means 'I believe p and p is self-refuting', a statement which exemplifies the paradox 'I believe p and p is false', called Moore's paradox after the Cambridge philosopher G. E. Moore. (As far as we know we are the first authors to notice that attacks on relativism cannot be refuted by relativizing the relativist's own claims.)

On the other hand, the really thoroughgoing global sceptics will not be worried by any refutation, because they reject the concept of refutation itself. If someone has already rejected the concepts of truth and falsity he or she might just as well reject the ideas of sound and unsound arguments and thereby the idea of refutation. In this way the sceptical position eventually becomes impervious to all rational criticism. For rational criticism relies on the notions of truth versus untruth, validity versus fallacy and reason versus irrationality. Modern sceptics, then, differ quite radically from their predecessors. Earlier sceptics, even Protagoras, and possibly even Pyrrho, believed in the power of reason; many modern sceptics are *irrationalists*.

Let us now return to Hume and his practical objections to scepticism. Hume's argument rests on the premise that reason, on the one hand, and human nature on the other, are in conflict. Reason tells us (or seems to tell us!) that personal identity is a myth and that morality is not based on objective truths but on sympathy and social convenience. Reason tells us (or seems to tell us!) that our five senses cannot give us indubitable information about the existence or nature of an external world. Reason tells us (or seems to tell us!) that induction is unsound and that deduction cannot generate new knowledge. In short, reason itself tells us that reason cannot show that our beliefs are rational or well-founded.

Hume writes: '[I am] ready to reject all belief and reasoning, and can look upon no opinion even as more probable or likely than another.' But he adds: '. . . it happens, that since reason is incapable of dispelling these clouds, nature herself suffices for that purpose.' In other words, our human nature makes scepticism impossible. We cannot live by our sceptical principles but must behave as nature dictates.

Hume's reasoning can be developed as follows. Global sceptics claim that a belief in objective truth is the result of merely optional ways of using language. Traditional education, they say, trains students in this option which involves the idea that assertions are not normally relativized. But, say the sceptics, students can be taught how to use the linguistic conventions of post–modernism in which every statement is qualified by a Protagorian relativization.

That sceptical linguistic conventions can be taught is indeed true but, as Hume might have said, such conventions cannot affect behaviour. Being taught sceptical ways of speech is not like learning ordinary informal logic. Ordinary informal logic, the language of objective truth and falsehood, is absorbed in childhood. It is absorbed as the child learns how to cope with reality; with parents and siblings and pets, with standing up and falling over, with roads and sidewalks, with food and drink, with fire; and later with items like money, and timetables, and friendship and enmity. The word *assertion* isn't a piece of verbal elastic which can be given a special sceptical sense; on the contrary, it denotes a human activity which meshes with all our other activities. The linguistic conventions of modern scepticism (if they actually exist) do not and cannot mesh with the rest of human life. College students can be taught jargon but they cannot be taught to *behave* as sceptics. If they tried to behave as sceptics they would not go to lectures, or write essays, or attend exams or even order meals. If all knowledge is impossible how can one know that the lecture timetable is accurate or that the meal isn't poisonous?

Global scepticism is quite ancient, yet it renews itself from time to time. It would be interesting to know why, for what new or old reasons, it reappears at intervals in human history. Attempts at explaining the phenomenon have recently been put forward by various authors. Hilary Putnam, for example, speaks of 'the appeal which all incoherent ideas seem to have'. Thomas Nagel claims that in modern times global scepticism appeals most to academics teaching in fields other than philosophy. Perhaps these academics are trying to acquire the label 'philosopher', which sounds more grand than 'assistant professor of spoken Dutch' or even 'full professor of Spanish'. Roger Kimball, in his book *Tenured Radicals*, suggests that the popularity of global relativism, at least in America, can be traced to the arrival there in 1947 of Paul de Man, a Nazi collaborator. The notion that objective knowledge is impossible was allegedly adopted by de Man as a smokescreen to disguise the facts of his life in Europe as an anti-Semite.

Modern sceptics make much of the fact that the origins of many ideas are cultural. Now, tracing the origin of ideas, be they coherent or incoherent, is a task for historians of philosophy and is not the same enterprise as examining the validity or otherwise of arguments, or the truth or otherwise of premises. To confuse or meld these three equally important yet very different tasks is part and parcel of global scepticism itself. For, as we have already seen, scepticism in our time claims that once the cultural or psychological origins of a theory have been described, everything that can be said about it has been said. Plato, Hobbes, Hume and others have shown by example that this just isn't so.

Part II
Ethics: The Philosophy of Value

8

Morality and Illusion

It is quite common to hear people say that morality as such is 'all a matter of opinion'; goodness, like beauty, they say, lies in the eye of the beholder.

Where does this idea come from? And what does it mean? We can best decide what it means after examining the theories of philosophers on the point. So let us consider its origins.

The idea that morality has no basis except in people's opinions is a very old one, are least as old as the works of Plato. The character Thrasymachus, in Plato's dialogue *The Republic*, affirms this kind of view of morality. Hence when modern philosophers reaffirm it they are reinventing the wheel. The popularity of the view may be partly due to its familiarity. But will the wheel roll?

Schopenhauer and Nietzsche

Although the idea that morality is in some sense an illusion is very old, its main historical thrust for us today probably comes from authors of the nineteenth century, and specifically from Schopenhauer (1788–1860) and Nietzsche (1844–1900).

Schopenhauer says that morality is not discovered but created. His admirer Nietzsche describes morality as a fiction – but a necessary fiction, a fiction that mankind cannot possibly live without. It is worth noting that Nietzsche holds that mankind believes in, and needs, several 'necessary fictions', of which morality is only one. His other 'fictions' are more metaphysical; they include the belief that events have causes and the belief in the existence of the material world. Nietzsche was not just a sceptic about ethics, he was also a sceptic about science, politics, the existence of the physical world and even reason itself.

Since Nietzsche's time the philosophical wheel we have been discussing has been reinvented several times, typically by the logical positivists during the first half of the twentieth century, and again by the empiricist philosopher J. L. Mackie in the second half.

Emotivism

The point of view of logical positivism is well expressed by A. J. Ayer in his famous book *Language, Truth and Logic*.

Ayer held that ethical philosophy has nothing to do with behaviour. Ethical philosophy is concerned only with the meanings of words. He goes on to argue that words like 'good', 'right', 'wrong' and so on, do not describe anything in the real world, they merely express emotion. Hence Ayer's theory is called the emotive theory of ethics, or emotivism.

According to the emotive theory all sentences containing ethical terms like 'good' and 'bad' do nothing except express the speaker's emotional states. Sentences of the form 'I approve of such and such' or 'I disapprove of so and so', which might appear to be about the speaker's attitudes, in fact are not about attitudes at all. They *express* attitudes, or emotions, but they are not about anything. Ethical words and sentences have no more significance than the expletives 'Boo!' and 'Bother!' and 'Hurrah!' A sentence like 'it is your duty to care for your parents' merely expresses the speaker's emotional desire to have you care for your parents. He or she might just as well have said 'Caring for parents – Hurrah!'

For this reason emotivism bears the nickname 'the boo–hurrah theory of ethics'.

It is part and parcel of the theory that ultimately there is no reason to prefer 'Boo!' to 'Hurrah!' in any particular case. I can say 'Boo!' and you can say 'Hurrah!' and either response will always be equally okay.

Opponents of this aspect of logical positivism respond to Ayer by saying that if he were right about ethics it would be impossible to have moral arguments. But people have arguments about morality all the time. They argue about who is to blame for this or that, and they argue about the rights and wrongs of racism and anti-racism, and personal decisions, and political decisions, and sexual conduct, and so on and so on and so on. These arguments and discussions would make no sense at all if moral statements could all be boiled down to 'Boo!' and 'Hurrah!' Yet moral discussions and arguments do seem to make sense.

More generally, emotivism does not fit human experience. It is virtually impossible to think of the works of Hitler and Stalin (for example) as things which cannot be objectively described as wicked and bad, and it is humanly impossible to regard the expletive 'Hurrah' as a suitable reaction to deeds of cruelty.

Relativity and 'Queerness'

Let us now turn to J. L. Mackie's theory.

Mackie identifies two arguments which he thinks can be used to show that morality is an illusion. The first he calls 'the argument from relativity'. Mackie believes that there are significant variations between the moral codes of different countries and different religions and different periods of history. These variations suggest to him the hypothesis that moral codes merely express different ways of life, and the hypothesis that no one way of life is morally better than another. A man is a monogamist not because he sees that monogamy is morally good, but merely because he lives in a monogamous society. Ditto for polygamy.

An opponent might object, for three reasons.

First, he or she might argue that differences in moral opinion prove nothing. After all, different scientists have different theories about the origin of the universe (say), or about the cause of AIDS, yet we do not conclude that scientific truth lies in the eye of the beholder; we do not think that science is 'all a matter of opinion'.

Second, the opponent of Mackie might object that it is simply untrue that people always accept the way of life of the country they belong to. Slaves in a slave society do not always accept the way of life represented by slavery, women do not always accept without question the polygamous way of life, or more generally the status of women in their own society, citizens living under dictatorships show by their actions (when not totally crushed) that they believe that dictatorships are morally bad in a objective sense, and not merely as 'a matter of opinion'. People living under oppressive dictatorships very often want to do more than simply say 'Boo!'

A third and perhaps more positive objection to Mackie's theory is the claim that differences in moral codes are not deep. All moral codes, it can be argued, have in common certain very general principles. It is these principles that represent true, objective morality. Physical differences in climate, and in work patterns, and so on, produce superficial variations in codes, but deep down humanity agrees on a truly objective set of moral principles.

Unfortunately this positive claim could only be proved or rebutted by amassing vast quantities of anthropological and historical evidence. Since this information is probably not available at present we will have to leave the claim up in the air. It might be true and it might be false. No one knows.

Yet even if it were true that all peoples at all times have held to a small central core of moral principles, it does not follow that morality is not an illusion. Some illusions are very widespread and it might be that morality is one of those. This shows that counting heads cannot prove that Mackie's thesis is false, and hence shows that counting heads cannot show that it is true. Thus Mackie's argument about relativity, and the suggested argument against his argument, both turn out to be irrelevant.

Mackie calls his second argument in favour of the theory that morality is an illusion 'the argument from queerness'. He says that if objective moral values did exist they would be very queer entities, different from anything else in the universe. Goodness for instance is not like redness: it cannot be seen with the eyes. It is not like smoothness, it cannot be felt with the fingers. It is not like weight, because it cannot be measured. Therefore it is 'queer'. Or rather, argues Mackie, since it would be queer if it did exist, it must be the case that it does not exist.

So maybe the first question to ask is: How do we know that 'queer' entities do not exist? Queerness, whatever that means, is not necessarily a bar to existence.

Next, if goodness really is 'queer' we must ask what entities or qualities are 'normal'. For instance, how are we to classify such qualities and entities as force, necessity, the gene, the electron, and Einstein's space-time continuum? None of these things can be directly seen or heard or tasted or touched, and not all of them can be measured. Does that mean that they too are all 'queer', and so illusory? Surely not. We know about these entities by means other than simple sight and touch.

Queerness itself seems to be in the eye of the beholder. Who is to say which entities or qualities are 'queer', and which are 'normal'? To a layman the Einsteinian space-time continuum certainly seems rather queer, nevertheless most educated people think that Einstein probably knew what he was talking about. Queerness is a more subjective notion than value itself: it is therefore not a strong foundation for Mackie's theory.

Mackie asks: If moral values are an illusion, why do people believe in them? Where does the illusion come from? And he answers: We have this illusion because the belief in values is upheld by society, and continually reinforced by society. Society cannot work without discipline, and the illusion of morality helps to maintain discipline. The need for discipline is universal in human communities, hence the belief in the existence of goodness, badness, rightness, wrongness, is also universal.

Mackie says that morality is rather like a system of law from which the legislator has been removed, an idea reminiscent of Nietzsche's well-known statement 'God is dead'. Ultimately, morality is an offshoot either of positive government legislation, or of religion, or of both. Moral objectivists often hold that human life has ends or goals. Thus for example utilitarians (see chapter 10) say that the goal of life is general happiness, and that a good person will work for the greatest happiness of the greatest number. Those who link morality to religion may say that the goal of human life is to achieve union with God (Christianity), or to enter Paradise (Islam).

Mackie believes that no goal can have objective worth, since all worth lies in the eye of the beholder. He mentions, too, the fact that, as far as religion goes, the god or gods with whom believers wish to be united are very various, depending on the society the believer belongs to. The idea that anything at all has objective worth is an error. Worth, like morality itself, is a human invention.

It is not necessarily an error to think that human inventions can contain objective truths. Cartesian geometry is a human invention – it was invented by René Descartes; differential calculus is a human invention – it was invented by Isaac Newton. These human inventions enable us to get at objective (mathematical) truths. Indeed one might easily argue that all abstract ideas are human inventions. Only human beings are aware of abstract ideas as far as we know.

Nietzsche holds that the fiction of morality is a necessary fiction. Mackie too seems to think that the 'error' is necessary. But it is not easy to understand how something necessary could be a fiction, an error, unless every useful abstract idea is an error.

Perhaps the explanation is this. Values are not physical objects, they cannot be seen or touched. Their reality cannot be tested by a direct use of the eyes and the ears. In so far as it makes sense to speak of the reality of an abstract idea, that reality must be connected, not with what can be perceived by the five senses, but with some other factor in our lives. Perhaps necessity is the best possible test for the reality of an abstract idea.

9
Egoism and Altruism

In the last chapter we considered questions about the reality of valus. In this chapter we will examine problems connected with ethical motivation, problems having to do with selfishness and unselfishness.

Let us begin by defining egoism and altruism.

Egoism can be defined either as (1) systematic selfishness, or as (2) the theory that bases morality on self-interest.

Altruism can be defined as (1) systematic unselfishness, the principle of living for the good of others, or as (2) the theory that bases morality on the good of others; the opposite of theoretical egoism.

Each definition has two parts. The first part refers to motivation (selfishness or unselfishness) and to a personal trait (the trait of being systematically motivated by selfishness or unselfishness, as the case may be). The second part refers to a philosophical theory which bases morality on self-interest, or on the interests of others (as the case may be). It is the theories, not the personal traits, that are of interest to philosophy.

There are four kinds of philosophical theory which have to do with egoism. We will call them 'ego theories'.

The first kind of ego theory purports to give an empirical description of human nature. We will call this the ego theory of cynicism.

A second kind of ego theory is trivially verbal, depending on confused definitions of the words 'desires', 'wants' and 'likes'. We will call this verbalistic ego theory, or verbalism.

A third kind of ego theory states that only selfish motives are rational. We will call this the ego theory of rationality.

A fourth kind of ego theory asserts that it is good to be selfish and bad to be unselfish. For want of a better term we will call this the 'Nietzschean' ego theory.

Ego Theories: Cynicism

Empirical ego theory purports to describe human nature. It has two varieties or sub-types, ordinary cynicism and theoretical cynicism.

Ordinary cynicism is the view that all human beings are whole-heartedly selfish. According to the cynic even apparently altruistic actions are selfish 'deep down'. He holds that if you look long enough you will discover hidden selfishness behind every human action.

This viewpoint at least has the merit of encouraging us to examine our motives rather carefully. But in the end it must depend on facts, and facts do not seem to support it. Human behaviour is indeed often selfish, but it can also be unselfish, even heroically self-sacrificing. Examples of heroes and saints are not numerous, but they seem to show that not all human behaviour is base. Most people seem to be a mixture of the selfish and the altruistic, the exact mixture depending on many circumstances. Cynics deny this, but their dogmatic denial necessarily ignores the evidence.

The notion that human beings are essentially self-interested, non-social, competitive and aggressive seems to get some support from one very great philosopher, namely Thomas Hobbes. In his book *Leviathan*, Hobbes seemingly argues that people only co-operate with one another for selfish reasons. This particular interpretation of Hobbes has had some influence on British and American moral and political phi-losophy. Yet there is reason to think that Hobbes did not really believe that people are purely selfish, he only thought he did.

John Aubrey relates an anecdote about Hobbes, as follows. A friend saw Hobbes giving alms to a beggar and asked him to explain why he had done that. According to Aubrey, Hobbes explained his appar-ently unselfish action by saying that the alms not only relieved the beggar's distress but also relieved Hobbes' own distress at the sight of the misery of the beggar. In other words, Hobbes claimed that he had a selfish reason for giving, namely, to relieve his own distress.

We might question whether Hobbes' explanation really does reduce his altruistic action to egoism. Might it not rather show that in giving alms his altruism showed itself in the very fact of his distress? Hobbes did not say he gave money in order to get money back, or in order to impress people, or because a powerful person had ordered him to, or even because he was frightened of human or divine punishment. These would have been egoistic reasons. But what he actually said was that he gave the alms in order to relieve his own (and the beggar's) distress.

Well, but is that egoism? Surely it is altruism; surely distress at another's distress is an altruistic feeling *par excellence*. If we deny that, it can only be on verbal grounds, it can only be because we refuse to *describe* distress at another's distress as altruism. In such case we will have left the area of empirical knowledge of human nature and entered the area of verbalism; for more on which see below.

Theoretical cynicism is a useful general label for psychological and psychoanalytical doctrines like the thesis of the pleasure principle. The thesis basically is that under the veneer of altruism every person is secretly motivated by a search for pleasure. Theoretical cynicism, like ordinary cynicism, is answerable to empirical evidence and, like ordinary cynicism, it might fail this test.

In modern times the idea that human beings are naturally selfish has become rather doubtful. This is because the whole question is now embroiled with the theory of the so-called 'selfish gene'. According to this theory the only really selfish thing is the gene. Human beings (and other animals) behave sometimes selfishly and sometimes unselfishly, depending on circumstances. Much or most human and animal behaviour is governed by the selfishness of their genes, whose 'aim' is to survive *qua* genes. Roughly speaking, when the situation is such that the sacrifice of an individual will give its genes the best chance of survival, then that individual will behave altruistically and die for others. In other situations selfishness on the part of the individual will be better for the survival chances of its genes, and in such cases it will behave selfishly.

The theory of the selfish gene is excitingly but confusingly expressed. Selfishness implies conscious choice and consciousness, and the gene is not conscious. We must take the word 'selfish' as a metaphor only.

If the theory of the selfish gene is true it rebuts any empirically-based idea that human beings are always motivated by egoism and selfishness, it rebuts both types of cynical ego theory. Altruism in the form of genuine self-sacrifice turns out to belong to the repertoire of natural human responses.

Ego Theories: Verbalism

Verbal ego theory rests on a misunderstanding of language.

It runs somewhat as follows. If you help another person because you like him and therefore want to help, or because you generally like being helpful, or because you desire the good of others, that is still selfishness. It is maintained that any distress, whether at one's own suffering or at another's, is always one's own distress and therefore egoistic in its very nature; any desire, even the desire for another person's welfare and happiness, is always one's own desire.

The objection to the theory is that someone's *feeling distress*, or *having a desire*, is not the same thing as the *content* of that distress, or the *content* of that desire. The content of a desire is what the desire is *about*. The content of distress is what the distress is *about*. The contents of just one person's desires differ from one another, though in each case, of course, that one person remains the person who is having the desire.

The verbal ego theory muddles up the truth that the desire, the wanting, the distress, etc. must *belong* to the person who feels them, with the completely different, and false, notion that the desire, the wanting, the distress, are all and always *about* the person who feels them.

The Ego Theory of Rationality

The ego theory of rationality asserts that actions which are motivated by self-interest are more rational than those motivated by altruism.

The superior rationality of self-interest is apparently taken to be self-evident by the philosophers who believe it. They allow that unselfish actions are humanly possible, but claim that self-interest is nevertheless the only *rational* basis for action.

Since the doctrine is taken to be self-evident it is not argued for, but treated rather as if it were axiomatic. Once such an axiom is accepted the question of 'the possibility of altruism' becomes enormously problematic.

It is not too easy to convince people that what they hold as self-evident is perhaps not self-evident after all. If some philosophers say that the rationality of self-interested action is as evident as the truth of the equation $1 + 1 = 2$, can one show them that it isn't so? It is no use trying to prove that egoism does not pay, for that line of argument does not overturn their axiom, but rather accepts it.

On the other hand, it can be seen, from that very consideration, that self-interestedness, if rational, is rational purely and simply on its own terms. It is rational because it produces good results for the self.

The fact that egoistic actions tend to benefit oneself rather than others is no reason to give up egoism if you believe that benefiting the self is self-evidently reasonable and benefiting others self-evidently unreasonable. The egoist says 'Naturally I'm not helping others – so what? I'm being rational according to my own definition of rationality, so I must be on philosophically safe ground.'

But is the ground safe? It seems not, for the reasoning can be turned upside down. The altruist can affirm that altruism too is rational – on its own terms. It is rational because it produces good results for others. The fact that altruistic actions generally tend to benefit others rather than oneself will not be a reason to give up altruism for anyone who believes that benefiting others is self-evidently reasonable and benefiting oneself self-evidently unreasonable. The altruist says 'Naturally I'm not furthering my own interests – so what? I'm being rational according to my own definition of rationality, so I too am on philosophically safe ground.'

What does common sense say here? It says two things. First of all, common sense tells us that an individual who ignores his or her own welfare for no good purpose, who is wilfully self-destructive for example, is probably mentally disturbed. At the other extreme common sense also tells us that an individual who tries always to act in a purely selfish way is completely unreasonable. Indeed unremittingly selfish behaviour counts as a standard case of unreasonableness, according to common sense.

A policy of total selfishness is perceived by common sense as basically unreasonable.

A policy of total altruism is seen by common sense as good, but probably unnecessary, and possibly quixotic. Altruism which has unachievable ends, for instance, is quixotic.

A policy of self-destruction is seen by common sense as mad, but so is a policy of destroying others.

Some people claim that selfishness and altruism are consistent with one another. Thus it is often said that a genuine and deeply felt altruism is the best way to obtain personal happiness. And on the other hand, contemporary right-wing libertarians insist that selfishness makes one more useful to society. Thus supporters of egoism secretly allow that usefulness to others is a good thing, and supporters of altruism secretly allow that one's own personal happiness is a good thing.

Let us now take another look at the idea of reasonableness.

Rationality or reasonableness means, roughly, acting and thinking in ways that will be effective as means to reaching chosen ends. However, we can also ask what ends are reasonable, though this is not an easy question to answer. Still, it seems clear that it is unreasonable to choose and pursue unachievable ends, or ends which you know are unachievable.

In real life the aims of a policy of pure selfishness are in fact not achievable. Pure, permanent, unalloyed selfishness cannot reach its own ends. It is impossible for an individual who belongs to a gregarious species either always to have or always to achieve only purely selfish ends, unless he or she lives alone on a desert island.

It looks as if permanent and long-term altruism is more achievable than long-term egoism. But we cannot be absolutely certain about this.

The idea that egoism is self-evidently more rational than altruism has had much appeal for modern philosophers. But their belief in the superior rationality of egoism has an ulterior, empirical basis. In so far as they agree that altruism is empirically possible they claim that it is the result of anti-natural training and education. This shows that they think egoism is rational because they secretly believe it is more *natural* than altruism.

The theory of the rationality of altruism also has an ulterior basis. The ulterior basis behind philosophical altruism is an assumed connection between reasonableness and objectivity. Self-interestedness is plainly subjective in a perfectly ordinary sense (= concerned with the subject), and altruism is objective in a perfectly ordinary sense (= concerned with people other than the subject). The basis for the idea that altruism is reasonable is probably the conviction that objectivity is more reasonable than subjectivity.

'Nietzschean' Ego Theory

'Nietzschean' ego theory is the idea that while current morality is not based on self-interest it would be better if it were.

The most interesting and important exponent of this kind of philosophical egoism is Nietzsche. In his own life he tried to adopt the attitude of a sceptical observer of humanity, uninfluenced by the opinions of ordinary people, a 'free spirit'.

Nietzsche asserts his value judgements with a great deal of passion and literary skill. His values are strongly hostile to Christianity and to Judaism; as to democracy, he regards it as nothing but a contemptible, secularized version of the religions he despises. Because of his passionately held convictions Nietzsche is a philosopher whom readers either hate or love.

Nietzsche has a relativistic view of truth and believes that theories are true only in so far as they are biologically useful for the human species, or more importantly, for a special, higher, kind of man. Nietzsche was no feminist and it is worth noting that when he speaks of man or men he means the male sex rather than the human race. His division of people into 'higher' and 'lower' excludes females because on his view all females are naturally slavish and 'lower'.

Nietzsche says morality is a means of preserving the community. Yet he also maintains that there are two opposed kinds of morality. One kind, slave morality, does perhaps preserve the community, though maybe only temporarily. The other kind, master morality, furthers the aims of outstanding individuals. The aims of outstanding individuals are never social or altruistic. Unfortunately it is not very clear what their positive aims, if any, are supposed to be.

In the slave morality, 'good' means useful, helpful, charitable, pitying, compassionate, altruistic. These virtues promote the needs and aims of all the ordinary members of society, including the weakest. In the slave morality, 'bad' means selfish, non-conformist, uncharitable, unpitying, cruel. According to Nietzsche slave morality is the fruit of the resentment felt by lower men towards higher men. It represents envy, inferiority and weakness. The main reason why he condemns Christianity and Judaism is because of the fact that in them the slave morality prevails.

In the master morality, 'good' means aristocratic, free, individualistic, and 'bad' means slavish, despicable, pitying, pertaining to the herd. The master morality represents self-esteem, individuality, genius and the freedom owed to outstanding men with healthy egos.

The higher type of man creates his own morality. The lower type accepts the herd morality because it benefits the ordinary and the weak. Ultimately the higher and lower moralities cannot coexist, because the lower is essentially universal and will not allow the free spirit, the man of genius, the right to egoism or the right to create new moralities.

Nietzsche says that moral codes fall into two main types, and perhaps each type is a 'necessary fiction' for those who believe in it. However this does not seem to mean that he thinks there are no ultimate values; far from it. He believes that moral codes themselves have value, presumably some special kind of non-moral value. Moral codes can be graded as better or worse. At the bottom are those codes that emphasize altruism, pity, helpfulness, unselfishness, self-sacrifice, and at the top are the codes that condemn the Judaic and Christian virtues and instead are based on genius, aristocracy of outlook, self-esteem and the freedom of the outstanding individual.

In his book *Beyond Good and Evil* Nietzsche explains that to go beyond good and evil means to go beyond herd morality in order to invent your own. However, you have to be a superior type of man to do this successfully. Women cannot do it at all, of course, being too slavish by nature. Most of the men who try will be discontented resentful slaves, so that their efforts will not go 'beyond good and evil' in the required sense. Such men will be merely criminal. For the herd, the herd morality is the only possibility.

What precisely is the content of Nietzsche's higher morality? As we have mentioned above, the details are vague and mostly negative. The higher morality is *against* altruism, *against* pity, *against* conformism, *against* weak and ordinary people, and *against* the traditional virtues recommended in the teachings of Western religions.

Nietzsche has been described as a prophet, and he did make some startlingly accurate prophetic statements. He prophesied that not long after his death mankind would enter into a series of 'earth-shaking' ideological wars. He died in 1900, since when the world has indeed been blighted by a great deal of ideological warfare.

He also prophesied that after his death there would be a reaction against nineteenth-century scientific rationality, an explosion of barbaric forces. With hindsight we might half agree, though the barbarisms of the twentieth century have actually been made more barbaric by their use of science and technology.

Nietzsche held that nineteenth-century culture was complacent, feebly Christian, sure of progress and tending toward democracy and mediocrity. The new barbarism, he said, will overturn all this. But eventually higher values will prevail. The explosion of barbarism is necessary, it will pave the way to a better kind of man.

Unfortunately for Nietzsche's posthumous reputation, Hitler was one of his greatest admirers. The Nazis claimed that their programmes of warfare and genocide represented Nietzschean ideals. But supporters of Nietzsche argue that he would have regarded Hitler as one of the barbarians he said would precede the higher morality and the coming of the Superman.

Can Nietzsche's ideas be disassociated. from those of Nazism? The answer to this question depends partly on how we are to perceive the higher man. What is the higher man like, who does the future Superman resemble?

Will the Superman resemble the great philosophers of the past? Nietzsche's attitude to other philosophers was not always respectful. He did not think much of Socrates, and his reverence for Schopenhauer dwindled away when he discovered that the great pessimist was fond of playing the flute. Although we may agree that the philosophers of the past were clearly men of genius, highly individual, highly unusual and sometimes extraordinarily wise and clever, it has to be accepted that few if any of them preached egoism and some of them were positively in favour of altruism. It seems then that Nietzsche would have to say that the Superman will not be like the great philosophers.

Who then are Nietzsche's 'higher types'? Where exactly are these men who create their own stern and unpitying moralities? They are not to be found in the ranks of the philosophers, nor even indeed among the painters and the poets (though some of these, especially the painters, have been influenced a bit by sub-Nietzschean novels about Bohemian life). No: the propagators of the stern and unpitying 'new moralities' are rather to be found among the dictators and their generals and prison warders and chiefs of police.

It is not so easy, then, for Nietzscheans to defend their hero. Perhaps he can only be defended by arguing that, in spite of his general attack on democracy and mediocrity, and in spite of his (shortish) personal experience of warfare, he was ultimately a non-political creature who had no idea about what political prisons, and Prussian generals, and dictators and other absolute rulers are like in real life, and who gave no serious thought as to how his ideas might be translated into political terms.

10
Utility and Principles

Ethical consequentialism is the theory that actions should be judged only by their results. Utilitarianism is the best-known variety of consequentialism, and the best-known utilitarian philosophers are Jeremy Bentham, James Mill and John Stuart Mill.

The utilitarian philosophy does not admit the need for any special moral principles, such as 'do not tell lies' or 'love justice' or 'keep your promises'. Instead utilitarians adopt the view that the right action is always the action which has the consequence of making as many people as possible as happy as possible (the so-called greatest happiness principle). The only absolutely and intrinsically valuable things in the universe are happiness and pleasure, and all other valuable things are only valuable in so far as they produce happiness.

In sharp contrast to utilitarianism are theories that emphasize the importance of motive, duty, rights and principles. Theories of this kind are usually called deontological (meaning: theory of duty).

The most famous anti-utilitarian philosopher is probably Kant. Kant holds that it is useless to pursue happiness and pleasure, either your own or another's, because you will almost certainly fail. He said furthermore that happiness is not intrinsically valuable. If it were intrinsically valuable, that is, valuable in itself, we would not feel upset when we hear about villains getting on in the world and being happy. But in fact the thought that some wicked person is happy and having a good time does upset most people. Kant's view is that the only absolutely valuable thing in the Universe is a good will. A good will is the desire and the determination to do what is right. Those with good will, who wish above all things always to do what is right, will follow certain principles of conduct. These principles, says Kant, are rational, and all rational beings can and ought to follow them, though of course not everyone does.

Kant's maxims include:

Be truthful.
Be honest.
Do not make false promises.
Be generous and benevolent.
Do not waste your talents.
Be prepared to punish murderers and others who deserve punishment.
Be kind to animals.
Do not commit suicide.

Kant says that a rational being will understand that moral rules have no exceptions. The rules are exceptionless in two ways. First, everyone, without exception, and not only those who want to be good, ought to be truthful, honest and so on. Everyone has those obligations even if they do not recognize the fact. Second, one should be truthful at all times, honest at all times, without exception. Circumstances do not alter cases. Even if some great benefit came from telling a lie, still, you ought not to tell that lie.

How can we decide between these two views of what is ultimately valuable in life? Well, we might begin by seeing how the two kinds of theory would operate in tricky situations, situations involving difficult choices. Utilitarian and deontological theories sometimes end up recommending the same kinds of action (though for different reasons), but it can also happen that they will yield conflicting advice. We might consider the differences and ask ourselves whether they show anything about the theories.

Example 1: Deathbed Promises

Suppose Uncle Keller is dying on a desert island and has no opportunity to make a proper Will. Luckily for him his niece Griselda is living on the same desert island, so he asks her to look after his estate as soon as she gets back to civilization. Griselda promises to carry out his dying wish, which is to give the whole estate of £500,000 to a provincial art gallery.

However, when Griselda gets back to civilization she realizes that she herself, as Uncle Keller's only living relative, will inherit his estate. Should she keep her promise? Or should she spend the money on something else? In order to get around the possible accusation of selfishness and bias, let us suppose that Griselda does not want to spend the money on herself, but would prefer to give the money to a children's hospital threatened with closure rather than to a struggling art gallery.

Well, should Griselda keep her promise?

A deontologist will say yes. Breaking promises is a bad principle of conduct, keeping promises is a good one. If Griselda does not like the idea of spending money on art galleries, she ought not to have made the promise in the first place. But having made it she is bound by it.

Second, it is even worse to break a promise made to a dying person than to a living one. For the dying person is in an extremely weak position, he has to trust you, since he will never be able to check up on you. To cheat the dying is a mean and horrible thing to do.

A utilitarian on the other hand will say: it all depends on how much happiness will be created by the art gallery versus the hospital. If the gallery produces more happiness than the hospital, then Griselda should keep her promise. If the hospital will produce more happiness than the art gallery, then Griselda ought to break her promise.

As to the idea that she ought not to have made a promise in the first place, that will not do at all according to utilitarian standards. By making the promise Griselda probably gave Uncle Keller a few last minutes of happiness; had she refused to promise he would perhaps have had a few last minutes of misery instead. Since on the utilitarian theory happiness is the only absolutely valuable thing in the universe, the right action for Griselda on the desert island was to make the promise, even if she later decides to break it – even if, indeed, she intended to break it all along.

As to the idea that it is specially mean to break a promise made to the dying, why so? A dying person will never find out that you have broken your promise, so he or she cannot be made unhappy by that knowledge.

Example 2: The Work of Mother Teresa

Most of the work of Mother Teresa and her helpers in Calcutta involved looking after poor and friendless dying people.

Now for the utilitarian this may seem like a complete waste of time. For the utilitarian, the poor and friendless dying can scarcely appear anywhere on the utility scale. If their needs appear at all on the scale of utility it will be very low down.

Of course, some happiness is brought about by the work. The workers perhaps feel happy doing the work, and the dying themselves are possibly somewhat happier, or at any rate more comfortable, at least for a short time, than they would otherwise have been.

The point though is that on a utilitarian estimate this happiness must by definition be short-term. Consequently on a utilitarian estimate it would have been better for Mother Teresa to have directed her efforts at caring for the living. Perhaps she ought to have got a job in an ordinary hospital. For efforts to help the living will make a difference in the relatively long term as well as in the short term.

At this point many people, whether utilitarians or not, may find within themselves a certain sympathy with deontological theories. Surely (they feel) people like Mother Teresa and her helpers are very good people. Surely such work is very noble. Who are we to say that it is misguided work? Is the world not a better place because it has contained Mother Teresa and her helpers?

Well, if this work is noble and valuable, where does its value lie? For it cannot lie in its utility. Its utility relative to other possible kinds of medical work is probably quite low.

Perhaps it lies in the motives of the carers, or in their moral or religious principles; perhaps it lies in the sacrifice of self. Perhaps it is the respect for humanity, however poor and degraded, the belief in the dignity, indeed the sanctity, of human beings, which makes the work noble. As human beings ourselves we like to believe in the dignity of human beings and who is to say that that is unreasonable? Utilitarians hold that the only absolute value in the universe is happiness: but who is to say that there can be only one absolute value? Who is to say that human dignity is not an absolute value?

Example 3: The Informer

Suppose the police have been on the trail of a notorious gang of drug dealers for a number of years but have not managed to secure any convictions. One day a member of the gang goes to the police and offers to provide them with all the information they need to catch the entire ring. Her motivation is not remorse for what she has done but rather malice against her former colleagues, with whom she has fallen out. In return for her help she demands immunity from prosecution. What should the police do?

The utilitarian answer, which is sometimes also the answer in real life in such cases, is to give immunity. It is judged that the overall benefit to the community outweighs any other considerations.

Deontologists, on the other hand, especially if they are Kantians, will insist that the informer be punished for her past crimes. Justice demands that similar crimes should be treated similarly, and particularly if there has been no genuine repentance. The cry of the deontologists is said to be 'let justice be done though the heavens fall'.

Yet to follow Kantian principles in this case might mean that the drug dealers would not be captured, and the consequences of non-capture could be very serious. In cases like this might it not be best to let one guilty person go free?

Example 4: The Rights of the Innocent

Suppose terrorists hold a plane full of passengers to ransom, but say that they will let all passengers go free provided that a particular local citizen is handed over to them to be killed. Perhaps this citizen belongs to a group opposed to their aims, or is rightly or wrongly believed to be responsible for some counter-terrorist activities. In any event they wish to kill this person; and if the local authorities do not co-operate with them in this aim, then, they say, will blow up the whole plane.

The local authorities know that the citizen is innocent of any crime and moreover has no connection with any counter-terrorist activity. But they have no time to argue the point with the terrorists. And they have no doubt the terrorists will carry out their threat if this innocent person is not handed over. Should they surrender an innocent life in order to save the lives of the passengers?

If the local authorities were utilitarians then for them this course of action would certainly be a possibility. It would depend, for them, on whether the utility of saving the passengers was or was not outweighed by the disutility of encouraging terrorism.

But if the local authorities were deontologists then for them such an action, that is, the action of handing over an innocent person for execution, would be morally impossible. They would cite the principle of human rights, in this case the right of the innocent not to be harmed, and would refuse to be involved in violating that right. If the terrorists violate the rights of the equally innocent passengers then that is their crime and not the responsibility of the local authorities. In short the deontologist's view is that it is always a moral crime to violate the rights of the innocent.

An Objection to Deontological Theories

Many people have objected that a complete refusal to consider the consequences of actions may lead to horrendous results. But that objection presupposes that results, i.e. consequences, matter a great deal; and deontologists would doubtless reply that results are not all that important.

A more significant objection is as follows. It is easy to say one must never tell lies and never harm innocent people, but what if these two moral rules (or any other two moral rules) come into conflict with one another? What if you are sheltering Jews in your attic, and Nazis come to your door and ask you if you know their whereabouts? Should you tell the truth and see the innocent people taken away to a death-camp? Or should you tell a lie and thereby save some innocent lives? Whichever you do you will be breaking one rule in order to conform to the other. In other words it is not always possible to keep all the rules at once.

This may seem to be a serious disadvantage of deontological theories in comparison with utilitarianism. Utilitarians assume that it is always possible, in principle, to know in advance which future situation would contain the most happiness for everyone, and always possible to know what actions will bring that situation about. In this belief they are probably wrong, because it is not really possible to predict the future, as we know from Chaos Theory.

Let us look again at conflicts between moral rules. The ordinary person in the street tends to rank moral rules according to relative importance. For most people in Western society, saving an innocent person from destruction would take precedence over absolute truthfulness, should these ever come into conflict.

Suppose we agree that moral rules must be ranked according to their importance. What makes one rule more important than another? Is it the fact that one rule produces more happiness than another? If the ranking rests on utility and the happiness principle that means that utilitarianism is the true theory after all.

Some Objections to Utilitarianism

Yet utilitarianism seems to have many defects. One classic objection is that it turns us into pigs.

Just suppose that happiness and pleasure are the only things of absolute value in the universe. Obviously then we should all try to produce, and also to get, as much of these absolutely valuable things as possible. But some kinds of happiness and pleasure are harder to obtain than others. For instance, the happiness of becoming a great chess player or a great ballet star is given to only a few. The most reliable and most common kinds of pleasure and happiness are the simplest and most animal: food and drink, sex, warmth and snugness, lazing around, fighting, gambling, simple games which everyone can understand, and so on. Even if we think that all these things are good in their way, it can hardly be said that any of them are particularly noble or dignified. Utilitarianism, it is argued, tells us that it is better to be a happy pig than an unhappy philosopher. For some people that idea goes against the grain.

Robert Nozick develops another anti-utilitarian argument. Utilitarianism, he thinks, implies that we ought to prefer illusion to reality. But in actual fact (he says) human beings prefer un-ideal reality to pleasant illusion.

Suppose someone invented a machine which simulated real life. You lie on the machine and it stimulates your brain in some way so that you have the illusion that you are experiencing all kinds of happy and pleasurable events. All the time, though, you are simply imagining it all.

Nozick thinks we instinctively rebel against the idea of illusory pleasures and would refuse to get on to such a machine. We would rather have a mix of real pleasures and pains than an existence based entirely on illusion, however pleasant the illusion might be. Also we would prefer to take the risk of looking for happiness ourselves, rather than having it provided for us by mechanical means which we have not chosen.

Another difficulty with utilitarianism is that it seems to tell us we ought to concentrate our moral efforts on people who experience happiness easily, and ignore those who are hard to help.

To take a simple example, suppose Morgan is good at making people happy, mainly because he tells such good jokes. He tells a joke to the Blob family and to the Grob family. The Blobs and the Grobs all laugh heartily, but while the Blobs say they feel a bit more happy as a result of the joke, the Grobs say they feel a hundred times more happy. This is because the Grobs are utility monsters, creatures that feel intense happiness at small things. It might seem that if Morgan is a utilitarian he ought to concentrate all his efforts on the Grobs.

This kind of choice can arise in real life. Of course there are no real utility monsters. All the same, people who are already reasonably cheerful are easier to make happier still than those who have lots of things wrong with their lives.

Consider the decisions that have to be made by those who spend our taxes for us, housing departments for instance. A housing department might well have to decide between spending money on making a few houses a great deal better (thus causing a lot of happiness in few inhabitants) or making a lot of houses slightly better (thus causing a small amount of happiness in a larger number of people). If the first lot of tenants are utility monsters like the Grobs, or even just more naturally cheerful than the average citizen, then it seems that a utilitarian housing department ought to spend the money on them. But justice may well suggest exactly the opposite, particularly if the larger number of people are a lot worse off than is considered acceptable in their own society.

G. E. Moore suggests an answer to this problem. He says that preventing misery is more important than creating positive happiness. Strictly speaking there is no rational support for this view, apart from a common-sense intuition that it is correct.

Ultimately neither deontological theories nor consequentialist theories can fully mesh with the common-sense intuitions of the person in the street. Perhaps this is because the theories we have been looking at are monistic. Maybe what is needed is a pluralistic theory. After all, why should a simple idea, for instance, the idea that the only absolute value is happiness, be the right one? Is there any reason to suppose that simple ideas are always better than complicated ones? Is monism more likely to be true than pluralism? In real life people do adopt principles of conduct, but they also take consequences into account. Perhaps then that is the best, or the only possible, way to carry on. At face value, too, pluralism might help resolve difficult questions and problem cases such as the case of the deathbed promise.

Yet in the end we will probably always be faced with difficult choices however much we wish to do what is right. Usually, indeed, it is pretty obvious what is the right thing to do. If someone does the wrong thing instead, well, the reasons for that are also pretty obvious: selfishness, weakness, etc. account for many bad decisions. But it might be that some questions have no right answers. It might be that some difficult decisions are difficult precisely because the arguments for and against are equal in weight. Human life might just be like that. Fortunately it is not like that all the time.

11
Life and Death

Some of the oldest problems in philosophy have to do with questions about life and death. In metaphysics the possibility of immortality, either of the soul or (after resurrection) of the body, and the hypothesis of earthly reincarnation, have been topics of philosophical enquiry for at least two thousand years. In moral philosophy questions are asked about the wrongness or otherwise of murder and suicide and euthanasia and abortion and of allowing people to die when they could be saved.

In this chapter there is space to discuss only two of these topics, namely, *murder* and *suicide*. A number of different points and arguments will be considered, some traditional, some philosophical, some from history and some from the law.

What is Murder?

Murder is killing but not just any killing: it is non-accidental killing of human beings by human beings. Thus the destruction of non-human animals, either by other animals, or by human beings, is not strictly speaking murder (of course). Secondly, the perpetrator of a murder must either know that his immediate action will bring about a death, or if he is ignorant of that fact then his ignorance must itself be culpable. A man who shoots at another man cleverly disguised as a tree, and whom he mistakes for a tree, is not a murderer; but someone who negligently fires a gun near a crowd of people, careless of whether or not anyone is hit, could well count as a murderer, other things being equal. It is useful to remember, here, that murder is in part a legal concept and that what constitutes murder under the law varies to some extent between different countries.

Very young children cannot commit murder because they are ignorant of death and of cause and effect. Older children who know about death and killing are, however, capable of this crime. A sane adult who claimed that he did not know that guns are dangerous, or that murder is wrong, would not and should not be believed.

This short account leaves many questions unanswered. Are there different types of murder? Is murder exactly the same thing as killing innocent people? Is war a kind of murder? Is self defence ever murder? Is murder bad by definition?

It would seem that there is more than one kind of murderous killing. In American law murders are classed as first degree, second degree or third degree, a classification representing differences which depend, partly, on the extent to which killings are intentional. In Britain culpable homicides are categorized as either murder or manslaughter. Murder entails either intention or very serious negligence; manslaughter is the result of negligence only. Each type of homicide can occur in 'extenuating circumstances'. Some cases of 'British' manslaughter would count as second or third degree murder in the USA.

We could also think of murders as comprising core cases and penumbra cases. At the core are deliberate peacetime non-defensive killings of human beings carried out by people of sound mind and not under duress. In the penumbra are some homicides caused by negligence, some judicial killings, and at least some acts of war. Beyond the penumbra lies manslaughter and beyond that non-culpable killings of human beings and other animals. First degree murder, as defined in the USA, would belong to the core while second and third degree murder would belong in the penumbra. In England some killings lie on the border between manslaughter and the outer penumbra of murder.

Christian and Jewish traditions teach that the deliberate killing of innocent people is always murder. From this it does not follow, of course, that *only* the killing of innocent people is murder. Consequently it turns out that the distinction between innocent and guilty will not invariably enable us to distinguish murders from other killings. It is possible, for example, to kill a man who happens to be a burglar, not while he is burgling, and not because of his burgling in the past, but simply for some private reason; such a deed, other things being equal, would be murder – at least in Western legal systems – even though the victim is not in any general sense an innocent man. The traditional account could perhaps be reworded: 'murder is the deliberate destruction of individuals who are innocent of the crime or other deed which is the reason given (if any reason is given) for killing them.' According to that version a professional criminal hanged after being framed by the police ought to count as a victim of murder. And so too should the non-combatants and neutrals targeted in modern warfare. Jurists, though, might disagree with the last two inferences.

Murder and War

There are further problems with the idea of innocence. It has been argued that, in the case of unjust war, volunteers and conscripted soldiers alike are none of them innocent; if the war is not just they are all murderers or something akin to murderers. This doctrine enables us to affirm that the excuse – made, for example, by those who have participated in genocide – namely, 'I was only acting on orders from above', is no excuse at all. Yet on the other hand the doctrine of general guilt places what in some cases might seem to be an intolerable strain on the important distinction between actions performed voluntarily and actions performed under duress.

Part of the point of the above doctrine about innocence and guilt is, or was, to provide a way of removing most kinds of military action from the category of murder. The medieval doctrine of justice in war claims, plausibly enough, that defensive war is allowable unless the means used are evil. The proviso about evil means, as expounded by Vitorio, Grotius and others includes the following: the deliberate military targeting of neutrals and non-combatants is never justified and is either murder itself or something as bad as murder.

The doctrine also states that aggressive war carried out in a righteous cause is allowable (though with the same provisos as in defensive war). Later versions state that aggressive military action is not criminal provided either that you are on the right side or do not know you are on the wrong side. This interpretation of the meaning of innocence emasculates traditional teaching on the just war because, given enough ignorance and self-deception on the part of aggressors, it permits any and every kind of international and inter-racial violence. Readers will agree, perhaps, that the modern age is now in urgent need of a revitalized account of justice and injustice in war. Until such an account has been developed it will be difficult indeed to explicate the relationship between warfare and murder.

Murder and Self Defence

Is there a right to kill in self defence? If so, how far does it extend? Does it extend to protection of one's property? Is there a right, or even a duty, to rescue others from homicidal attacks, if necessary by killing their attackers?

The right to defend one's life is taken to be absolute by many philosophers and most notably by Thomas Hobbes. Hobbes writes: 'a man cannot lay down the right of resisting them that assault him by force, to take away his life', and 'a Covenant not to defend myself from force, by force, is always Void.' He says that a condemned man ought not to be punished for escaping from prison or for attacking the hangman. Virtually all governments, on the other hand, place stringent limits on when a citizen may kill in self defence. Governments argue that the right of self defence has been replaced by arrangements for police protection and legal redress. All the same even judges and politicians allow that a citizen has a right to defend his or her life, if need be by killing, when it can be shown that protection by the agents of the state cannot be counted on. However, in Britain and Europe the courts only very rarely acknowledge that such a state of affairs has been reached. In the USA, on the other hand, there seems to be a contrary assumption.

Traditional Western teaching on self defence rests on the premise that every human being has a natural right to life, a right which, however, is subject to certain limitations stemming from the community's need to impose penalties (which might include a death penalty) for serious crimes. The right to life carries with it the right to defend one's life against direct attack provided the means of defence are not evil. One's motive must be to protect oneself, not to harm one's attacker. Killing the attacker is not permissible if escape is possible. The right to kill when rescuing another person from direct attack is subject to the same provisos and limitations.

Killing a direct attacker when that really is the only way to preserve one's life does not count as murder in the jurisdictions of the West.

Newspaper reports of case law from the USA and France seem to indicate that these nations allow citizens to kill intruders as a way of defending private property.

Why is Murder Bad?

Is murder bad *by definition*? If not, then a substantive explanation of its wrongfulness is needed.

Consider the following definition: 'biological paternal uncles are fathers' brothers'. This truth rests on rules of language governing the uses of the words *uncle, father, brother*, etc. And since the underlying rules are merely verbal it would be rather foolish to ask 'But *why*, exactly, are all biological paternal uncles the brothers of fathers?' The answer is trivial: 'that is just what the words mean'. Similarly, if murder is bad by definition then it is pointless to ask 'But *why*, exactly, is murder bad?'

Now, when attempts are made to justify some particular type of killing there is a tendency to give the deed a new name – as it might be 'mercy killing', or 'political assassination' or 'freedom fighting'. The tendency to rename killings which are felt to be justified, the tendency to juggle with *words*, seems to support the view that murder is bad by definition. That conclusion, though, is not at all satisfactory. The belief that murder is wicked surely rests on more than merely verbal considerations.

Why is murder condemned in every civilized nation? There are three connected reasons, having to do with, respectively, *intrinsic value, subjective value* and *natural rights*.

Socrates says that some things and states of affairs are good as means to ends, others are good as ends in themselves (i.e., intrinsically good) and yet others are esteemed both as means and as ends. All human beings, whether they realize it or not, treat some things and some states of affairs as ends. Examples are not hard to find. Health and happiness are everywhere held to be intrinsically good; so too, probably, are beauty and strength. Many people consider that learning and knowledge and experience have intrinsic value.

Human life itself is intrinsically valuable. It is impossible to think of human life in general as being good *solely* as a useful means to some further purpose. Certainly no one thinks of his own life or the lives of those he loves in that way. The intrinsic value of human life is a matter of reason and common sense. If human life were not intrinsically good very little else could be; perhaps nothing else could be. How, for example, could the health and happiness of human beings matter if human beings themselves did not matter?

The intrinsic value of human life is traditionally given a religious explanation and for that reason life is sometimes said to be *sacred*. The religious connection comes, of course, from the biblical story of Creation. In the Book of Genesis it is said that God made man in his own image. Human life is sacred because mankind is akin to God. Nevertheless it is possible to understand intrinsic value, and the intrinsic value of human life, without relying on a religious explanation.

The term *subjective value* has to do with the fact that each human individual normally places a high value on his or her own life. There are exceptions to the rule, of course, for some men and women seem not to care whether they live or die. However, very often such individuals are nearing the end of life anyway; others are mentally ill. It has to be admitted, though, that serious misfortune can make people wish to die whether or not they are old or ill. These phenomena will be discussed further in the sections on suicide.

A third reason why murder is condemned has to do with the importance, in history and in philosophy, of the theory of natural rights. Thomas Hobbes, as we have already seen, argues that the right to life cannot be given up; it is inalienable. John Locke, whose political ideas are thought to have laid the intellectual foundations of the American and French revolutions, asserts that every man has a natural right to life, to liberty and to property. It is clear that the right to life must be fundamental since any exercise of the other natural rights depend on

one's being alive in the first place. Murder violates this most fundamental human right.

What is Suicide?

It has been claimed that suicide can be noble or even saintly. The death
of Socrates is sometimes cited in support of this view. Another
instance given in support comes from the history of Captain Oates,
one of Scott's companions on the ill-fated British expedition to the
Antarctic. In 1912, on the trek back from the South Pole, Oates walked
into a blizzard, believing, it seems, that by removing himself from the
shared tent he would help save the lives of the other members of
the party. In this he was mistaken, since all his companions died soon
afterwards, but his intention has been widely regarded as wonderfully
good.

These examples do not show that some suicides are noble but rather
that not all self-destructive actions are suicide. A love of risky and dangerous activities − rock-climbing for example − is not in itself an
indication of suicidal tendencies. Driving fast cars *can* lead to death but
that does not mean that those who drive them are actually seeking to
die. Joining the army carries a risk of dying young but it is not suicide
for all that. Even the soldier awarded a posthumous medal for gallantry,
after throwing himself onto a hand grenade in order to protect his
comrades, has not committed suicide, though here we could speak of
'suicidal courage'. (*Suicidal courage*, however, is really a simile. It means
something like *courage having the appearance of suicide*.)

It is clear that Socrates' death was not suicide. Giving hemlock,
for the Greeks, was a mode of execution. Doubtless if a condemned
man were to refuse to take the poison he would be put to death in
some other more painful manner. Socrates' quietly swallowing hemlock was analogous to a modern person's walking quietly to the
scaffold.

For an act to count as suicide it is not enough for it to end in death
and not enough, even, for it to involve a conscious choice of death.
Socrates would not have taken hemlock if he had been given a free
pardon by the Athenian authorities; Oates would not have walked into
the snow if a rescue party had arrived in time to save the expedition;

the brave soldier wanted only to protect his comrades. These people did not wish to die 'come what may'.

Is Suicide Always Wrong?

Opinions about suicide tend to be all-or-nothing in character. In traditional Jewish and Christian teaching the Mosaic law against murder is absolute and is commonly taken to cover self-slaughter. At the opposite extreme is the idea that suicide is either never wrong at all or wrong only when it has bad consequences. Thus utilitarians believe that it should only be condemned when it leads to the grief or the impoverishment of the survivors; others argue that because my life is my own I may do whatever I like with it, however unfortunate the effects of my demise might be on those who outlive me.

The view to be expressed hereunder is less extreme than those just mentioned. Suicide, though usually unreasonable, and sometimes bad, is not so invariably. In defence of this position we will discuss certain important counter-examples and then consider the meaning of the slogan 'my life is my own'.

Suicide *in extremis*

Although having a wish to die 'come what may', and acting on that wish positively and all by oneself, is a sufficient condition for suicide, it is perhaps not a necessary condition. There are cases of self-destruction which should be counted as suicide, and are so counted by most people, even though the individual chose to die, not 'come what may', but in order to avoid a terrible alternative. During the war against Nazi Germany British secret agents sometimes carried capsules of poison which they would swallow if captured. Such individuals did not wish to die 'come what may', rather they wished to die quickly as an alternative to being tortured to death slowly and betraying their comrades when under torture. It seems reasonable to describe such deaths as *justifiable suicides*. Cancer patients swallowing overdoses of morphine, in the days when techniques of pain control were more limited than they are now, surely fall into the same category.

So far, then, it seems that justification is possible for those *in extremis*.

'My Life is My Own'

Can it be argued that suicide is *always* allowable? Some have claimed that, just as one has a right to destroy personal possessions such as old newspapers or teapots or outworn clothing, so too one has a right to destroy one's life. For life is a possession and each person's life belongs to that person alone.

Supposing for the sake of argument that I do own my own life, does it follow that I have a right to self-destruct? My right to destroy some trifling object, such as a newspaper or a kettle, need not be questioned; but does that mean that I may rightly destroy anything at all which I happen to own? I might happen to own a wonderful collection of works of art, for example, yet to destroy those belongings, that collection, would be a dreadful thing to do.

Human life is valuable and every human individual is unique. It is questionable whether ownership confers an absolute right to destroy things which are valuable and unique.

In any case the notion of *owning* one's own life seems rather peculiar. *Ownership* in this context looks suspiciously like a metaphor for *power* or *right*. Other cases of 'owning' a life are worse than peculiar. In ancient Rome fathers had a legal right to kill newborn infants, a right based, no doubt, on the idea that the infants belonged to them. The right of a husband to kill an adulterous wife was also doubtless based on the notion that her life was owned by the husband. Modern Western societies, influenced as they are by Christianity and, later, by feminism, have decided that ancient ideas about ownership, which conferred on fathers and husbands absolute rights over the lives and deaths of their families, were barbaric.

It can also be argued that my life is not wholly my own, not even metaphorically, It can be argued that my life belongs, partly, to the society into which I was born and which has nurtured me in various ways. This view of the matter has been taken by many states, ancient and modern.

In some countries, though, and notably in Japan, suicide is not regarded with disfavour. It seems that a Japanese businessman about to be disgraced by public revelations of crooked dealing will be thought well of if he avoids the shame of punishment by killing himself. From a Western point of view a suicide of this type looks not much better than running away from a policeman. In the West the suicide of a crooked businessman is not seen as an honourable way of making amends to his victims but a dishonourable way of avoiding retribution. Which view is more rational? Well, the death of the businessman can make only a symbolic restitution, even in Japan, whereas facing the music might provide an opportunity to make restitution in a literal sense. We can tentatively conclude, then, that avoiding shame and punishment is not an ethically rational basis for self-destruction.

Suicide and Utility

The utilitarian position on suicide is roughly as follows: serious misery provides sufficient reason for self-destruction provided that no one else will suffer from the death of the suicidal individual. Moreover only the person concerned can judge the degree of his own unhappiness and pain. It is right for passers-by to delay a man's attempt at suicide, but only for such time as is needed to ascertain whether or not he has dependants, or comrades who will grieve for him, and to ascertain, also, whether he is of sound mind and knows what he is doing. If he has no friends and dependants, and is sane, and has decided that his misery is serious and incurable, then he should be allowed to destroy himself.

There is a fundamental error in this position, embodied in the premise that only the unhappy individual knows how bad his situation is. Common experience tells us that even profound unhappiness can turn out to be temporary. This is especially the case when a young man or woman decides that life is not worth living. It can easily happen that older people with more experience are in a position to tell suicidal young persons that their states of mind are temporary and less serious than they seem.

The actions of very old people have a somewhat different significance from those of the young. A decision to refuse medical treatment need not be regarded as suicidal in intent, or even as resembling suicide, in the old and frail. Such a decision is likely to be due to the recognition that natural death is rapidly approaching anyway and should be accepted with equanimity.

Conclusions

The lines between more culpable and less culpable killings are drawn differently in different jurisdictions, but, in the West at least, the variations are not gross. In general the boundaries between murder and other kinds of killing are not completely sharp but they are not seriously hazy either. The worst uncertainties have to do with warfare and capital punishment. It is by no means clear when, and to what extent, warfare and capital punishment resemble murder. (According to pacifists the answer, of course, is 'always; and completely'.)

Neither suicide nor murder is bad by definition. The reasons why these actions are bad have to do, firstly, with the intrinsic value of human life, secondly, with the subjective value of human life, and thirdly, at least in the case of murder, with the concept of natural rights.

It is conceivable, but unlikely, that murder might occasionally be a lesser evil than some alternative. It is rather more likely that suicide is neither invariably irrational nor invariably bad.

Utilitarians are right to insist that thoughts about the grief of survivors should weigh heavily against any desire for self-destruction.

The notion that I own my own life is peculiar. No one *literally* owns anyone's *life*. In this context ownership is, at best, a metaphor for power or law or right; and power and law and right need a basis, a justification.

Common sense and experience both indicate that degrees of unhappiness cannot always be accurately estimated by unhappy people. Happiness and misery are states which come and go in virtually every life and this fact by itself means that suicide, when not positively cowardly, is often unreasonable.

Part III
Political Philosophy: The Philosophy of State and Citizen

12
Authority and Anarchy

To many readers the word 'anarchy' will suggest a situation of social chaos and unrestricted violence. Anarchist *theorists*, though, do not say that a situation of social chaos is a good thing to aim for. The theory of anarchism is that we, the human race, would be better off if there were no states. Anarchists argue that there are simpler and better methods of organizing human society. According to theorists like P. J. Proudhon, serious violence and social chaos are not caused by individuals, or small groups of individuals, but by the State itself. Proudhon defined government as follows:

> To be governed is to be watched, inspected, spied upon, directed, law-driven, numbered, regulated, enrolled, indoctrinated, preached at, controlled, checked, estimated, valued, censured, commanded, by creatures who have neither the right nor the wisdom nor the virtue to do so . . . [it] is to be . . . registered, counted, taxed, stamped, measured, numbered, assessed, licensed, authorized, admonished, prevented, forbidden, reformed, corrected, punished. It is, under pretext of public interest . . . to be placed under contribution, drilled, fleeced, exploited, monopolized, extorted from, squeezed, hoaxed, robbed: then, at the slightest resistance, the first word of complaint, to be repressed, fined, vilified, harassed, hunted down, abused, clubbed, disarmed, bound, choked, imprisoned, judged, condemned, shot, deported, sacrificed, sold, betrayed, and to crown all, mocked, ridiculed, derided, outraged, dishonoured. That is government; that is its justice; that is its morality.

Proudhon was gaoled for holding these opinions.

Left-wing and Right-wing Anarchism

The difference between left-wing and right-wing anarchism is this: left-wing anarchists, such as those of the nineteenth century – Prince Kropotkin is an example – believe that the future ideal (stateless) human society will be held together by voluntary democratic co-operation. There will be little or no private property, except for personal goods like clothing, because land and the major means of production will be communally owned.

Right-wing anarchism is a branch of a modern political theory sometimes called *capitalist libertarianism*. Capitalist libertarians usually want a minimal state, but a few are anarchists and want no state at all. These right-wing anarchists believe that the ideal human society will be based on an absolute right to private property, and will be held together by voluntary co-operation based on economic exchanges, both between individuals, and between small and large business corporations. Right-wing anarchists, and their close cousins the 'minimal statists', hope for a situation in which the operations of capitalism will be left alone and more or less unfettered. Capitalism, they say, always brings enormous benefits to everyone involved, though legislation and taxation reduce the effectiveness of the system and hence the benefits that flow from it. If taxes and anti-monopoly legislation and other such restrictions could be abolished, then the natural operation of the capitalist system would get rid of shoddy goods and pollution and inefficiency quite automatically.

Can the State be Abolished?

Supposing for the sake of argument we decided that governments are bad things: could we get rid of them? We cannot just run away from government because there are no places left on earth to run to. Virtually every piece of the earth's surface now falls within the borders of some national state.

In the past, left-wing (socialist) anarchists argued that the only way to get rid of the state is to assassinate rulers or to have a general revolution. Here though we should notice one important exception, namely Gandhi. Gandhi was a kind of leftish anarchist who believed that the best society would be one based on voluntary co-operation between small groups (villages or communes). But he was against all violence, including violent rebellion; instead he advocated techniques of passive resistance.

Modern right-wing (capitalist) anarcho–libertarians tend to recommend non-revolutionary modes of operation. Some hold that the state could be abolished by democratic political means. Others believe that as governments take over more and more control of our lives they will become more and more inefficient and will eventually collapse spontaneously. Some anti-statists recommend a policy of converting the elite. Anarchists should try to persuade intelligent people, and people in positions of power and influence (generals, big businessmen), to stop co-operating with governments. When the elite has been converted to anarchism the state will die.

Old-fashioned Marxism says that only violent revolution can remove capitalism and capitalist governments. Marx held that after a successful anti-capitalist revolution a new but transitory state would be formed, the dictatorship of the proletariat. This proletarian state would then soon wither away, leaving communism, in which there is no state as we know it. Well, history seems to have shown that the dictatorship of the proletariat (so-called) does not gently wither away. On the contrary, it is a type of government which extends its tentacles into every aspect of human life. Marxist revolution, then, does not bring in either anarchy or liberty, and in any case violent revolution for whatever cause must always be a risky policy.

Could states and government be abolished democratically? There is something odd about the idea of standing for election on the platform of abolishing government. Would anyone vote for candidates whose aim it was to abolish the institutions they were asking to be elected into? Would anyone believe that their policy was not in fact phoney and hypocritical?

Is there any real likelihood that the state will wither away of itself? Inefficiency is not enough to make a state wither away. The vast, unwieldy Ottoman Empire, which according to historians was amazingly inefficient and corrupt, lasted for several hundred years. Its eventual collapse was not followed by a situation of statelessness but by the immediate appearance of a group of smaller and somewhat more efficient states.

Is there anything that non-violent anarchists could do to encourage the state to wither away? Some ideas, such as the suggestion that anarchists should nobble the elite, have an air of fantasy. More generally, it is not really very surprising that political ideologists (both statists like B. F. Skinner, and anti-statists like Ayn Rand) should couch their theories in the form of Utopia novels and science fiction. For nobody knows what the real political future will be.

The State and the 'State of Nature'

Why do we have states? And why should we obey the state? Is there any obligation to obey? Or is our obedience simply due to fear? Is the state something special, or is it no better than a band of robbers, having the undoubted power to boss us around, but no right to do so?

One ancient answer to the first question is this. Mankind lives under governments for the same reason that the bee lives in hives – because it has to, because it can do no other: it is the nature of the beast to live in a hive (if a bee) or in a state (if human).

But this does not seem right. First of all, what is natural is not inevitable, nor is it always the best option. It is natural for cows and sheep and goats to roam free in the wild, but all the same, and if we ignore the meat industry for the moment, it is obvious that cows (free-range dairy cows, that is) and other animals (Angoras, say) live longer and have an easier life as a result of being domesticated. In the same way we can argue that although it is natural, perhaps, for human beings to live in states, it is not absolutely inevitable. And they might actually be happier if they could roam wild in the woods and forests.

Second, the human species is so extremely versatile that it is difficult anyway to say what is natural or unnatural for it. Versatility itself is the real nature of the beast.

Some people say that for mankind *whatever is possible is natural*. We think this might be going a bit too far. It would be *possible*, perhaps, for people and rats to live together in symbiotic colonies in the Antarctic wastes, subsisting together on a diet of rat's milk. But it would hardly be *natural*. The fact remains, though, that it is not easy to say what is natural and what is unnatural for the human species.

Finally, while bees always live in hives, history and anthropology show that human beings do not always live in states. Some human beings live in patriarchal groups ruled by polygamous old grandfathers, some live in larger tribes, with or without kings and priests and judges, and a few even live as hermits. The reason most people nowadays live in nation states is that nation states are big and powerful, and have a strong tendency to wipe out any small independent tribes or clans that they happen to come across.

Hobbes and Locke

Thomas Hobbes, who lived through the English Civil War, says that the state has nothing to do with the natural condition of mankind. He holds that the *natural* condition of mankind – 'the state of nature' – is wild and savage and dangerous, the main danger being other people. In the state of nature 'The condition of man . . . is a condition of war of everyone against everyone' and life is 'solitary, poor, nasty, brutish and short'. People *create* the state in order to escape from the horrors of their *natural way* of life. Hobbes says that the first state was created by a contract according to which individuals agreed between themselves to set up a king who would have a monopoly of power over them and whose prime purpose would be to keep the peace. He argues that keeping the peace is always the primary function of the state, and one which can only be carried out if the king or other ruler has absolute power. Hobbes thought that any curtailment of the power of the ruler would lead to civil war.

Hobbes' view of the state, and of the state of nature, was challenged by other philosophers, one of the best-known being John Locke. Locke says that people prefer to live in peace, and can actually do so even in a state of nature. He says that human beings have certain natural rights, the rights to life, liberty and property. The state does not exist merely to preserve the peace, it also has positive duties to maintain and uphold natural rights. A monopoly of power is inconsistent with this programme; therefore the powers of the state must be limited, and divided in some way between different agencies or institutions.

Locke's ideas deeply influenced the American revolution. *The Declaration of Independence* makes explicit reference to natural rights, the existence of which is said there to be 'self-evident'.

Locke and Hobbes disagree about how people would actually behave if there were no state. Hobbes thinks there would be nothing but fighting, Locke thinks there could be peace. This is really a question of fact, so we ought to be able to settle it by looking at the evidence. Unfortunately the evidence is ambiguous. The versatility of the human species extends to its social arrangements, which are quite various. Some clans and tribes live peacefully, others go in for intermittent fighting, others again live entirely by preying on their neighbours. We simply do not know how human beings would live in a 'state of nature'. We do know however that they have many different ways of arranging their lives, some warlike, some peaceful.

Hobbes speaks about civil war as if it were the greatest conceivable catastrophe that could befall a nation. We today are much less frightened at the prospect of civil war than at the prospect of international nuclear war. War has changed, and so too have states. Hobbes' own justification of government obviously could not take into account the kind of danger for mankind which flows from our century's developments in military technology. And civil war itself has also changed. In our time civil wars, especially those involving guerrilla action, can easily spill into other countries. And even after the end of the Cold War it can happen that a civil conflict, so-called, is really a clandestine struggle between bigger states fought out on the territories of smaller ones. In such cases local people are used as mercenaries or puppets in undeclared disputes between external powers. One only has to consider the Lebanon or Central America, to see that these things are so. For such reasons anarchism is – at least in theory – a more plausible option for us today than it was for Hobbes in the seventeenth century.

The State and its Authority

We will end this chapter by discussing a modern theory, a sort of up-to-date Hobbesism, put forward by G. E. M. Anscombe in her paper 'On the Source of the Authority of the State'.

Anscombe says that there must surely be *some* difference between a state and a voluntary association. And there must surely also be *some* difference between a state and a gang of bandits. But what can the differences be?

The chief difference between a voluntary association and a state is that you can resign from a voluntary association, but it is never possible to resign from the state.

Anscombe exaggerates here, for there are some organizations which you can *join* voluntarily but cannot easily *leave* – the French Foreign Legion for instance, or indeed any volunteer army. And, on the other hand, it is sometimes possible to obtain permission, from a particular state, to leave its confines and transfer one's allegiance to another state.

Still, in the main and generally speaking, there is this difference between states and voluntary organizations, that everyone has to belong to some state or other, but one can usually avoid joining a voluntary organization.

It is harder to pinpoint the difference between a state and an efficient gang of bandits such as the Mafia. Anscombe even suggests that there might not be all that much difference. The state and the bandits both use force in order to make you obey. States, like bandits, can be arbitrary in their behaviour – she mentions the rule of the Great Turk in the fifteenth century as an example of arbitrary government. Bandits, like states, can sometimes be benevolent; states, like bandits, are often quite malevolent.

However, in the end Anscombe decides that there *is* a difference between states and bandit gangs. The difference is that the state has authority.

She defines authority *as the right to make decisions and the right to be obeyed when obedience is relevant.*

But where does this right come from?

Anscombe argues that there are three kinds of right: (1) customary rights, (2) contractual rights and (3) 'task rights'.

The authority of the state is a 'task right'.

Example of a Customary Right

In your own house you have a right to make 'polite requests' of your guests, for instance, 'Please don't use the upstairs bathroom, that's reserved for Grandma.' These 'polite requests', Anscombe says, are really prohibitions which you as householder have a customary right to impose on your guests. The right of the state to obedience is not like this. For one thing, the authority of the state is always backed up by force if need be, whereas customary rights are usually maintained by a sort of silent, almost unconscious, acceptance and agreement.

Examples of Contractual Rights

Contractual rights include the rights generated by formal and informal business contracts, and by promises in general, and by marriage and divorce (and so on). Contracts are usually voluntary. The authority of the state is not a contractual right because we the citizens have never promised or contracted to obey the state; we are born within the boundaries of this or that national state and soon find that we have to obey whether we like it or not.

'Task Rights'

Task rights are generated by the prior existence of a task, the carrying out of which is desirable or necessary. For instance, it is necessary for the survival of the race that the task of rearing children be carried out. The right of a parent or guardian to rear a child is generated by the need that the task be carried out. The overall right in this case consists first, in not being prevented from rearing the child, second, in being allowed to take decisions on behalf of the child when it is too young to make decisions for itself, and third, in being allowed to make the child obey one when it is old enough to obey but not yet old enough to know how to avoid harming itself.

Task rights presuppose the existence of necessary or desirable tasks. Anscombe argues that the authority of the state, its right to make laws, prevent crimes, punish criminals and so on, stems from the necessary tasks that arise as soon as lots of people start living together in groups. These necessary tasks are, first, to protect people from one another (as in Hobbes' account), second, to enforce contracts made by the people with one another, third, to maintain and protect whatever customary rights seem desirable and useful, and fourth, to organize large-scale ventures of benefit to the community – for example, to build roads and railways, and to organize an army to defend the community from outside attack.

Anscombe holds that the state is necessary, and has authority, i.e. the right to be obeyed, because the tasks are important and real. However, she concedes that in a tiny community the tasks might be carried out by voluntary co-operation instead. She also concedes, for what it is worth, that one major task would vanish if human beings were extremely virtuous and never tried to harm one another.

Let us agree for the sake of argument that the tasks carried out by the state are necessary tasks, and that only a large-scale organization like the state could carry them out. Does it follow that any and every reasonably efficient state has the right to be obeyed? Is there never a right to rebel, even against the most cruel and tyrannical rulers? Surely that does *not* follow.

Anscombe's answer to our problem is incomplete. There is more to the authority, the legitimacy, of the state, than the efficient carrying out of a task. Carrying out the task is a necessary but not a sufficient condition of state authority.

In our next chapters we will discuss some suggested additional conditions of rightful authority. These conditions, *liberty* and *equality*, are two of the traditional ideals of Western democracy.

13
Liberty

Liberty or freedom is one of the fundamental ideals of modern democratic states. But what is freedom?

On 6 January 1941, in a message to the American Congress, President Roosevelt referred to what he called 'The Four Freedoms':

> We look forward to a world founded upon four essential human freedoms. The first is freedom of speech and expression – everywhere in the world. The second is freedom of every person to worship God in his own way – everywhere in the world. The third is freedom from want . . . everywhere in the world. The fourth is freedom from fear . . . anywhere in the world.

'Positive' and 'Negative' Liberty

Some philosophers have tried to distinguish between positive freedom, or 'freedom to do . . .', and negative freedom, 'freedom from . . .'. Roosevelt's message mentions two 'positive' freedoms, freedom to speak and worship, and two 'negative' freedoms, freedom from fear and from want.

However it seems to us that the difference between 'freedom to do . . .' and 'freedom from . . .' is of no great philosophical importance. This is partly because 'freedom to do . . .' and 'freedom from . . .' are often

116

only two sides of one coin. Thus in a social or political context 'freedom *from* censorship' means the same thing as 'freedom *to* say and write what one chooses', 'freedom *from* religious oppression' means the same as 'freedom *to* worship as one chooses, or not to worship at all'.

In short the main difference between 'freedom to do . . .' and 'freedom from . . .' is usually merely verbal. We will therefore ignore this supposed distinction between 'positive' and 'negative' freedom.

Political Liberty

Not all freedom is political. Take Roosevelt's 'freedom from fear'. Roosevelt himself was doubtless talking about fear engendered by tyrannical political regimes, but people have other fears as well. They long to be free from fear of disease, fear of loneliness, fear of failure, fear of pimples, fear of psychological hang-ups and breakdowns. Because of this some political philosophers have got bogged down in irrelevant questions about psychology. For example, they ask whether one is free to do X if one has a psychological inhibition about doing X. This might be an interesting problem; but its connection with *political* freedom is somewhat remote.

Our discussion will be about those kinds of liberty which are clearly political, which have to do with the relationship between the individual and the state.

Political liberty is a big subject, so we will confine ourselves to just three basic questions.

The first question is: How many kinds of political liberty are there?

The second is: Are the different kinds of political liberty connected? In other words, if a society has one kind of freedom, will that ensure that it has the other kinds as well, or not?

The third question is: Which kind of liberty is the most important?

There are four kinds of political liberty: national liberty (as opposed to colonialism), the political liberty of representative government (as opposed to autocracy), economic liberty and individual liberty. The first three of these are collective in nature, pertaining to groups.

National Liberty

> The mountains look on Marathon,
> And Marathon looks on the sea,
> And musing there an hour alone.
> I dreamed that Greece might still be free.

Byron dreamed that Greece might be freed from the centuries-old Turkish colonial yoke. For many people, for much of history, liberty has not meant civil rights, or democracy, or even representative government; rather it has meant *national* liberty – that is, freedom from the domination of foreign overlords.

Why do nations hate foreign rule? Partly because colonial tyranny is often even worse than home-grown tyranny. Thus although no doubt many governments and most tyrannies practise some economic exploitation on the citizenry, it seems fairly certain that colonial government involves more exploitation than other kinds of rule, since economic exploitation is normally the reason for colonizing a country in the first place.

Colonialism creates hierarchical societies in which the original inhabitants occupy the lower tiers and may even be forbidden the use of natural amenities like beaches and rivers and the land itself.

Colonial rule is generally worse than local tyranny from the point of view of language, religion and culture. Colonialism often involves some destruction of local cultures and local religions, and can even destroy languages.

Nevertheless the generalization above has exceptions. The worst crimes of colonial tyranny are genocide and torture, but at different times, and in various parts of the globe, there have been local oppressors who were just as bad in these regards as any foreign tyrant. For instance, Caligula and Pol Pot made things worse for their own people than most colonial rulers make things for colonized people. George III's silly behaviour to the settlers of America pales into insignificance when compared with the actions of men like Pol Pot.

Political Liberty as Representative Government

The quest for liberty has often been a war of words, and sometimes a war of swords, against the absolute powers of monarchs or dictators.

The powers of monarchs or dictators become limited when those who are governed acquire some form of representation, so that, other things being equal, increases in the representation of the people go with decreases in the power of the sovereign. This is one reason why political representation is associated with liberty.

All government imposes restrictions, heavy or light, on those who are governed. Now, freedom is generally preferable to restriction – other things being equal. What kind of government allows most freedom? It would appear that those who govern themselves will allow themselves plenty of liberty, or anyway as much liberty as is compatible with other good things, like civil peace.

But what exactly is self-government? Is parliamentary government enough? No: it depends on who sits in parliament. Is representative government enough? No: that depends, primarily, on whether all the people are represented or only some of them. It also depends on such things as whether political parties are permitted to exist; whether the voting system is reasonably fair, or (like 'first past the post') pretty unfair; and whether it is easy or difficult to gerrymander the electoral divisions or otherwise rig the system. It depends too on whether the system itself is genuine, or merely a front for other interests such as the armed forces or foreign communist or capitalist investors.

What about democracy? In a large society direct democracy, in which everyone votes on every political issue, is most likely impossible. It seems then that the ideal of liberty *qua* self-government cannot take the form of direct democracy in a large, modern nation state. The closest we get to this ideal is representative government with regular elections in which every adult has a vote and no one has more than one vote, in which political parties and political independents are neither of them illegal, and in which the voting system is not rigged.

The city-state of Athens is said to have been the original 'democracy' and it did indeed have a form of direct government by citizens. However, it is notorious that the only people who counted as citizens were free adult males, and also notorious that the economy was founded upon slavery. Athens did not really have a democracy, rather it had a kind of non-elected representative government in which the adult free males were the representatives of the people. The adult free males made laws not only for themselves but for everyone else in the city as well.

Economic Liberty

Economic liberty is usually understood to be the freedom to own private property, to buy and sell goods, and to sell one's labour. But there can be no such thing as private property in the first place, nor contracts of sale, nor contracts of employment, without government. Both economic liberty and its opposite are essentially political in so far as both of them presuppose the existence of government.

The American philosophers Ayn Rand and Robert Nozick, whose theories are discussed again in the next chapter, treat economic liberty, which they identify in the main with capitalism, as absolutely central. They believe that economic liberty is the most important kind of freedom, both in itself and as a genuine foundation of all the other kinds of liberty. They strongly imply that communism lacks freedom of speech and freedom of religion, and so on, *because* it restricts economic liberty.

Can any Collective Liberty Guarantee the Others?

Unfortunately the answer to this question seems to be no. The battle for freedom is not over when one kind of liberty has been achieved.

Take national liberation. History shows that a successful fight for national liberation can be followed by any kind of government. It will be good luck if the new nation ends up with a democratically elected government; it is just as likely to have a military dictatorship or other one-party arrangement. National liberation is no doubt a *necessary* condition for the political liberty of self-government, but it is certainly not a *sufficient* condition.

Now consider liberty as representative government. Some of the most famous defenders of this kind of liberty – the Founding Fathers of the United States for instance – deliberately restricted its advantages to members of their own race and sex. So the benefits of full citizenship, even in democracies so-called, have not always been available to all the people born within the state's borders. There is no objective non-selfish reason for this type of restriction on liberty. The facts of the case are blatant. The most famous democracy on earth did not abolish slavery until ninety years after its foundation, and did not give the vote to women until well over one hundred years after. The many assassinations of black voters in the Southern states of the United States, and the man-handling, gaoling and force-feeding of suffragettes in Britain, both testify to the strength of the feeling, found in the great democracies, that self-government is not for everyone.

Even genuine majority rule cannot guarantee individual liberties such as freedom of speech. Majority rule too often combines with intolerance of minority opinions, and there have been times when it has been dangerous to speak openly against majority ideas in a democracy. Only a very long tradition of tolerance of minorities is any kind of protection against majoritarian intolerance.

Does representative government guarantee full economic liberty of the kind Ayn Rand and Robert Nozick think desirable? It does not – some nations which have representative government and full parliamentary democracy (the Scandinavian countries for instance) run their economies on a mixture of capitalism and socialism.

What of economic liberty? Does economic liberty, does capitalism, guarantee political liberty? Nations which have a considerable degree of economic freedom often have other freedoms too. That is greatly to their credit of course. However, economic freedom does not positively guarantee political freedom (representative government), still less can it guarantee freedom of speech or freedom of worship. Rand and Nozick suppose that economic freedom causes and upholds the other kinds of freedom, but they generalize from one case, that of the United States, without bothering to look at the rest of the world. They do not understand that not all capitalist states have been democracies. The economy of South Korea is run on capitalist lines and the same is true of most of the nations of South America. Capitalism is possible under Islam even though most of the independent Islamic nations do not permit full freedom of worship and few of them can be said to have fully developed systems of representative government.

It seems then that the various kinds of collective liberty cannot guarantee one another, nor can they guarantee the freedom of the individual. National liberation cannot guarantee political liberty. Political liberty too often has self-restricting conditions and tends anyway to foster majoritarian intolerance. Economic liberty is compatible with political dictatorship and with serious restrictions on freedom of speech and freedom of worship.

National liberty, representative government and economic freedom are *collective liberties*. They exist for nations and societies and groups, and presuppose the existence of these. It is time now to look at a different ideal, the ideal of individual liberty. It comes later in history than the liberties discussed above and it is closely connected with the concept of a right.

Individual Liberty and Natural Rights

In the second of his *Two Treatises on Civil Government*, John Locke outlines a theory of 'natural rights'. He claims that there are three natural rights, the right to life, the right to liberty and the right to property. Thomas Jefferson substituted the pursuit of happiness for Locke's original third natural right, the right to property.

Locke's *Treatises*, and the Declaration of Independence, have strongly influenced American philosophers, many of whom hold that the concept of a right is the fundamental concept of ethics.

Although the doctrine of the natural rights of man has had very important short-term and long-term effects on ethical and political thinking, it must be admitted that it has some weaknesses.

One defect is that the doctrine is pretty vague. In what way can a right be natural? Surely not in the same way that instincts (for instance) are natural. Usually the meaning of 'natural' is left more or less unexplained.

It can also be objected that to claim that men have a natural right to liberty does not tell us in what the right consists, nor does it tell us how to protect this right. For instance, does the doctrine entail that convicted criminals have a natural right to liberty? If so, would giving all criminals a free pardon be a good way of protecting their natural right to liberty?

Thirdly, the history of the eighteenth and nineteenth centuries shows that the rhetoric of natural rights can easily coexist with slavery, and with drastic limitations on political and social rights like the right to vote and the right to study.

In spite of its relatively good long-term practical track record, the doctrine of natural rights is not precise enough to rely on all by itself. We need to look at other ideas about freedom too.

Individual Liberty and Civil Rights

Individual liberty is the freedom of the individual from interference from other people, most especially freedom from undue interference from government. As an ideal it assumes that some areas of the life of the individual ought never to be interfered with by any government. *Which* areas these are we can deduce from the liberties themselves. The essential individual liberties are generally held to be: freedom of speech and expression; freedom of information; freedom of worship; and the right to marry, or not, as one wishes. The 'free' areas, then, are the individual's private life (as it is called), and the life of thought and reason.

Defenders hold that these freedoms need to be protected by law, and that they must be extended to minorities.

Many Western philosophers and other thinkers have defended the ideal of individual liberty, in various ways. Benjamin Constant, for example, held that liberty of religion, of property and of opinion, are fundamental to a decent society. Others have emphasized freedom of speech and the freedom of the press; others again stress the importance of education, without which it is not easy to exercise liberty of thought and opinion.

The names of authors who have written about individual liberty are quite numerous, but the following deserve a special mention: John Milton, Tom Paine, Mary Wollstonecraft, Thomas Jefferson, J. S. Mill, F. D. Roosevelt.

Milton's defence (1644) rests on the idea that truth and knowledge are of supreme value. Religious freedom is in his view a necessary condition of religious knowledge, and indeed there can be scarcely any knowledge at all unless there is freedom of expression: 'Where there is much desire to learn there of necessity will be much arguing, much writing, many opinions; for opinion in good men is but knowledge in the making.' He also says that truth always overcomes falsehood in a fair fight:

> Though all the winds of doctrine were let loose to play upon the earth, so Truth be in the field, we do injuriously, by licensing and prohibiting, to misdoubt her strength. Let her and Falsehood grapple; who ever knew Truth put to the worse, in a free and open encounter?

123

Milton also says that, for the individual, the liberty of thought is more precious than any other freedom: 'Give me the liberty to know, to utter, and to argue freely according to conscience, above all liberties.'

Two hundred years later, in 1859, J. S. Mill said much the same things in his well-known essay 'On Liberty'. Thus he states that truth cannot be discovered if men, who are fallible, place limits on what is permitted to be discussed; only open discussion of ideas can lead to truth and to new knowledge.

Mill also defends liberty of thought and expression because it is valuable to the individual; he argues that to limit freedom of ideas is to limit what is essential to, and best in, mankind. Without freedom of thought people become cramped and degraded. Civilization cannot advance without liberty, and societies that lack individual freedom are characterized by mediocrity and a general withering of human capacities.

Liberties Compared

Can we decide which liberty is most important, overall? Probably not. The character of a society is determined by its freedoms, but also by innumerable other factors, so that in one place empirical observation, and the study of history, will give one kind of answer, and in another place another.

Yet it is worth pointing out that without freedom of thought and expression we cannot even ask the question, still less try to answer it.

14
Equality

Is equality an ideal worth defending? Before we tackle this question we had better make it clear what kind of equality we are talking about.

Confusions about Equality

It has to be admitted that the rhetoric of equality tends to cause confusion. For example, egalitarian rhetoric sometimes begins with the premise that all people are equal anyway, then draws the conclusion that all people *ought* to be equal. Clearly in such reasoning the word 'equal' must be being used in different senses, but what different senses?

It could be argued that anti-egalitarians are the main victims of the confusions in egalitarian rhetoric. Pointing to this rhetoric they note that people are obviously not equal, and ask: What then can be the sense in saying they ought to be? They not unnaturally conclude that the ideal of equality is both baneful and impossible. The fact that the rhetoric itself, as we have already noted, fails to distinguish between different kinds of equality ought really to serve as a warning to anti-egalitarians not to fail in the same way.

Different Kinds of Equality

Obviously no government, however powerful, could make all its people equal in height, or equal in confidence, or beauty, or mountaineering

125

skills. As to brain power, if politicians could do anything about that they would no doubt begin by arranging for a big increase in their own.

But governments can make people pretty equal in other respects. To take the worst case, a government can get close to making its people equal in ignorance, or equal in mental or physical slavery. We know from experience that governments can make people equal in regard to the duty to pay taxes.

Governments can also make people equal in other more worthwhile ways. Governments can give all citizens an equal right to vote, an equal right to run for parliament, an equal right to trial by jury. Political equalities of this kind are not impossible at all. You might as well say that elected democratic government is an impossible form of government. But it is not impossible; it happens.

What of economic equality? No government has managed it, but it has seemed to some that maybe citizens might be made equal in respect of material goods and income. For material goods can be moved around from one person to another, unlike beauty, brains, confidence or mountaineering ability.

When we speak of equality we will mean either political equality or equality in respect of material goods and income.

Are these ideals of equality worthy of our respect? Most Westerners, including a number of anti-egalitarian philosophers, accept that political equality is a condition of political liberty, and hence a worthy ideal. It is economic equality that causes most dispute, partly because it is itself an ambiguous concept, and partly because it appears to carry a number of evils in its train.

Economic equality is an ambiguous concept because of its relationship to needs, deserts and wants. This comes out when we ask the following questions, for which no one as yet has found a satisfactory answer:

Should people who are unequal in respect of beauty, or intellect, or business ability be made (or left) economically equal?

For instance, do the beautiful and the clever and the able possibly *deserve* higher incomes than the other citizens?

Or, alternatively, do the less beautiful and less able and less clever people perhaps *need* higher incomes than the others?

It looks as if the attempt to bring about economic equality invariably incurs evils such as totalitarianism and economic inefficiency. Even though this must depend somewhat on how much equality is demanded, and what steps are taken to implement it, and how this ideal is mingled with, and affected by, the other ideals of the society, yet it remains a sheer empirical fact that governments wedded to the ideal of economic equality have in the recent past shown themselves to be not only subject to corruption but capable of tyranny. Still, the facts should be treated coolly. It won't do to think of Clement Attlee and F. D. Roosevelt, say, as if they were early versions of Pol Pot.

Against Equality: The Possibility of Tyranny

It looks as if the process of achieving a society without economic inequalities may involve a fundamental problem. It looks as if the only way to bring about economic equality is through a phase of extreme inequality. The scenario goes like this: first of all there has to be a revolution; after the revolution the people hand over all power to Comrade Joe, who, in order to organize the redistribution of property, has to be made more equal than everybody else. (The manner in which this happens is brilliantly described by George Orwell in his novel *Animal Farm*.) Joe and his cronies, usually referred to as 'the Party officials', organize the redistribution of assets from a position of unequalled power. And history shows that because of this concentration of power the 'interim' phase of inequality never gives way naturally to equality.

Second, the process of *maintaining* equality is at odds with liberty. An initial revolutionary redistribution of assets, however successful, not only *does* not, but *cannot*, produce a permanent state of equality. The egalitarian dream of final and lasting equality can never be reached, hence the government has to become more and more involved in more and more excessive interference in the lives of the citizens. To maintain equality a government needs to tinker constantly with the economic infrastructure in order to thwart those who are cunning, and ambitious, and more economically skilful than their compatriots. Strict codes have to be laid down about what people can and cannot do with their entitlements. Either that, or the government would have to pay for brain operations to confuse the mental order of those with moneywise minds.

Against Equality: Nozick on Liberty and Property

The American author Robert Nozick has been deeply influenced by the political philosophy of Ayn Rand, a strong supporter of right-wing capitalism. In his book *Anarchy, State and Utopia* Nozick claims that if a government seriously wanted to bring in economic equality it would have to outlaw capitalist acts between consenting adults.

As a typical example of Nozick's thinking we will repeat his little story about the basketball player, Wilt Chamberlain.

Wilt Chamberlain is immensely skilful, and many of those who go to watch the matches do so especially to see him. Not being one to miss a trick, Wilt says he will only play if his fans put an extra sum of money into the Wilt Chamberlain appeal box. An egalitarian, says Nozick, would deem this unfair, because basketball is a team game, and Wilt Chamberlain ought not to be paid more than any other member of the team. On the other hand, he insists, for the egalitarian to forbid the fans to pay extra to see their hero is a gross infringement of their liberty.

Nozick takes issue with the whole idea of redistribution of property. He complains that high-sounding moral arguments are thrown about without anybody stopping to consider that the goods under discussion are owned by real people. The hard-earned booty of real people is talked about as though it was manna from heaven that happened to fall into Comrade Joe's lap.

There are several different theories about what constitutes the just acquisition of goods. If you believe that all property is theft, then you need have no qualms about redistributing assets. Assets for you would indeed be like manna from heaven, to be handed out to those who need them. Or if you believe that the system whereby goods are acquired in a particular society is corrupt, then you will naturally want to make a case for re-cutting the economic cake. You will argue that in a better society the cake would have been cut differently in the first place.

Nozick has a different view. He holds that all property is justly acquired unless it has actually been taken (stolen) from someone else by force or fraud or blackmail. If no such theft has been perpetrated either by the current owners or their ancestors, then any attempt to relieve them of their property is an interference with their right to freedom. Tax on earnings, for instance, is no different from forced labour; hence governments that tax rich people in order to help poorer ones violate the rights of many of their citizens. A state should be 'minimal', concerning itself only with prevention of crime and defence against external enemies.

Nozick's account of how property is justly or unjustly acquired follows some thoughts to be found in Locke's *Second Treatise on Civil Government*. But as a matter of fact if Nozick's theory of government were ever put into practice it would wreck itself on the reef of what he calls his two 'necessary Lockean provisos'. These provisos are:

1   If your property is inherited from ancestors who stole it in the first place then *ceteris paribus* the property must be handed back to the former owners or their descendants.
2   If the property was not stolen, but yet it can be shown that at the time of acquisition not enough unowned land and goods were left for other people, then the state must redistribute – now.

These two provisos would involve the state in costly historical research (presumably paid for out of taxes), leading every so often to tremendous upheavals in the economic regime. To start with, much property in the United States would have to be handed back to the American Indians, and that would probably lead to armed revolution by the non-Indians. Hence Nozick's 'Lockean' interferences with property arrangements might well turn out to be no less destructive of civil order and political liberty than the interferences of hardline economic egalitarians.

Defending an Ideal: Equality of Opportunity

Some egalitarians prefer a restricted doctrine, the doctrine of equality of opportunity. The idea here is that everyone in the community should have a chance to succeed. Making this possible ought to be the responsibility of the government, which can use taxation to pay for creating schools and other educational institutions. Whether or not these or those people in fact succeed as a result of such measures is less important than that the measures be implemented and, of course, that they work.

Equality of opportunity is seen by its proponents as more consistent with other values, such as liberty, than are stricter egalitarian doctrines.

Equality of opportunity does not involve tampering greatly with individual liberty. There is no need for government to maintain incomes at a fixed level or discourage competition. Equality of opportunity does not sacrifice efficiency in services and enjoyment of life on the altar of an impossible ideal.

It is doubtless true that nobody likes to be taxed. Still, not a few taxpayers acknowledge the value of universal education and healthcare, the value of social housing programmes, and even the value of giving all citizens a chance to reach for the skies. Taxpayers may argue about the extent to which these ideals should be state funded, but most agree in principle that some minimum state funding should be undertaken.

Most citizens of the Western nations are not Ayn Randians or Nozickeans. They accept the possibility that on some occasions a group might well be morally obliged to part with something which it legally owns. It is only a small step from here to accepting that in certain circumstances a government might have the right to deprive some persons of a portion of their income for the sake of the greater public good.

Now, there would be no point in being committed to a programme for the promotion of equal opportunity, if as a matter of fact persons from certain social groups still failed, in large numbers, to achieve any success. For example, there would be no point in a scheme to encourage women to become engineers if no more women went into engineering as a result of the scheme. On the other hand, to make sure the scheme itself works might lead to more and more tinkering, more and more interference with liberty.

Anti-egalitarians claim there is no hard and fast distinction between equality of opportunity and 'strict' equality. They hold that inside the commitment to the equality of opportunity is the seed of a desire for universal success. But universal success is impossible, and the desire for it can only lead to constant state tinkering and interference with liberty.

Defending an Ideal: Law and Values

Egalitarians sometimes defend their ideal by referring to the rule of law. Equality is connected with the idea of social rules and laws because laws *qua* laws have to be couched in general terms. A law or rule which applied only to one person would not be a law at all.

Now since the usefulness of having laws is well documented and widely supported, it might seem that we have found the right place to look for a defence of equality. But there are two problems. First, egalitarians look for a defence of more than mere legal equality. They wish to defend political and economic, and possibly social, equality as well. Second, the equality before the law that follows from the logic of rules alone allows much less legal equality than the egalitarian usually seeks. For while all those accused of breaking a particular law may be treated in the same way, it is possible for the law itself to discriminate unequally between certain groups in the relevant society. The pass laws in South Africa were of this kind: those convicted of pass law infringements were all treated in the same way, but white people did not have to conform to these laws in the first place.

Can the ideal of economic equality be related to other values, the value of humane treatment for instance?

The ideal of humaneness, of kindness and gentleness and mutual respect, is of course consistent with a belief in a hierarchical society. It is logically possible for those in lowly social positions to be accorded dignity and respect in a hierarchical society. On the other hand, although it is *possible*, it does not always happen in practice. It rather depends on just how steep the hierarchical ranking is. If the ranking is so steep that many people must live and die in the streets then that very fact makes dignity problematic and respect unlikely. Usually those who want more humane treatment of the poor and lowly soon find themselves calling, if not for complete economic equality, then at least for a great deal less *inequality*. And as a matter of fact reduction of inequality is an ideal which Western peoples are pretty strongly attached to. Furthermore it is an ideal which freedom-loving modern nations can pursue with success – Sweden and New Zealand are two examples.

Sameness and Worth

It is sometimes said that the pursuit of equality leads to a boring sameness. But sameness is not what political and economic egalitarians want.

They know as well as anyone else that sameness, if it means equality of talent, intellect, height, weight, beauty, cannot be brought about by government decree because it cannot be brought about at all.

Egalitarians often say that persons are of equal worth. What does this mean? It means, in part, that lack of sameness does not require lack of political or economic equality.

Egalitarians tend to upgrade the idea of need and downgrade the idea of desert, while anti-egalitarians of course go in the reverse direction. Egalitarians argue that those who are cleverer or more talented do not actually *need* more food and drink and motor cars than other people. Nor for that matter do those who are less clever. And generally speaking this is undoubtedly true.

But the main meaning and importance of the saying that all persons are of equal worth is the idea that a human individual is more than just a node or location of achievements and abilities. Human beings primarily have worth as human beings, and only secondarily as mountaineers or businessmen or jockeys or philosophers or whatever.

The notion that all human beings, whatever their race, age, sex, status or achievements, are of equal worth is not some new dangerous revolutionary theory. It is a conception of humanity which modern egalitarians share with traditional Judaeo–Christian thought and to some extent with modern Western democratic ideology.

How Minimal is the Minimal State?

Ayn Rand, Nozick and other right-wing libertarians argue that the best kind of state is a minimal state, one that confines its attentions to a very few areas. These include defending the nation from outside attack, and playing some part, possibly, in the maintenance of law and order. (We say *possibly*, because Nozick claims that even police protection ought ideally to be paid for directly by those who wish to buy such protection and can afford it.)

Nevertheless the minimal state is still a state, and Nozick agrees, of course, that the very fact of living in a stage entails the sacrifice of a few liberties. We obey the law against murder because we agree that no one ought to be at liberty to kill the next-door neighbours. This is a constraint of a sort, but it is not one that ordinarily offends us.

The distinction we draw as citizens is between those constraints we accept as necessary and those we think are superfluous.

The conflict between the egalitarian and anti-egalitarian positions is really a disagreement about where to draw the line of state power.

One answer is: the line of state power should be drawn at the barest necessary minimum. All attempts to pursue equality must be given up.

The other answer is that there is no such thing as 'the barest necessary minimum' because it all depends on what you think is necessary. For instance, is anyone really willing to tolerate *any* and *every* possible degree of inequality that might come about as the result of current property arrangements? Will the citizens of a modern affluent state happily tolerate the sight of thousands of out of work tramps dangerously roaming the streets? Will they tolerate having children living on garbage? The 'necessary minimum' of state power cannot be located by reference to liberty alone. The value accorded to the liberty of the taxpayer or potential taxpayer must be weighed, at least in a democracy, against the value placed on other things, e.g. on the lives of the children in the society, on education, on national defence, on the citizens' longevity and last but not least (for Nozick), on the rights of people whose ancestors our ancestors robbed.

Liberty is a very important value, but it is not, and could not be, our only value; it is not, and could not be, the only marker of the necessary minimum for state power.

15

Marx and Marxism

Intellectually invigorated by a powerful cocktail of Hegelian metaphysics and Ricardian economics, Karl Marx produced penetrating sociological insights into the industrialized England of the nineteenth century. During the twentieth century his ideas contributed more to the political and cultural map of the world than those of any other thinker.

But what did Marx really believe? What exactly is the Marxist philosophy, the philosophy to which so many states have sworn allegiance – at least until recently?

Absolutely authoritative answers to these questions, even if available, would be beyond the scope of this chapter. Moreover Marxists are hampered by the fact that there are apparent inconsistencies between the so-called 'early' Marx of *The German Ideology* and the 'late' Marx of *Capital* and *Grundrisse* (*Foundations*). Interested non-Marxists, on the other hand, are hindered by the fact that when they look to experts for help in understanding Marx's writings they often discover that some, at least, of those experts write books in 'Marx-speak', an opaque and self-sustaining language which makes appreciation of complicated economic and political arguments very difficult.

This chapter aims to give an introduction to the main ideas of Marx which will, we hope, be neither insultingly simplistic nor unnecessarily complex.

When Marx discusses societies he draws a distinction between what he calls their *economic bases* and their *political, cultural and legal super-*

structures. He holds that the nature of a society's economy determines the character of its legal, political and cultural life. According to Marx beautiful poetry and complex legal and social customs cannot arise when people are constantly struggling against starvation and trying to cope with severe climatic conditions. He claims, moreover, that the kind of society an individual happens to be born into will place fundamental limits on his or her personal development and possibilities.

It is certainly true that human beings do not create themselves or their personalities by some kind of mysterious, undetermined action. We do not decide which historical epoch to spend our lives in nor can we choose the geographical and political circumstances into which we are born. The problems we face are often largely determined by the conditions of our life, and we solve those problems using ideas and solutions which we find to hand and which themselves are partly conditioned by circumstances. On the other hand, although human beings are undeniably products of circumstance they are also changers of circumstance. Marx is far from believing that we are the passive victims of determinism. He stresses the possibilities of dynamic change and revolutionary practice. Thus Marxism cannot be identified with mechanistic determinism, a fatalistic doctrine which denies human purpose and activity. On the contrary Marx argues that the circumstances that shape consciousness themselves depend, in part, on human actions. They include human relationships which have been created historically by the actions of manking. In the *Third Thesis on Feuerbach* he writes:

> the materialistic doctrine concerning the changing of circumstances and upbringing forgets that circumstances are changed by men.

In the same work he even gives some credence to idealism, a theory usually regarded as the exact opposite of materialism.

The Influence of Hegel

Marx's interest in Hegel centres largely on that philosopher's *Phenomenology of Spirit*, and especially on the very abstract and metaphysical section entitled 'Self Consciousness'. Here Hegel describes the relationships that exist between one human consciousness and others. It is important, however, to understand that he is not describing actual or even merely possible people: rather, his topic is the relations that hold between different archetypal human spirits, which in turn are manifestations of the (so-called) World Spirit. Each relationship is said to contain internal inconsistencies, or tensions, which make it unstable and eventually lead to breakdown. After breakdown a new relationship arises out of the wreckage of the old, producing solutions for whatever problems caused the initial collapse, but later developing its own tensions and inconsistencies. The momentum caused by the repeated replacement of one set of relationships with another is the basis of the Hegelian Dialectic which can aptly be called a dialectic of the spirit. Its imagery is somewhat reminiscent of the Christian triad: Innocence, Fall and Redemption. The primitive Spirit, which is Hegel's starting point, is, as it were, pure and whole, but lacks self-knowledge. A struggle for self-knowledge brings about division and internal turmoil, leading to reconciliation and to a higher and more satisfactory kind of wholeness.

Like other young intellectuals of his generation Marx was captivated by Hegel's philosophical and historical vision. However, he outgrew his initial attitude to the older man in the 1840s, a decade during which he came to believe that spiritual relationships are not, after all, the things which shape societies. Material conditions external to the spirit, for example the kinds of work men do, and the wealth which their labours produce for themselves and for others, are the things which matter. In other words the progress of history is not determined by self-consciousness. According to Marx self-consciousness increases as our control over the environment increases, not the other way around. Moreover until the human race achieves complete control of its material circumstances the relations between human beings will inevitably take the form of mastery and servitude. Yet mastery and servitude themselves continually evolve, taking new forms with every stage of the historical process. The momentum of this process is not as Hegel perceived it; the tensions which appear at every stage in the history of mankind are features, not of spirit, but of material forces. As nearly everyone knows Marx's theory is called dialectical *materialism*.

Productive Forces, the Division of Labour, and Forms of Ownership

According to Marx the internal structure of any state depends on the extent to which that state's productive forces have been developed. It follows that once we know what type of economy a country has we should be able to discover a great deal about its cultural and other internal characteristics.

The nature of the economy is revealed, interestingly enough, not only by what the country produces, but also, and more importantly, by the degree to which the division of labour has taken place. New productive forces are necessarily accompanied by developments in the division of labour: in other words, by changes in the overall character of the workforce as a whole. Moreover all the various stages of development, Marx tells us, can be regarded as so many different types or forms of *ownership*.

The first form of ownership is *Eden*. Eden is a stage in the history of humanity in which production is still undeveloped. In Eden people live by hunting and fishing, and perhaps by rearing animals, and by agriculture – but agriculture in an extremely elementary form. The division of labour at this stage is very simple, being based on slight extensions of the 'natural' division of labour to be seen in the family.

The second form of ownership is *slavery*. Now according to Marxist theory slavery already existed in Eden as a kind of latency implied in the structure of the family itself. However, full-blown slavery only emerges as populations grow, societies become more complex, and inter-tribal contact – in the form of trade and warfare – increases. Complex tribal communities, and feudal States of the kind familiar to us from the history of Europe in the Dark Ages, are slave societies according to the Marxist system of classification. A complex tribal community can be defined as one which has arisen from the union of several tribes; such a union can come about as the result either of agreement or by conquest, and will typically develop into a polity or city. In *The German Ideology* Marx states that these groups retain at first some traditional forms of communal ownership existing side by side with private property consisting of both movable and immovable items. This latter kind of ownership appears first as an abnormal arrangement subordinate to communal traditions but eventually supplants them.

Feudal society develops around the division of the people into owners and non-owners of land. In a feudal community both the enserfed peasants and the nobles who possess the estates are perceived as having their own special relationships to the land. The hierarchical social structure is supported and enforced by the bands of armed retainers employed by the nobility for that purpose.

The third form of ownership is *capitalism*. Wherever there is trade there will appear a merchant class, a class quite different from that of the owners of land. Capitalism represents the victory of this new class, which is often described as the middle class or bourgeoisie. Under capitalism the middle class, or one of its sections, owns the means of production and the control of moneys: it owns factories, banks, shipping firms, and so on.

The fourth stage of ownership is *socialism*. Marx holds that socialism becomes possible once there exists an industrialized and semi-educated workforce. The industrial underclass, the proletariat, work for small reward, and the surplus they produce goes to enrich their masters, the bourgeoisie. Proletarians need to work, of course, in order to keep body and soul together, for they have nothing to sell except their labour. They need their capitalist masters (or at least they believe they do) because it is the masters who provide the wages. It is important to remember though that the capitalists need the workers just as much as, or even more than, the workers need their jobs. Obviously without a workforce there will be nothing produced and nothing to sell. A socialist revolution can occur, according to Marx, when the workers realize that they have power over those who employ them. At this point in the historical process the workers rise up against the bourgeoisie and take control of the means of production. Just as the capitalist revolution can be described as the victory of the bourgeoisie over the feudal landowners, so the socialist revolution can be called the victory of the proletariat over the middle-class controllers of industrial production.

The rule of the working classes, which will be the outcome of socialist revolution, might be thought to be Marx's idea of the pinnacle of human historical development; but it is not that. Just as earlier societies developed tensions leading eventually to their downfall, so too will socialist societies crumble under the stress of their own internal contradictions. The 'dictatorship of the proletariat' is itself the first sign of destructive tensions within. The final stage of human development will be achieved, according to Marxist theory, only when this dictatorship is overcome. At that point in history the state will wither away, there will be no more private ownership and no more class divisions.

There are few positive descriptions by Marx or anyone else of what the communist state (or rather, non-state) will be like. In some early passages the younger Marx describes a sort of Idyll in which people spend a lot of time fishing and writing poetry. Otherwise descriptions of the Marxian Utopia are negative: there will not be any class struggle, there will not be any exploitation of man by man, there will not be any private ownership of the means of production, and there will be no social evils or social problems.

From Eden to Communism: One Road Only?

There is some debate about whether Marx held that all societies must develop according to the sequence Eden, Slavery, Capitalism, Socialism, Communism. There is evidence to suggest that he did not want to insist that there can be only one route to his Utopia. In *Grundrisse* he appears to make a more limited and pragmatic point, namely, that non-Communist societies invariably contain social divisions which lead to instability. Hence only Communist societies can be stable.

This simpler conception unfortunately leaves us with a picture of human societies as consisting of irrational systems which keep repeatedly breaking down and repeatedly being replaced by new social and economic arrangements. Such a picture gives no assurance that human beings will ever hit upon Communism – the only arrangement, according to Marxism, which can guarantee stability.

It is therefore more comforting, perhaps, to believe that the teleological sequence: Eden, Slavery, Capitalism, Socialism has to occur everywhere, and that it will necessarily produce Communism everywhere in the end. On the other hand this inflexible teleological model does not correspond to actual historical events. According to the model Capitalism must come before Socialism; yet as is now well known, the successful Socialist revolutions of this century did not occur in the industrialized countries of Europe and North America but in nations with a largely agricultural workforce: Russia, China, Cuba.

Another question which emerges here is: Why do human beings choose to leave Eden? Why do they go through centuries of struggle in order to bring about a distant future Communist society? One might indeed be forgiven for thinking that to live at the bottom of the social heap in Eden — if Eden has a top and a bottom — sounds much more pleasant than occupying the bottom place in a slave society, or under Capitalism, or even, dare it be said, in a Socialist State.

Marx's response is that when Nature is generous there is no history and no dialectical momentum. The inhabitants of a generous Eden tell us nothing about themselves, and if there are ever any significant changes in their situation these will come to the community from outside, not from internal tensions.

Nevertheless even a generous Eden might have to face the problems associated with a rapid growth of population. Population growth is likely to be followed by expansion in production and more aggressive technologies. Animals will be raised rather than hunted, vegetables planted rather than merely gathered; and the result might well be the generation of a surplus of goods above what is needed to sustain the producers. The generation of surplus is the catalyst which leads to the formation of a new social class whose task it is to handle the surplus and to organize the more complex productive arrangements. The new class will take from the producers as much of the surplus as it can get its hands on, and this in turn can well lead to the emergence of a class or sub-class of well-fed people who have no tasks at all. The organizational and non-working classes dominate society as a whole, thus destroying the community as a whole.

Ideologies

Ideologies are belief systems. In Marxist theory the word *ideology* often has pejorative overtones suggesting that the beliefs in question are suspect — or, in Marx-speak, that they are 'rooted in false consciousness'. All corrupt, i.e. non-Communist, societies are supported by their respective ideologies. All hierarchies are justified by ideology, and those who accept the local ideology will naturally defend the hierarchy even if they themselves live at the bottom of the heap. The defence might consist of the idea that there is a natural order in which the poor and lowly are downright inferior to other people. Or it might consist in the idea that without hierarchy society would break down.

Lenin, in *What is to be Done?*, argues that the way to counter ideological beliefs is to create a 'vanguard group' whose task will be to introduce correct beliefs. Without the efforts of such a group the proletariat might never break out of its ideology-ridden world. Lenin advocated the inculcation of whatever ideas best enable workers to restructure society in such a way as to make it serve their own interests. He held that a radical critique of society has to involve a critique of its ideology; the two operations are inseparable. He also said that he wished to exclude from the process of inculcation all desires to enslave, to exploit and to dominate other people.

The Frankfurt School

Marxist philosophy was developed in Germany during the 1920s by Theodor W. Adorno, Herbert Marcuse and others at the Institute for Social Research in Frankfurt; the Institute, however, was closed down when Hitler came to power. Its professors fled to the USA and inaugurated a reincarnation of the 'Frankfurt School' in that country. Marcuse in particular became a big name in America. After the war the Institute for Social Research was set up once again in Frankfurt and here Adorno in particular taught many people who were destined to become well-known philosophers.

The philosophy of the Frankfurt school is called *Ideologiekritik* (*Critique of Ideology*). It asks the quasi-Leninist question: How can the transition be made from humanity's present situation of ideological delusion and economic and social bondage to eventual enlightenment and emancipation? The answer is that people must subject themselves to a critical procedure which will make them search out the origins of their beliefs about the world. We might, for instance, be less inclined to believe in the virtues of a hierarchical system, in which, perhaps, we ourselves are doomed to poverty, if we were shown that the only people who benefit from our holding such beliefs are the aristocrats of capitalism.

It seems though that *Ideologiekritik* can only get started if and when ordinary people come to share certain basic assumptions with their Marxist counsellors. Ordinary people will have to acquire the assumption or fundamental meta-belief that their beliefs about society have the function of legitimating oppressive but unnecessary social institutions.

The first aim of the Frankfurt-style Marxist 'therapy' is to encourage people to imagine a model of society which fulfils all their criteria for an ideal community and which does not depend on oppressive institutions or on a ritual enslavement of certain groups. The next step is to discuss the matter until those involved come to see that the model they have described is not merely an idle dream but could actually come about in reality. Philosophical counselling will show people that the 'ideal' society is not only possible but necessary – necessary, that is, for the full development of human potential. In the end those who have attained enlighhtenment through *Ideologiekritik* will become members of the Marxist-Leninist vanguard group. They will go out and convince everybody else that revolutionary change is both necessary and desirable.

Unfortunately for the Frankfurt school (and its kindred souls), several years of philosophical instruction in its methodology have not so far brought about even one single successful revolution anywhere in the world. It would appear, then, that *Ideologiekritik* is not a reliable way to bring about social change.

As it happens, some members of the school have given a lot of thought to this problem. Adorno maintains that enabling a forum for discussion in which participants can modify their beliefs and thereby attain their own concept of a rationally satisfying existence is a good way of restructuring society. However, he at times appears to fear that ideological delusion might be so deep – especially under capitalism – that it cannot be removed. To put this another way: it might turn out that Adorno will never be able to persuade a critical mass of people to agree with his premises, namely, that living in an advanced capitalist society involves (1) keeping half the world in poverty so that the others can maintain consumerism; (2) squandering the Earth's natural resources for the same purpose; (3) manufacturing goods which are designed to fall apart because that is the only way to keep the engines of capitalism moving. Nor will people necessarily believe that other ways of managing an economy would be any better.

Marx's Legacy

Nowadays Marx's theory might seem to be nothing better than an intellectual curiosity, hidebound by an antiquated belief in progress and obsessed with the living conditions of the English urban working class. Yet it would be unwise, and parochial, to underestimate the power of Marx's Utopian vision. More than one generation of thinkers, not only in Europe but all over the world, have been influenced by his thought. In the twentieth century probably all the most prominent figures of Europe's intelligentsia were readers of Marx. Jean-Paul Sartre, Simone de Beauvoir, Michel Foucault and Antonin Gramsci – not to mention Herbert Marcuse, Theodor Adorno and Jürgen Habermas – were all at one time inspired by his writings. It is notorious, too, that Marx's ideas have been borrowed, and transmuted, by some of the most notable political figures of the times. Marxism was adapted by Lenin to fit what he perceived as the requirements of Russian State Socialism and by Fidel Castro to meet the needs of the Cuban revolution. Mao Tse Tung propounded a Chinese version and Gramsci a European one. The agents of State Socialism everywhere paid a merely ritualistic lip service to the idea of the class struggle, claiming that the victory of the pro-letariat had been realized in their own societies – a claim completely at odds with Marx's own predictions about the withering away of the state and the flowering of a classless non-statist community.

This chapter has hinted at the broad appeal of Marxism and alluded to the large array of theories which can all be loosely described as Marxist. The common thread running through these diverse annals – all the way from the academic theses of Frankfurt to the crude popu-lism of China's Cultural Revolution – is the thought of one man who said he wanted to remembered as a thinker not as a philosopher.

16
Politics and Sex

The Ideology of Sex

The ideology of sex covers a number of related topics, the most important of which is the traditional difference in social and political status between women and men.

Other topics are marriage; the rights and wrongs of divorce, abortion and contraception; homosexuality; and sexual behaviour in general.

Philosophy and Sex

Readers might be surprised that a philosophy book should contain a chapter about sexual matters. Is sex a suitable subject for philosophy?

The difference in status between men and women to be found in most societies is sometimes expressed in legislation, and conversely, changes in the status difference are sometimes brought about by changes in the law. Now, law and the laws are the subject matter of jurisprudence (philosophy of law): it follows that any status difference based in law is potentially a suitable subject for philosophers to think about.

Second, traditional morality and traditional religious teaching both contain quantitites of imperatives telling the two sexes how to behave. The validity or otherwise of particular ethical imperatives is (or ought to be) part of the subject matter of moral philosophy.

Third and most importantly, sex is a suitable subject for philosophy because the ideology of sex is mixed up with ideas about nature, that is, with theories about the natural and the unnatural, the normal and the abnormal, and 'nature versus nurture'. Such ideas are essentially philosophical in character, and it is chiefly these that we will be discussing.

It is an ancient commonplace that not all the differences between human beings are natural. Many differences are social or institutional. One of the most striking examples of a structured social difference, or set of differences, is the Hindu institution of caste.

It is also a commonplace that unreflective people often make no distinction between natural differences and social ones. In the minds of many unreflective people the distinction itself scarcely exists. This distinction however is crucial to our topic. It will be discussed below.

But first, do real philosophers write about the status of women? Do real philosophers write about sexual topics?

Well, yes, they do. The status of women, and the nature of women, were considered suitable topics by Plato, Aristotle, Rousseau, Schopenhauer and J. S. Mill, among others. In recent years a considerable number of philosophers, especially in France, Canada and the United States, have interested themselves in feminism, which of course raises those same questions about status and nature.

Sexual topics generally have also been widely discussed by philosophers during the last thirty or forty years or so. In that time many philosophers have published papers about abortion. A somewhat smaller number of people have published work on the morality of contraception. The British philosopher Roger Scruton and the American philosopher Thomas Nagel have separately attempted to define sexual perversion. More recently still the philosophical journals have begun to publish articles on certain ethical questions which have arisen in connection with the AIDS epidemic.

Philosophy and Feminism

What is feminism? Feminists claim that traditional social arrangements are unjust to women. The injustice consists in such facts as the following:

145

Historically women in most societies have had no political power and still today have less power than men.

Women have had, and in many societies still have, inferior education.

Women have been allowed fewer possible roles in life and fewer opportunities for interesting work outside the home.

It is claimed that in most societies women work harder than men, and for lower wages, or even for no wages.

Women as a sex are encouraged (successfully) to have low self-esteem.

Feminists aim to end these states of affairs by argument and, where possible and relevant, by political action.

Feminism is not especially new. Mary Wollstonecraft, the suffragettes and the suffragists, Virigina Woolf and Simone de Beauvoir were all feminists. And if you have sharp eyes you can often see feminist ideas lurking unexpectedly in plays and novels by ladylike and seemingly conventional authors.

As a social phenomenon feminism comes in waves. The current wave has had marked effects on employment and on higher education.

Expectations and the Sexes

Sex and sexual differences structure life in many ways. The first question asked about a new baby is 'Is it a boy or a girl?' In traditional societies the birth of a boy causes rejoicing, the birth of a girl is a disappointment.

The *status* difference itself is naturally perceived differently by men and by women. For one thing a woman might resent the status difference whereas a man can have no personal reason to feel resentment. When women accept rather than resent the status difference they are nevertheless possibly more likely to be surprised at its particular manifestations than men are. Men are perhaps more likely than women are to assume that members of the other sex will think and act very differently from those of their own sex.

No doubt every society expects men and women to behave differently to some extent. In our own society women are assumed to be kinder than men, and to understand better the complexities of close relationships and human needs. They are believed to have a better grasp of psychological realities, and a better understanding of human flourishing, human personality, human psychological growth. Men are assumed to be less emotional than women. They are expected to be better able to understand machinery and the complexities of modern technology. They are also thought to have a better understanding of political and economic realities.

At least one anthropologist has maintained that assumptions and expectations about male and female human behaviour differ from one society to another. Thus Margaret Mead writes:

> In every known society mankind has elaborated the biological division of labour into forms often very remotely related to the original biological differences that provided the original clues. Upon the contrast in bodily form and function, men have built analogies between the sun and moon, night and day, goodness and evil, strength and tenderness, steadfastness and fickleness, endurance and vulnerability. Sometimes one quality has been assigned to one sex, sometimes to the other. Now it is the boys who are thought of as infinitely vulnerable and in need of special cherishing care, now it is the girls . . . Some peoples think of women as too weak to work out of doors, others regard women as the appropriate bearers of heavy burdens 'because their heads are stronger than men's' . . . Whether we deal with small matters or with large, with the frivolities of ornament and cosmetics or the sanctities of man's place in the universe, we find this great variety of ways, often flatly contradictory one to the other, in which the roles of the two sexes have been patterned. But we always find the patterning . . . We find no culture in which it has been thought that all identified traits – stupidity and brilliance, beauty and ugliness, friendliness and hostility, initiative and responsiveness, courage and patience and industry – are merely human traits.

Feminists attempt to look at the socially stressed differences between men and women with fresh eyes. They are critical of common assumptions about what is natural and acceptable behaviour in men and in women, and point out that these common assumptions often work against women's interests. Kate Millett, in her book *Sexual Politics*, argues that the accepted notions about masculine and feminine roles and temperaments, and the socialization of boys and girls to conform to these, guarantee that power in society will remain in the hands of the males.

One Sex or Two?

Simone de Beauvoir, writing in 1949, remarked:

> In truth, to go for a walk with one's eyes open is enough to demon-
> strate that humanity is divided into two classes of individuals whose
> clothes, faces, bodies, smiles, gaits, interests and occupations are mani-
> festly different.

Yet on the other hand there is a deep-rooted and contrary idea that
humanity is really a one-sex species. One way in which this deep-
rooted and presumably subconscious idea manifests itself is in the supposition that women are simply anomalous men. Women are childish
men, or sick men, or castrated men. You can see this strange thought
in the writings of several thinkers, including Aristotle, Schopenhauer,
Freud and Otto Weininger.

The idea that humanity is a one-sex species, or could be turned into
one, also appears in certain feminist writings, those that support what
might be called the *androgynous ideal*.

According to the androgynous ideal the best possible state of affairs
would be one in which sex roles, including the roles of conception,
pregnancy and mothering, were abolished. All institutional and inter-
personal relationships could then be free of power, domination and
unfairness. The androgynous ideal could be brought about in the near
future by the use of artificial insemination, and by scientific arrangements enabling infants to be born and bred in laboratories.

This particular branch of feminism claims that the allegedly special
psychological characteristics of men and women are the result of social
engineering. Our task should be to unlearn the underlying ideologies
so that women can be allowed to be strong and courageous, logical
and analytic, and less interested in unworthy and boring things like
babies. In return men can be allowed to be caring and sensitive if
anyone still thinks that those traits are valuable.

Different Types of Feminism

The androgynous ideal seems to presuppose that traditional female roles
are inherently dull, boring and not worthwhile, whereas traditional

male roles are held to be interesting and humanly significant. But there are two schools of feminist thought about this.

The other school of thought argues that men and women really do have different natures and that the female nature and psychology is as valuable as or more valuable than the male. Women have special characteristics and abilities and capacities, and a distinctive feminine thought style which is more intuitive, more emotionally honest, and more creative and lateral than male thinking. There is a genuine alternative to the scientific, rational, logical, analytic thought style of men. The feminist task is not to try to bring about the androgynous ideal but rather to make sure that society recognizes the true value of the specifically feminine abilities and virtues which for centuries have been consistently undervalued by patriarchal societies.

There are also two schools of thought within the feminist movement about the need for equality in the workplace.

One view is that equality with men in the workplace is an essential feminist goal. The other school of thought is that such equality ought not to be pursued. The sexual difference must be recognized by society, albeit in new ways, because treating men and women *equally* means treating women *unjustly*. Women have to bear children, and for the most part they have to care for children. Indeed most women enjoy caring for their children. To insist on equal conditions of employment (employment outside the home, that is) would mean that women in fact would need to work for far longer hours than men do, as happened in the old Soviet Union.

But it is surely plain that if 'equal' work conditions lead to an unjust, unequal division of labour, then those work conditions were not really equal in the first place. The difference between the two views seems in the end to rest on a confusion about the meaning of the word 'equal'.

Sex and Gender

Many men, and some women, while agreeing that man-made laws and customs do indeed create and enshrine a status difference between men and women, nevertheless insist that those laws and customs, or anyway some similar ones, are made necessary by natural differences. Sex itself is a natural difference which laws and other social institutions must respect.

However the evidence of anthropology, not to mention ordinary knowledge of history, shows not that laws and customs always create and enforce some one set of social distinctions between men and women, but rather that different societies create different social differences. The social differences do not reflect the universal natural difference but rather interpret its importance in a variety of ways. The sex difference of itself cannot necessitate all the many and various social and political norms which it is used to justify.

In order to adumbrate this point modern feminists draw a distinction between sex on the one hand and what, for want of a better word, they have called *gender* on the other.

The sex difference is a difference found in nature, but its natural importance is confined in the main to the contexts of reproduction and sexual love.

'Gender', on the other hand, is not a fact of nature at all. It is made up of a huge collection of laws, customs, psychological theories, methods of bringing up children, recommendations, rules, etiquettes, and so on. Gender, in short, is not nature but nurture. Sex roles, such as insemination and pregnancy, are based in physiology, i.e. in nature, but gender roles are artefacts. Every individual is brought up to fit into his or her society's male or female roles, and most individuals unthinkingly accept the idea that differences in gender roles are just as natural as physiological differences.

So much for the feminists' account of sex and gender. Purists and pedants will object that the word 'gender' has to do with grammar. So we need to explain why the word 'gender' is an appropriate label for certain social structures.

Gender is the grammatical classification of all nouns into masculine and feminine (and, in some languages, neuter as well). English of course has this classification but uses the masculine and feminine genders in a realistic fashion, that is, only in relation to human beings and other animals. In English an inanimate object is not referred to as 'he' or 'she' but as 'it'. In French, on the other hand, everything, including all inanimate objects, is either grammatically masculine or grammatically feminine. Other languages have three genders but still allow inanimate objects to be 'he' or 'she'.

Gender is indeed a grammatical notion. But the extension of meaning from grammatical classifications to other social artefacts is not inapt at all. Grammatical gender is an artificial analogue of natural sex, a sort of imaginary sexuality invented by the human race. Grammatical gender mimics natural sexual difference.

In the feminist concept of gender we find an essentially similar type of analogue. In other words, the feminist concept of gender is the concept of a social, i.e. an artificial, distinction which mimics a natural one.

This case incidentally shows that using a word in a new or extended way need not bring all discussion grinding to a halt. That only happens if people fail to grasp that the meaning of a word has been deliberately extended or altered. In the present case the extended meaning is obvious, and not inapt, and not too difficult to understand.

Discrimination

Discrimination means drawing distinctions. There seems nothing inherently bad about drawing distinctions between people – after all, people really are different from one another, as individuals, and also *qua* members of different nations, races, classes and sexes. What is objectionable is unjust discrimination. But that at once raises the question: What makes this or that discrimination unjust?

There is a clue to the answer to be found in the answers to another question (suggested by Nietzsche in a different context), namely: Who benefits? If we find an ideology that discriminates between people we may not be able to decide whether it is just or unjust until we have discovered who benefits from it, how they benefit, and whether there is some reason, good or bad, for the existence of these benefits.

Much ideology is special pleading, as Nietzsche pointed out. As such it tends to have an air of ad hoccery about it. Here is an example. In 1857 the American Supreme Court produced a supreme piece of *ad hoc* special pleading when it ruled: 'blacks are beings of an inferior order – and so far inferior that they have no rights which the white man is bound to respect.'

Answering the question: Who benefits? cannot by itself decide which distinctions and discriminations are just, which unjust. But it is not a bad place to start.

151

Part IV
The Philosophy of Science

17
The Methods of Science

The idea of science conjures up different pictures for different people: mad professors in white coats, bunsen burners in school laboratories, the triumphs of organ transplants, the horrors of environmental pollution.

Perhaps, though, we all agree that science is both especially important and at the same time different from other spheres of enquiry. That is probably because science has been responsible for vast far-reaching changes in our lives. Even if one feels hostile to science one has to agree that it is an astonishingly successful enterprise.

Why is science so successful? Does it owe its success to its method or methods? Is there such a thing as a specifically scientific method? And if so, what is this method?

We will begin by finding out what the word 'science' means.

Until the nineteenth century science meant any branch of theoretical knowledge or learning; but it has increasingly come to refer only to those branches of knowledge which have to do with the material universe. Nowadays the ideal or paradigm science is the science of matter. Yet at the same time scholars working in other fields like to call their own subjects sciences. Thus it is claimed by practitioners that anthropology, economics, linguistics, philology and psychology are sciences. In spite of these claims, which are not unreasonable, we will take the word 'science' to refer in the main only to disciplines which study the physical world, including of course those physical things which are living organisms.

Observation and Experiment

Most scientists and philosophers of science would probably agree that one vital component of scientific method is the use of experiments. It is often held that intellectual progress occurs at times when scientists perform experiments and look critically at the results, whereas there will be intellectual stagnation at times when experiments are performed uncritically or not performed at all.

Those who believe that this is the case say that the claim can be supported by many examples from history.

The Greek physician Galen (AD 130–201), for instance, discovered things about the structure of muscles by dissecting dead bodies, in other words, by experimenting. Galen was responsible for pioneering many new medical techniques. Later on, in the so-called Dark Ages, it was assumed that the ancients, including Galen, had made no mistakes. So physicians did not bother to find out for themselves how muscles worked. These centuries are generally held to have been a time when science, including medical science, made little or no progress.

The assumption that the Greeks did not make mistakes was called into question during the Renaissance. Vesalius (1514–64) performed his own experiments and found that some of Galen's descriptions appeared to match the muscles of dogs rather than the muscles of human beings. Presumably Galen had dissected different kinds of animal, but the fact had been forgotten or otherwise lost sight of. The questioning spirit of the Renaissance, exemplified by Vesalius, enabled great strides to be made in science generally – although it has to be admitted that medical science as such did not make much progress until the nineteenth century.

Yet it would be simplistic to conclude that scientific progress depends entirely on the willingness or otherwise to perform experiments. While it seems that the medievals' admiration for their predecessors went too far, and amounted to a disregard for the evidence of their own senses, it would be unrealistic to insist that scientists ought to reperform every experiment performed earlier; for that would leave no time for new experiments.

Theories and Inferences: Hempel and Popper

Scientific method is more than observation and experiment. Scientists formulate theories which are intended to explain experimental results and to make it possible to accurately predict future observations.

But how do we get from observations to theory? And how are theories used in science?

Carl Hempel gave an account of how scientists operate which is very well known and which was widely accepted until quite recently. Hempel said that science was based on the *hypothetico-deductive* method. What this means is that scientists are supposed to begin by making and recording observations in whatever field they happen to be investigating; next, they formulate a hypothetical covering law; third, this hypothetical law is then used as a premise in a deductive argument.

Let us take a simple example.

Step one: set up a battery and some wires and try to send electric currents through various objects made of silver, iron, copper, brass and other metals. Observe and record that all the objects conduct electricity.

Step two: formulate a hypothetical law: 'all metals conduct electricity'.

Step three: use this law as a premise in a deduction, for example: All metals conduct electricity. Mercury is a metal. Therefore the mercury fillings in teeth will conduct electricity.

Hempel's covering law model is by no means a complete account of scientific thinking. To begin with, it leaves out or anyway minimizes the role played in science by unobservable (theoretical) entities such as gravity and magnetism. Second, it does not seem suited to explain particular events like someone's buying a ticket to Paris. For since people visit Paris for an enormous variety of different reasons there can be no covering law to explain this phenomenon. Yet going to Paris is not *inexplicable*.

Karl Popper (1902–94) is perhaps the most famous philosopher of science of the twentieth century. His account of scientific reasoning may aptly be called the falsification theory.

Popper holds that scientists formulate 'highly falsifiable' theories which they then test. In a way scientists can be said to spend much of their time trying to show that their own theories are false. When all the scientist's theories have been shown to be false except one, then he or she can conclude, at least for the time being, that the remaining theory is the correct one. But no theory is safe for all time. Every theory is ultimately only a hypothesis, and hence permanently open to the possibility of refutation.

There are some objections to Popper's account. One is that it is not possible to test each and every theory, since human ingenuity is capable of constructing an indefinitely large number of these. Next, Popper cannot really explain why exactly it is that some theories are rejected as obviously false and not worth testing at all. As a matter of fact we rely on common sense to tell us which theories are too silly to bother with. For example, suppose a young person were to formulate the theory that one can always obtain a ticket to Brighton by dancing in front of the ticket office. The theory is clearly highly falsifiable but only someone bereft of common sense would be bothered to test it.

A third problem is that the falsification theory seems to rule out from science too much that scientists themselves want to keep in.

Consider two important matters: the doctrine that every event has a cause, and the theory of evolution.

The doctrine that every event has a cause is extremely deeply rooted in all Western scientific tradition. It is so important that scientists do not allow it to be falsified, as it were. No failure to find a cause in a particular case ever counts as a falsification of this doctrine, which is thereby *treated* as unfalsifiable. Even in the case of quantum physics, where causal descriptions seem to be inapplicable, scientists say only that here the ideas of cause and effect lack explanatory power.

Darwin's theory of evolution also seems to have a privileged position, though for a somewhat different reason. The theory of evolution is not just *treated* as unfalsifiable, rather, it is not at all easy to see how it *could* be falsified. On Popperian terms, then, the theory is not scientifically respectable. Yet it explains such a wide range of data that biologists would be most loath to give it up. And even if someone could think of a way to test it, and the test indicated falsehood, could the theory of evolution be dropped overnight?

Popper's account on the face of it implies that as soon as a scientist makes one or two observations which do not fit into current theory then the theory will be abandoned as false. But in fact it often happens that theory takes precedence over observation. Who would abandon the heliocentric theory of the solar system on the basis of a few empirical observations?

Kuhn and Feyerabend

Popper wrote his magnum opus *Die Logik der Forschung* in 1934 and it was translated into English (as *The Logic of Scientific Discovery*) in 1958. Since then Thomas Kuhn and Paul Feyerabend decided – independently of one another – that the best way to find out about the nature of scientific method is not to philosophize in one's study but rather to observe and record the activities of real scientists past and present.

Kuhn's observation of scientists and investigations into the history of science led him to distinguish two different varieties of scientific enterprise, normal science and revolutionary science.

Normal science does not construct new theories, nor does it test the adequacy of older ones. Normal science simply assumes that current theories are true. It proceeds by determining 'known facts' or 'true facts' with more precision, by investigating unexplained happenings with the aim of fitting them into current theory and by resolving small theoretical ambiguities. The methodology of normal science is a matter of forcing nature into various currently accepted theoretical boxes – by fair means or foul fudge.

Now and again, says Kuhn, a scientific revolution takes place. Such revolutions are extremely rare though, and occur only when existing theories turn out to be very unsatisfactory indeed. For a while a number of different theories (and a number of different scientists) might compete, until one comes to be preferred to the others. The triumph of a theory will be due to a variety of factors: its capacity for explaining recalcitrant facts, its usefulness in solving problems and making accurate predictions, and last but not least the clout and prestige of the scientists who invented it and support it. An individual's scientific prestige, says Kuhn, is often assumed to be the result of, and proof of, exceptional ability; but in fact it can also be due to such things as having powerful friends in the worlds of business and politics. For a theory to succeed, its inventor must have access to money for research and a relatively high position in the academic hierarchy, as well as ability.

Kuhn also has some comments to make about his predecessors in the field. He claims that Hempel, Popper et al. misdescribe what scientists actually do. He says that these distinguished philosophers of science have been taken in and hoodwinked by the authors of students' textbooks.

Textbooks written for science students simplify drastically. They suppress many historical facts, particularly those that are deemed to 'confuse the issue'. They set out current theories as if these were the final truth. And one way or another they always enhance the myth that science is constantly progressing and constantly overcoming the weaknesses and failures of earlier generations.

Science textbooks never reveal the fact that older theories which are still used (such as Newton's) often contradict current views. Instead they incorrectly describe these earlier theories as simpler and more specialized versions of modern ones. Accepted older theories are said to be consistent with current theories even when this is not the case.

On the other hand, when modern scientists have completely rejected an earlier theory, then the textbooks will describe the rejected theory as *unscientific*. Thus they directly foster the belief that it is impossible for a *scientific* theory to be false, and indirectly foster the belief that *true* scientists are pretty well infallible.

Kuhn concludes that Popper, Hempel and others have described, not the real methodology of science, but fictional states of affairs existing only in the pages of the textbooks given to science students.

However, he argues that the textbooks have to be as they are. The distortions to be found between their covers are necessary for the training of young scientists, whose minds have to be closed off to theories that are not productive at the moment. But science textbooks do not tell the truth about the history of science and they are a bad basis for philosophy of science.

We turn now to the ideas of Paul Feyerabend. In order to make some estimate of the value of Feyerabend's theories it will be useful to have some idea of his personality. It seems that Feyerabend was a colourful and extrovert character, with a pronounced sense of humour. Judging from his books it would appear that he enjoyed poking cruel fun at establishments, hierarchies and pomposities of all kinds. Scientists and philosophers of science are not used to being ridiculed, and this flamboyant individual provoked a certain amount of hostility, which in turn sometimes led to misunderstandings of his work.

The Methods of Science

Feyerabend concentrates on what Kuhn called revolutionary science, the enterprise which leads to the birth of new theories and the death of old ones. His main claim is that scientists have no special methodology, hence the title of his best-known book – *Against Method*. Science, he says, has anarchistic features, and it has no rules of procedure which are used in all cases. The human mind is enormously creative and it responds to intellectual challenges in ever new and unpredictable ways. Even the idea that observation and experiment are of primary importance in science is not always applicable since what counts as relevant observation partly depends on what theory one is working with. New theories force scientists to reinterpret their observations. Not only that, says Feyerabend, but sometimes a new theory will be used in the absence of any supporting facts at all. Feyerabend's evidence for this startling thesis consists of detailed examinations of primary sources in the history of science, including the science of the twentieth century. He claims that sometimes empirical observation takes precedence over theory, but sometimes theory takes precedence over observation.

Feyerabend's account of what science is like is looked upon with deep distrust by many philosophers of science.

Science is standardly described as more rational than other human activities, highly rule-bound, very self-critical and consciously aiming at total self-consistency. Scientists like this description of their work and want it to be true. That scientists are perceived as embodying the virtues of cool rationality, consistency, reasonable self-criticism, etc. is one of the reasons why they are so respected in our society (another reason, of course, is that applied science creates power and wealth). Feyerabend's version of science shows it as creative, unpredictable and not especially rational. His idea of the scientist is somewhat similar to conventional ideas about the artist, as depicted in the Romantic tradition: someone inspired and anarchic and egotistical; and by association of ideas perhaps also bearded, unwashed and socially misfitted.

Well, who is right? Is science anarchic as Feyerabend maintains? Is it rule-bound as suggested by Hempel and Popper? Is there such a thing as scientific method at all?

Perhaps the best way to look at the matter is through the eyes of Kuhn. There are at least two broad varieties of scientific activity, normal and revolutionary (and there might possibly be more than two).

Feyerabend's historical researches show that revolutionary science does indeed have many anarchic features, and also shows that revolutionary scientists have to be both creative and open-minded.

Normal science on the other hand is fairly rule-bound, and normal scientists must not be too creative or too open-minded; they have to stick to the current theories.

As to methods, normal science follows what could indeed be called a method or methods. Sometimes a 'normal' scientist works like a Hempelian, sometimes like a Popperian, and sometimes like neither. Do these methods have anything in common? Only some rather obvious features. Working in accordance with any of these methods involves:

1   Collecting observations, perhaps also conducting experiments, and recording the data and the results.
2   Careful scrutinizing, i.e. thinking about, the data and the results.
3   Acknowledging that if a large body of facts turns out to be inconsistent with the current theory then everything, including the theory itself, will have to be checked.

The overall method described is obvious and rather banal. Its generality means that it fits many different branches of science. It also fits several other kinds of enquiry – for instance history and anthropology and economics – as well as the sciences of matter. Methodology, therefore, does not really explain the special successes of the physical sciences. Hence the question about the successfulness of science which was raised in the earlier part of this chapter remains unanswered. That does not mean the question will never be answered, for just as every generation produces new scientific discoveries so every generation produces new philosophical insights.

18
Causation

A cause has been variously defined as that which produces something, or as the origin or motive of an action, or as that which explains why something occurs or comes into existence. Some of these definitions are somewhat anthropomorphic, for the idea of causation probably has roots in human efforts to produce things or bring about changes in things.

In 1912 Bertrand Russell reflected that the word 'cause' seldom if ever crops up in the discussions of physicists. Yet the concept is not redundant, even in physics, and even if the word is not often used in that science. For physicists still sometimes ask: Why did such and such happen? and then they are asking about causes.

Moreover the notion of cause is not redundant in other sciences. It occurs frequently in the applied sciences. It is perfectly in order for physicians and pharmacists and pathologists and vulcanologists and meteorologists and oceanographers to enquire into the causes of phenomena.

Aristotle's Four Causes

Aristotle held that there are four kinds of cause, which he illustrated with the example of a sculptor making a marble statue.

The four causes are as follows:

1   *Efficient causes* bring about changes. In the example the efficient cause is the sculptor.

2   *Material causes* are the stuffs in which changes occur. In the example the material cause is the marble.
3   *Formal causes* are the distinctive shapes or forms or properties belonging to the final result. In the example the formal cause is the shape of the completed statue.
4   *Final causes* are purposes or ends or aims. In the example the final cause is the sculptor's intention to produce a work of art.

Aristotle's concept of an *efficient cause* corresponds roughly to the modern understanding of what a cause is. Two of his other three senses of the word cause are now archaic. We would not today say that the marble, or the shape of the statue, were causes. The fourth sense, that is, the idea of the final cause or purpose, is more problematic. In the physical sciences (physics, chemistry, astronomy), and the applied sciences which are based on them (e.g. engineering), no one ever speaks of causes as if these included purposes. Inanimate matter does not have purposes. But in the life sciences (biology, zoology, genetics) Aristotle's final causes still seem to have a place. In explaining the behaviour of organisms, scientists do sometimes speak of purposes. The purpose of the heart is to pump blood. The purpose of pain is to warn of danger. The function of antibodies is to fight disease.

We looked at a modern application of the idea of purpose in chapter 9, the example of the 'selfish' gene which strives always to preserve itself.

The concept of purpose, therefore, has not been entirely abolished from science. But as its appearances in scientific explanation are nevertheless somewhat problematic we will from now on concentrate on explicating the notion of efficient cause.

Things or Events?

Are causes things or events? And do causes cause things or events? Most philosophers in the past have held that there can be no creation *ex nihilo* except for God's creation of the world. It is argued therefore that the ordinary idea of cause is the idea of change in existing things. Thus causes do not create hens (for instance) but rather bring about the changes which transform eggs into chickens. This leads on to the view that causal explanations refer always to changes in things. Events, not persons or things, are causes; effects too are events, not things.

But there remains a kind of ambiguity in the meaning of cause. Things and persons as well as events and changes *can* be perceived as causes, in spite of philosophy. This ambiguity may be at the root of some of the philosophical problems associated with the idea of causation.

Universality, Uniformity, Power and Necessity

It is assumed that causation is universal, that is, that every event has a cause. But this assumption is only an assumption since it cannot be proved. It is simply taken as a maxim – both in applied science and in ordinary life.

It is also assumed that causation is uniform, that is, that like causes produce like effects. This principle too is unprovable. Yet it seems part of our nature to accept it as a given. Indeed the non-human animals appear to share our belief that like causes produce like effects.

Universality and uniformity will be discussed more fully in the next chapter. Here we will consider the problem of power and necessity.

It cannot be denied that the idea of cause is connected in our minds with the ideas of power and necessity. We feel in ourselves certain powers to bring things about, we can produce new artefacts, such as new clothes, by knitting or sewing or whatever, and we can destroy things, e.g. by throwing a crate through a window, and we can some-times induce other people to change their minds or their ways by arguing with them. We seem to see analogous powers in other animals and in inanimate objects; thus we believe that the cobra has the power to kill us, and that the sun has the power to warm us. Moreover, we feel that the very idea of cause involves necessity. Surely if a cause oper-ates, the effect must necessarily follow?

Hume's Theory

Let us begin the examination of power and necessity by looking at David Hume's theory of causation.

Hume seems to say slightly different things about causation at different times. But on the most obvious interpretation his theory is reductive in character; that is, he wishes to *explain away* the element of power and necessity that we think we see in the relation between causes and effects. Roughly speaking he claims that any necessity here lies only in the mind of the observer.

Cause and effect, says Hume, is a matter of, first, an observed constant (i.e. repeated) conjunction of events of one kind with events of another kind; second, contiguity in space and time; third, cause must precede effect. Human observers watching constant conjunctions of similar events are induced to expect the same things to happen over and over again. *The idea of necessity is nothing more or less than this induced expectation.* Because we expect similar effects to follow similar causes we come to think that the effect must necessarily follow the cause, that the cause has forced the effect to come about. But, Hume asks, can we see this forcing, this necessity? No, we cannot, all we can see is one thing following another. We can feel an expectation. We cannot see or feel necessity.

If Hume is right about constant conjunction then some particular event *A* causes some particular event *B* only if every similar *A* is followed by a similar *B*.

If Hume is right about contiguity then there cannot be causation at a distance. Either the cause and effect, *A* and *B*, must be adjacent in space and time, or the spaces and times between *A* and *B* must be filled with a chain of events (a causal chain) in which each event (or link) is adjacent to the next one.

Hume's theory has been subjected to a number of criticisms.

To begin with, contiguity does not seem to be needed for the operation of cause and effect. There are several examples of action at a distance, and of action across a vacuum. Gravitational attraction, for instance, is thought to occur across a vacuum and at a distance.

Next, as Russell points out, constant conjunction, even between contiguous events, is by no means enough to give us causes. The fact that night is constantly followed by day does not show that night causes day. There is endless repetition of night and day, with no way of telling the supposed cause from the supposed effect, for we cannot say which came first, night or day. Russell notes that in this and similar examples we look for a cause external to the cycle; this third item, we may decide, is the cause of two others. Thus the rotation of the earth is the cause of both night and day.

Moreover, constant conjunction can be found where there is coincidence. It is easy enough to think of actual or possible examples. Here is a possible example.

Suppose that the number of X-rays taken each day in a certain hospital varies from day to day but is always the same as the number of male patients who fall in love with one of the nurses on that day. Thus suppose that when six patients are X-rayed on Tuesdays, it so happens that six (different) patients fall madly in love with a nurse on Tuesdays; and similar conjunctions occur on all the other days of the week. Although we have here a constant conjunction of like pairs of events, most probably it is only a coincidence and not cause and effect.

Another more fundamental objection to the theory about constant conjunction is that it presupposes that all events that can be explained in causal terms belong to classes of similar events. In other words, the theory entails the conclusion that one-off events cannot have causes and cannot have effects either. For if a sequence of two events is one-off, there is by definition no repeated conjunction of events. So much is obvious.

As an example, suppose it is claimed that the arrival of the con-quistadores caused the fall of the Inca empire. Now the arrival of the conquistadores only happened once, and the fall of the Incas only happened once. In this and many other historical cases there is no rep-etition and hence no constant conjunction. Thus on Hume's theory the arrival of the conquistadores did not cause the fall of the Incas. On Hume's theory unique events cannot have causes and cannot have effects. Yet it is surely true that the arrival of the conquistadores *did* cause the fall of the Incas.

Some philosophers of history have argued that if we widen our viewpoint we can always discover a constant conjunction whenever there appears to be a cause operating. For instance in the case above we may find a constant conjunction between *A*s, i.e. attacks by strong armies on weaker armies, and *B*s, i.e. the collapses of empires. However this conjunction, like most generalizations about human affairs, has many exceptions. It seems unlikely that it could have anything to do with causation as Hume understands causation.

Power, Manipulation and Recipes

The twentieth-century philosopher Douglas Gasking finds a new approach. He argues that the concept of causation is essentially connected with human manipulative techniques. The cause and effect relation is best described as the 'producing by means of . . .' relation. The concept of cause and effect has to do with general rules for doing things. Gasking calls these rules *recipes*.

According to Gasking a statement like 'adding water to sodium causes it to fizz' means that by applying to sodium the general technique for making things wet you will also be using, or discovering, another general technique, a technique for making a particular kind of substance, namely sodium, fizz.

Can Gasking's analysis of causation be applied to inanimate causes? Can it be applied to events (as against things or persons)?

Consider an example of each.

First, an inanimate cause: the sun's light causes plants to grow. And second, an event cause: the breaking of the dam caused the flooding of the village.

Gasking points out that we can in fact manipulate the environment even when dealing with the sun, and in two ways. We can simulate the characteristics of natural sunlight; and we can also show, by carrying out experiments, that plants deprived of sun do not grow.

Causes which are events seem a little more problematic. After all, events do not perform manipulations. Yet it could be argued that events are often themselves elements or parts of human manipulations. This would be obvious in the case of the broken dam if the breaking had been deliberately engineered by some person.

Our understanding of events as causes, on Gasking's theory, would boil down to something like this: we correctly say that one event caused another when that event either is itself a human manipulation or could have been.

Can Gasking's account of causation cope with the complexities of historical events such as wars, and the downfall of empires, and so on? Probably not. It is surely impossible to give recipes for the downfall of empires, and in general very difficult to give recipes for manipulating human affairs. Such recipes as exist are hit and miss.

But that might show that we are wrong in the first place to speak of the causes of wars and such. It might show that a different kind of explanation is needed when dealing with historical events and such-like human matters.

On the other hand, it could be argued that the fundamental question about cases is not, as Gasking claims, the question: How can I make such and such happen? (make sodium fizz, make plants grow). The fundamental question is: How and why do these things happen? Until that question has been answered the answer to the first question will depend on chance and luck.

Possibility and Necessity

Let us now re-examine the notion rejected by Hume, the notion of necessity.

What is necessity? In the context of the discovery of causes necessity cannot mean logical or mathematical necessity. The conclusions of logic and mathematics, which follow necessarily from axioms or other premises, are deduced from those premises or axioms. But the laws of cause and effect have to be unearthed by means of experimentation or discovered through observation. Unlike the theorems of pure mathematics and of logic they cannot be deduced while one sits in one's study. The necessity of cause and effect, then, must be different from logical or mathematical necessity.

Can we speak instead of physical necessity? Hume's answer is that physical necessity is spurious, a thing of the mind. Contiguity and conjunction can be perceived, necessity cannot. Experience alone can tell us about the real world. Experience tells us that ice does feel cold to the touch, but it does not tell us that ice *must* feel cold. That *must* is in the mind, not in the real world.

John Stuart Mill accepts the bones of Hume's account of causation, the three conditions of constant conjunction, contiguity and the temporal precedence of cause before effect. But he tightens it up by adding a fourth condition, namely that the cause and the effect must be constantly conjoined *not merely in actual circumstances but in all possible circumstances.*

In his book on logic Mill sets out rules for distinguishing genuine cause and effect from coincidences and other sequences not representing causal regularities. These rules are rules for experimental testing of causal hypotheses. First, the experimenter should attempt to prevent the supposed effect from following the supposed cause; this establishes whether or not the supposed cause can possibly occur without the supposed effect following. Second, the experimenter should attempt to produce the supposed effect by means other than the supposed cause; this establishes whether or not the supposed effect can possibly occur without the supposed cause having preceded it.

In these ways one can establish whether or not the supposed cause and effect are *constantly conjoined in all possible circumstances*.

Mill's refinement of Hume's account is useful. Although it does not directly introduce the element of power and necessity, nevertheless by insisting on a more solidly-based constant conjunction it does introduce necessity indirectly. For if something happens in all possible circumstances that is tantamount to saying it happens necessarily.

Is 'Cause' an Ambiguous Word?

Russell was probably right when he suggested that the concept of cause is not suited to pure science. The reason is that it is not a particularly precise notion. The concept of cause is made up of elements that are not entirely compatible with one another.

For one thing modern thinking about causes is still affected to some extent by an Aristotelian hangover, so that in some contexts references to purposes, aims or functions count as types of causal explanation.

More importantly, events and changes are regarded as causes, but so too are things and persons. Things and persons, though, are radically different, of course, from events and changes. Our own control and manipulation of the environment generates simultaneously the idea of ourselves as causes, and the experience of the exercise of power. The experience of power becomes part of the idea of cause and effect. On the other hand, when we think of events and changes as causes there is no room for the notion of power. Events and changes do not manipulate anything, they do not exercise power. Events as causes relate to the idea of necessary connection. Necessity is connected with possibility and impossibility; if some state of affairs is physically impossible then its negation or opposite is physically necessary. Mill's refinement of the concept of constant conjunction introduces necessity indirectly.

Because his idea of uniformity as constant conjunction in all physically possible circumstances involves necessity, it fits our ideas about events as causes. But it does not fit so well with the idea of persons as causes because persons do not behave uniformly.

Hume considered that the concepts of power and necessity go together. But this seems to be wrong. Power goes with persons, necessity goes with events. These two somewhat disparate elements make up the concept of cause.

19
Induction

Reasoning and 'Truth Preservation'

In philosophy a distinction is drawn between inductive reasoning and deductive reasoning. Both kinds of reasoning can occur in any sphere and much actual reasoning is a mixture of both. However, reasoning in logic and mathematics is almost always deductive, whereas in science and in ordinary life inductive reasoning is possibly more common than deductive.

Deduction consists in drawing conclusions which follow with certainty from their premises. It is said to be 'truth preserving' because the conclusion of a sound deductive inference is guaranteed to be true provided that its premises are true. Here is a traditional example:

1 All men are mortal.
2 Socrates is a man.
3 So Socrates is mortal.

If the premises (i.e. 1 and 2) are true then the conclusion (i.e. 3) must also be true.

Induction consists in collecting particular facts and then generalizing from those facts. Thus it is based on experience, observation and experiment. Inductive reasoning as such is not truth preserving because the generalizations it forms are open-ended or universal; for instance, they apply to the future as well as to the past and the present. Of course generalizations based on observation of facts often are true, as far as we know. The point is that the truth of a finite number of statements about particulars (e.g. 'this swan is white', 'that swan is white', 'this third swan is white', etc.) is compatible with the possible falsehood of a universal generalization based on them ('all past, present and future swans are white'). Since collecting facts, however many, does not guarantee the truth of the resulting universal generalizations, some philosophers have held that inductive reasoning as such must be *unsound*.

It will be argued at the end of this chapter that the traditional account of induction is somewhat misleading. But for the time being we will accept the traditional way of distinguishing induction from deduction as broadly correct.

Some inductive reasoning is indeed unsound in that it produces very shaky generalizations. Consider for instance the generalizations 'all swans are white', 'all men are bullies', 'all women are hysterical', 'all Alsatian dogs are unmanageable'. One knows that these generalizations are easily overturned. On the other hand, the generalizations formulated by Kepler and Tycho Brahe about the paths of the planets have not been overturned and do not seem to be shaky.

(These generalizations, i.e. Kepler's laws of planetary motion, are:

First law: The orbit of each planet is an ellipse, with the sun at one of the foci of the ellipse.

Second law: The radius vector of each planet sweeps out equal areas in equal times.

Third law: The squares of the periods of the planets are proportional to the cubes of their mean distances from the sun.)

The Problem of Induction

Inductive reasoning can be about almost anything you like, though as it happens it often has to do with predicting future events.

The question as to whether induction as such is sound or unsound was first raised in modern times by Hume, and it has since been discussed, in an elegant and economical fashion, by Russell, in his book *The Problems of Philosophy*.

Here is a comparison, taken from Russell:

Everyone believes that the sun is going to rise tomorrow. But how can we know what is going to happen tomorrow? Tomorrow has not arrived yet.

People believe that the sun will rise tomorrow because it has always risen in the past. In other words, we all believe that the future will resemble the past. But how can we be *sure* that the future will resemble the past? Russell compares our confident prediction about the rising of the sun with a chicken's confident belief that the farmer will go on feeding it forever. But one day the farmer decides to have chicken for dinner, showing that the faith of the chicken in the farmer's benevolence was misplaced. The chicken's future did not resemble its past. Similarly, our faith that the future will resemble the past might also be misplaced, for all we know. It appears then, from the chicken example, that inductive reasoning must be very risky.

The problem of induction can be expressed as a dilemma:

Either inductive reasoning is circular, or it can be reduced to deduction.
If it is circular it is unsound.
If it is reduced to deduction it is no longer induction.

How circular? Well, suppose we predict that the sun will rise tomorrow. What is the reason for our prediction? It is that we know the sun has always risen in the past. Reminded of the chicken, we ask: Is our reason a *good* reason? Perhaps we then reply: Yes, it is a good reason, because we know that in the past the future has always resembled the past; past pasts have resembled past futures.

It can be seen that the second reason merely repeats the first reason in a new form; hence the 'justification' offered for the reasonableness of the first reason is tightly circular.

Attempted Solutions

Russell and others have outlined and criticized a number of possible solutions to the problem, as follows.

Induction

The 'laws of nature' solution

We know the sun will rise tomorrow because we know the solar system obeys Kepler's laws of planetary motion, which are laws of nature.

Russell objects that the laws of nature themselves are only discovered by observation. If we cannot be sure that the sun will rise tomorrow then we also cannot be sure that Kepler's laws of planetary motion will still be working tomorrow. The fact that the sun has always risen so far is compatible with its not rising tomorrow; the fact that Kepler's laws have always held so far is compatible with them not holding tomorrow.

The 'uniformity of nature' solution

It might be thought that inductive inference is unsound because it is incomplete. If we compare our examples of deductive inference and inductive inference, we see that the first (deductive) inference has three parts:

1   All men are mortal.
2   Socrates is a man.
3   So Socrates is mortal.

Whereas inductive inferences have only two bits, for instance:

1   The sun has always risen in the past.
2   So it will rise again tomorrow.

Or for instance:

1   The laws of planetary motion have held in the past.
2   So they will hold in the future.

Russell suggests that inductive inferences might be 'completed', by adding another premise, the *uniformity of nature premise*. This would turn the inductive inference into something resembling a deductive inference, and deductive inferences are truth preserving. So the uniformity of nature premise seems to guarantee that the laws of nature will be as true tomorrow as they are today.

The inferences about the sun's rising now run as follows:

1 Nature is uniform.
2 The sun has risen every day for millions of years.
3 So the sun will rise tomorrow.

Or in a more sophisticated form:

1 Nature is uniform.
2 The planets obey Kepler's laws of planetary motion today.
3 So the planets will obey Kepler's laws of planetary motion tomorrow.

This solution has flaws. It appears to abolish induction altogether, by turning it into deduction. Second, the uniformity of nature premise is extremely vague. It does not say *how* uniform, nor does it explain what is to count as uniformity. The third fault is more complicated. It is this.

Suppose for the sake of argument that the uniformity of nature premise is true. Now, it can be seen from comparisons that even if it is true it is not *self-evidently* true. 'Nature is uniform' is not like 'every vixen is a female fox', which is self-evident and true by definition. Nor is it like 'everything is itself and not another thing', which also is self-evident.

It follows that the uniformity of nature must have been discovered from experience. But if it was discovered from experience it was based on induction. But if induction is unsound then the uniformity of nature premise cannot be relied on. Even when induction has been reduced to deduction an element of circularity remains in the reasoning.

The 'probability' solution

The proposal here is to introduce a general premise about probability into the reasoning. If that is done the inference will look something like this:

1   When something has happened in such and such circumstances a certain number of times, call it N times, then there is a probability that that thing will happen again in the same circumstances.
2   The sun has risen N times in the past.
3   Therefore it is probable, or more probable than not, that the sun will rise again tomorrow.

The probability solution is of the same general type as the uniformity of nature solution in that it supplies the inductive inference with an extra premise. It is also open to all the same objections, plus some others.

One such further objection is that the idea of probability is here undefined and unclear. The only really precise notions of probability are those of mathematical probability and statistical probability.

Mathematical and statistical probabilities are expressed as percentages or as fractions. Thus we can calculate that the probability of drawing an Ace from a full pack of cards is 1 in 13, and that the probability of a tossed penny falling heads is 50 per cent. Another example of a slightly different type is the Gallup poll. A Gallup poll of, say, voting intentions is made by questioning a 'typical sample' of a known total. For instance, in the elections to the Cambridge City Council, if a 'typical sample' of voters is questioned it can turn out that 34 per cent of electors will vote Green, 33 per cent will vote Red and 33 per cent will vote Blue. It is important to note that one could not know whether the sample was typical, nor whether it was large enough to rely on, if one did not know the size of the total number (of electors in the city).

A precise concept of probability requires that one knows at least two magnitudes. For otherwise one could not express the probability as a percentage or as a fraction.

In our first example the magnitudes were: the number of Aces in a pack and the total number of cards in a pack. In our second example the magnitudes were: the number of sides on a penny (two) and the number of heads on a penny (one). In our third example the magnitudes were: the total number of voters, the number in the 'typical sample' and the numbers within the sample who say they intend to vote Green, Red and Blue respectively.

When we generalize about the sun's rising we do not have two magnitudes, in fact in this case we do not know *any* magnitudes. We believe that the sun has risen millions of times, but we do not know the exact total of the times it has risen, nor the total of the times it will rise. Obviously then we cannot know whether our sample is typical. We cannot say 'probably the sun will rise tomorrow' because we do not know for how long the earth is going to go on spinning and hence we do not know how often the sun is going to rise or how often it is going to fail to rise. Our experience might only be of a tiny untypical sample of the behaviour of solar systems.

In these contexts the word 'probably' does not have anything to do with mathematical or statistical probability. Most likely it has something to do with human expectations and human psychology. We just cannot help believing that the sun will rise tomorrow. This tendency seems not unlike the tendency of the chicken to believe in the benevolence of the farmer.

'Reliabilism'

How then can we justify or defend our belief that accurate predictions about the sun and the planets really are possible, that the future is bound to resemble the past in many ways, and that generalizing from experience is often a sound way to acquire knowledge?

Some contemporary philosophers say that induction needs no justification because any fool can see that it is a *reliable* way of acquiring knowledge. This answer is called 'reliabilism' and it is reminiscent in some ways of Ramsey's suggested solution to the problem of knowledge (see chapter 6).

The reliabilist solution does at least prompt the question: If induction is 'the' reliable method of acquiring knowledge about the world, where are the unreliable ones? When we try to answer this question we find that induction has no rivals. It is not a method at all, but a compendium of all the methods that seem to be successful for the time being. Since it is a compendium or totality it is misleading to say that it is either a, or the, reliable method.

In order to illustrate this point one needs to consider some of the different things that are called induction, and to ask when, how and whether induction could be given up in favour of another method.

Our contention is that induction cannot be given up because it is a compendium of everything. It is not just difficult to give up induction, it is inconceivable. The reliabilist theory is therefore an empty platitude, similar to the platitude that something is more than nothing.

Comparative Reliabilities

Empirical generalization is not always reliable. Many generalizations turn out to be false in the long run, many scientific theories turn out to be false in the long run. Deduction *per se* is not better, for not all deductive reasoning is sound, some is and some is not, it depends on the reasoner, and on his or her choice of inference rules. If all induction and deduction were one hundred per cent reliable that would mean that mankind is omniscient.

'Induction' is an ambiguous word. It can refer to particular methods of investigation, such as collecting samples, or using a telescope, or inventing new scientific instruments for special purposes. Or, on the other hand, it can simply mean *any method of enquiry which is not deductive.*

Particular methods, of course, can be comparatively reliable or unreliable *vis-à-vis* one another. Also, particular investigators can be more or less reliable (successful) compared to one another. But it makes no sense to say that deduction as such is more (or less) reliable than induction as such. Whether either is reliable or unreliable in a *particular* case depends either on who is doing it and how clever they are, or on the particular method being used, or on the particular rules of inference being applied. Some methods, some rules of inference, are more shaky than others.

What Happens when Theories Fail

Let us consider some imaginary examples. First let us imagine you believe that you can predict the future by reading tea leaves. This theory is likely to let you down quite soon. When it does, do you say 'Oh, so induction is unreliable'? Of course not. Instead you say 'There is no connection after all between future events and the patterns in tea leaves.'

Scientists too, like disappointed tea leaf readers, sometimes discover that things they thought were connected are *not* connected. Science sometimes discovers that some patterns are just *not* there. Such a discovery is not like formulating generalizations on the basis of facts, rather the reverse: it is discovering that some generalizations are false. But this is never taken as indicating that induction is unreliable. On the contrary, the discovery of a lack of connection, a discovery that a certain generalization is impossible, is itself taken to be an example of 'the' inductive method. In other words, induction discovers regularities and connections, and it also discovers irregularities and lack of connection.

Imagine next that scientists start to fail *over and over again* in all kinds of different fields. Will they then say 'Oh, so induction is not a reliable method after all'? Not at all. Most likely they will say 'The world is more complex than we thought' or 'We are less clever than we thought' or 'Maybe we need to completely rethink our methods' or even 'Maybe there is something in Eastern mysticism after all — let's give that a try'. And in trying something else instead, be it mysticism or whatever, experience, observation, in some guise or other, will have to come into play again. Even guesswork is a kind of induction, and one that sometimes succeeds.

No failure of a generalization or of a theory would or could show that induction, as such, is unsound or unreliable.

There is nothing self-contradictory about supposing that all our former generalizations, all our former science, and all our particular scientific methods turned out to be inaccurate or unsuccessful. What is more, it is not absurd to suppose that, if that happened, we might not be able to form any new hypotheses or generalizations.

What would this show? Would it show that induction *as such* is not justified? No. If it happened it would be taken as showing only that the human race is not clever enough to do science after all. It could not show that nature positively lacks uniformity, only that the human race cannot discover (much) uniformity.

Chaos and Description

To show that the universe has no uniformity is impossible. It is possible to *say* 'the universe is a chaos', but only if that proposition is false.

It would be impossible to say *truly* that the universe is a chaos, because if the universe were genuinely chaotic there could be no language in which to say so. Language itself depends on things and qualities having enough persistence in time to be pinned down with words, and that very persistence is a kind of uniformity. Of course this is no guarantee that the universe might not become a chaos, but if it does we will not be here to see it.

Part V
Logic: The Philosophy of Inference and Argument

20

The Subject Matter of Logic

Formal logic studies deductive inference. It does not study inductive reasoning. The subject matter of logic is that aspect of strict or deductive proof which is concerned with validity and soundness.

Induction, Deduction and Proof

Inductive reasoning is based on observation and experiment. Basic induction consists in collecting facts and then generalizing from the facts.

Deduction, on the other hand, consists in drawing conclusions which follow with certainty, either from axioms, or from statements of facts which are assumed to be already known.

When logicians speak of proof they mean *deductive proof*. But when ordinary people, or scientists, speak of proof they usually mean *very strong evidence*. These two senses of the word 'proof' in a way encapsulate the difference between deduction and induction.

The difference, as we noted in chapter 19, has to do with 'truth preservation'. However overwhelming the evidence, the truth of the conclusion of a piece of inductive reasoning is not guaranteed. A reasonable inductive inference is *compatible* with the falsehood of its conclusion. Even if the facts are indubitable, it is still possible for the conclusion of an inductive inference to turn out false. This is because inductive reasoning collects finite quantities of evidence from the past and the present, and then draws conclusions in the form of universal generalizations. Such generalizations cover an indefinitely large number of further facts and may well apply to the future as well as to the past and the present.

We have already considered inductive reasoning in chapter 19, so we will say no more about it here.

Deductive proof is 'truth preserving'. The conclusion of a valid deductive inference has to be true if its premises are true. Why is this? Simply because 'valid' is defined that way. The definition of validity is this: *An inference is valid if it is impossible for its premises to be true and its conclusion to be false.*

From now on when we mention proofs we will mean deductive proofs.

Logic studies deductive inferences in general, rather than deductive proofs. Deductive *proofs* are a sub-class of valid deductive inferences.

Deductive inferences as such can start with true premises, or with mere hypotheses, or with false premises. Now, a deductive inference can be valid even if its premises are false, or fallacious even if its premises are true. This can be seen from the definition of 'valid' given above.

Here is an example of a valid deductive inference which is not a proof. It is valid, but it does not prove anything because it starts from a false premise about Napoleon:

Napoleon was Japanese.
All Japanese are Asian.
So Napoleon was Asian.

If a valid deductive inference starts from true premises it will be a proof. Here is a traditional example:

All men are animals.
Socrates is a man.
So Socrates is animal.

Technically speaking any deductively valid inference with true premises is a proof, though in practice the title of 'proof' will be withheld if the conclusion is already known, or is more credible than the premises.

Must genuine proofs always start from true premises? No, for there is an important exception, namely, proofs by *reductio ad absurdum*

(RAA). A proof by RAA starts from a premise known or suspected to be false, the aim of the proof being, if you like, to show that it is true that the premise is false.

Reductio ad absurdum proofs are not uncommon in mathematics. We set out a famous example below*.

The Methods of Logic

How exactly does logic study deductive reasoning? Basically, it sets out general rules for testing validity. But before setting out such general rules it classifies linguistic entities, and introduces linguistic novelties. It may also introduce artificial languages.

Logic classifies linguistic entities, that is, words and sentences, so as to make it easier to classify inferences and arguments.

Logic introduces linguistic novelties for a number of reasons. One reason is to clear away ambiguity and vagueness. Another reason is to make it easier to express new ideas. A third reason is so as to have a kind of shorthand which will make the expression of complicated inferences less cumbrous.

Logic also devises technical or semi-technical vocabularies. The technical vocabulary of the older traditional logic is simple and is used mainly to *describe* the structures of inferences. The technical vocabularies of modern logic are much more complex. They are rather like complete artificial languages. The idea is to have a means of expressing inferences in such a way as to *display* their structures in a perspicuous fashion. These artificial languages of modern logic are supposed to be simpler, and more exact and definite, than ordinary natural languages. Exactness, definiteness and perspicuity make it easier to detect fallacies and easier to distinguish between different types of inference.

In the following chapters we will outline the basic features of traditional logic and of modern logic. We will also explain why traditional logic gave way in the twentieth century to modern logic.

---

*Euclid showed that there is no highest prime number with a *reductio ad absurdum* proof, as follows:

There is a highest prime number, call it P.

There is a large number which $= 1 \times 2 \times 3 \times 5 \ldots \times P$. Call this number Q. It is the product of all primes from 1 to P.

Q is clearly not a prime number, since it is divisible by every prime number up to and including P.

There is a larger number still which $= Q + 1$. Call this number R.

R must be a prime number because it cannot be divided without a remainder (of 1) by any number up to and including Q.

So P is not the highest prime number, because R is a prime number and is larger than P.

Clearly the process can be repeated forever, starting with:

There is a highest prime number, R.

There is a larger number which $= 1 \times 2 \times 3 \times 5 \ldots \times R$.

(And so on and so on and so on.)

Conclusion: there is no highest prime number.

21
Syllogistic Logic

Let us begin with the general definition of validity:

An inference or argument is valid if it is impossible for its premises to be true and its conclusion to be false.

The Greek work syllogism simply means valid argument. But a long time ago it came to mean something slightly different. For logicians the meaning of the word is narrower than the original Greek in one respect, and wider in another.

It is narrower in that syllogism now refers, primarily, only to inferences or arguments which conform to a certain general pattern. This pattern consists of two premises and a conclusion. It is wider in that syllogism now refers not only to sound arguments of the above-mentioned pattern, but also to unsound ones.

The simple-seeming pattern for the syllogism in fact allows a large number of variations. A syllogism can look like this:

All men are mortal.
Socrates is a man.
So Socrates is mortal.

Which incidentally is valid, since if the premises are true the conclusion cannot fail to be true also.

Or it can look like this:

No ravens are white.
Some ravens have albino genes.
So some things with albino genes are not white.

Which incidentally is also valid – if the premises were true the conclusion would have to be true too.

Or it can look like this:

Some animals are deer.
Some animals are carnivores.
So some deer are carnivores.

Which is obviously invalid – the premises are true yet the conclusion is false.

Syllogistic logic is often called Aristotelian logic because Aristotle himself was responsible for most of it. However, certain additions and developments are due to later philosophers, among whom are Zeno, Cicero and Boethius, and the medieval authors Abelard, Duns Scotus and William of Ockham.

Some inferences have just one premise. These are said to be simple or direct. An example: all swans are pure white (premise), so no swans are black (conclusion).

Traditional logic maintains that all arguments are either simple and direct or else are syllogistic. It assumes that any inference which appears to be more complicated than a syllogism can be reduced to a syllogism or sets of syllogisms. In nineteenth-century textbooks of logic there are exercises in which the pupil has to transform complicated-looking inferences into syllogisms or sets of syllogisms.

Symbols, Shorthand and Technical Terms

It is possible to classify and to some extent to formalize syllogisms by using symbolism. The symbolism used in syllogistic logic is quite simple, involving about a dozen technical terms, not all of which are essential for understanding the system. Quite a few of the technical terms, or the ways they are used, are post-Aristotle.

Propositions and quantifiers

A proposition is defined as a sentence which can be true or false. Propositions are contrasted with sentences of other types, for instance questions, prayers and commands, which cannot be true or false.

The four expressions 'some', 'all', 'no' and 'some . . . are not' are called quantifiers.

Traditional logic classifies propositions into four types. The difference between one type of proposition and another depends on which of the four quantifiers is used.

The shorthand used to refer to the four kinds of proposition consists of letters of the alphabet, as follows:

A   propositions begin with 'all'.
E   propositions begin with 'no'.
I   propositions begin with 'some'.
O   propositions contain the expression 'some . . . are not'.

The technical terms for the four kinds of proposition are:

A   Universal Affirmative ('all').
E   Universal Negative ('no').
I   Particular Affirmative ('some').
O   Particular Negative ('some . . . are not').

Examples
A   All Sudanese are Perfect.
E   No Sudanese are Perfect.
I   Some Sudanese are Perfect.
O   Some Sudanese are not Perfect.

Terms

Inferences, of course, are always *about* something – Poles, maniacs, perfection, cities, prime numbers or whatever. Terms are words used to refer to the subjects or topics of inferences. Traditionally the letters S, M and P are used as shorthand for terms.

There are three terms in a syllogism. Starting with the conclusion these are:

The Subject (S) of the conclusion.
The Predicate (P) of the conclusion.
The Middle Term (M), which appears in both premises but not in the conclusion.

In our examples we will from now on use words beginning with 'S', 'P' and 'M' in order to help remember which is which.

Premises and conclusion

As we have already seen, a syllogism consists of three propositions. It starts with two premises from which a third, the conclusion, is to be inferred. The sentence in which S and M appear is called the minor premise, and the sentence in which P and M appear is called the major premise. The sentence which contains both S and P is the conclusion and it is always placed last, of course. The conclusion is usually preceded by some such word as 'therefore', 'hence' or 'so'.

Here are two syllogisms, one sound, the other unsound. The truth of the premises will be taken for granted 'for the sake of argument'. We ask: Assuming the truth of the premises, does the conclusion follow? Which is to say: Assuming the truth of the premises, could the conclusion be false?

Example 1
All Poles are Maniacs.
No Sane people are Maniacs.
So no Sane people are Poles.

Given the truth of the premises the conclusion could not be false, hence the inference is valid. This is made intuitively clear by an Euler diagram:

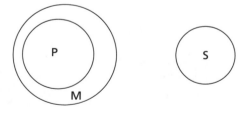

Example 2
Some Maniacs are Peruvians.
No Maniacs are Sane.
So no Sane people are Peruvians.

Given the truth of the premises the conclusion could be true, see diagram 2a, or it could be false, see diagram 2b. Hence the inference is unsound.

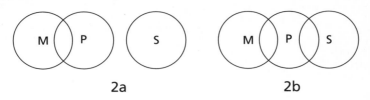

2a   2b

Classification of Syllogisms into 256 Forms

Syllogistic logic classifies arguments according to their various possible forms. The classification gives ways of sorting out the sound from the unsound. According to the theory of the syllogism, validity depends on two things, the figure of the syllogism, and the mood of the syllogism.

Figures and moods

The *figure* of a syllogism is the arrangement of its terms, S, M and P. There are four possible figures.

The *mood* of a syllogism depends on the combination of the quantifiers, that is, the combination of A, E, I and O propositions. There are 64 possible combinations of A, E, I and O, that is 64 possible moods. Hence there are 4 × 64 = 256 possible forms which syllogisms can take. Nineteen of these 256 possible forms are valid and 'strong', five are valid but 'subaltern' or 'weak', and all the rest are invalid.

Figures

The four possible arrangements of S, M and P (the figures), are as follows:

First figure:
MP
SM
SP

Second figure:
PM
SM
SP

Third figure:
MP
MS
SP

Fourth figure:
PM
MS
SP

Moods

The moods of the syllogism can be designated by means of the alphabetical shorthand mentioned ealier (A, E, I, O).

Thus if the premises and the conclusion of a syllogism all begin with the quantifier 'all' the mood of the syllogism is designated AAA. This signifies that each proposition in the syllogism is a universal affirmative.

If the first premise starts with 'no', the second with 'some' and the conclusion with 'some . . . are not' the mood of the syllogism is designated EIO. This signifies that the first premise is a universal negative proposition, the second premise a particular affirmative proposition and the conclusion a particular negative proposition.

As already stated, there are sixty-four moods of the syllogism – AAA, AAI, AII, III IIA, IAA, EEE, EEA, EAA, and so on, up to the sixty-fourth.

Examples – two for each figure
(Readers might like to try to decide which of the inferences below are sound and which unsound, and which moods they belong to. Answers are at the end of the chapter, at ★.)

194

First figure

MP	All men are proud.	All men are proud.
SM	Some soldiers are men.	No sows are men.
∴SP	So some soldiers are proud.	So no sows are proud.

Second figure

PM	No Poles are male.	No priests are married.
SM	Some soldiers are male.	Some Serbs are married.
∴SP	So some soldiers are Poles.	So some Serbs are not priests.

Third figure

MP	No mobsters are pretty.	All mobsters are pretty.
MS	Some mobsters are suave.	No mobsters are suave.
∴SP	So some suave men are not pretty.	So some suave men are pretty.

(We have assumed for the sake of argument that all mobsters are male.)

Fourth figure

PM	Some prigs are modest.	No prigs are modest.
MS	All modest folk are sensible.	All modest folk are sensible.
∴SP	So some sensible folk are prigs.	So no sensible folk are prigs.

The figure and the mood of a syllogism can be represented simultaneously by combining the symbols for the figure with the symbols for the mood. Any syllogism can be represented in this way. The total number of possible forms, as we have already noted, is 256.

Thus this:

MaP
SaM
∴SaP – represents a syllogism of the first figure in the mood AAA.

And this:

PeM
SiM
∴SoP – represents a syllogism of the second figure in the mood EIO.

Distinguishing Valid from Invalid Forms

The valid forms can be distinguished from the invalid by inspection, or by the use of mnemonics, or intuitively by using Euler diagrams, or by formulating and using general rules.

Aristotle himself begins his discussion by distinguishing a number of valid and invalid forms by direct inspection of examples.

Medieval scholars invented a mnemonic which learners used to help them distinguish the nineteen strong valid forms from the five weak forms and the remaining 232 invalid forms. Each line represents a figure. The first three vowels in each word represent a mood.

1 BARBARA, CELARENT, DARII, FERIOQUE – prioris; (First figure valid moods: AAA, EAE, AII, EIO)

2 CESARE, CAMESTRES, FESTINO, BAROCO – secundae; (Second figure valid moods: EAE, AEE, EIO, AOO)

3 Tertia: DARAPTI, DISAMIS, DATISI, FELAPTON, BOCARDO, FERISON – habet; (Third figure valid moods: AAI, IAI, AII, EAO, OAO, EIO)

4 Quarta insuper addit – BRAMANTIP, CAMENES, DIMARIS, FESAPO, FRESISON. (Fourth figure valid moods: AAI, AEE, IAI, EAO, EIO.)

This mnemonic is not very easy to memorize. It seems to be in a foreign language, perhaps Latin, but really it is only Latin-sounding gobbledegook. So we thought we would construct a modern version, but quickly found that the task is by no means a simple one! Perhaps some readers might like to see if they can improve on our version.

Here follows our new mnemonic. The first three vowels of each word gives the mood of the syllogism; ignore 'U', of course, and the fourth vowel if any. The rule 'girls 1, boys 2, places 3, famous people 4' gives the figure.

1 Four girls:
BARBARA, BERNADETTE, HERMIONE and LAVINIA (AAA, EAE, EIO, AII),

2 Met four boys:
ALPHONSO, ELIOTT, GERVASE and LAWRENCE (AOO, EIO, EAE, AEE).

3   They travelled to six places:
    the ATLANTIC, the PACIFIC, the EQUATOR; then ETHIOPIA,
    MIAMI and MONACO (AAI, AII, EAO, EIO, IAI, OAO).
4   Where they saw five famous people:
    CLARENCE in the wine-butt, King MELCHIOR, the prophets
    ISAIAH and MALACHI, and the scholar MELANCTHON (AEE,
    EIO, IAI, AAI, EAO).

Example
MELANCTHON–EAO in the fourth figure (PM, MS, therefore SP).

No princes are mad.
All madmen are sick.
So some sick people are not princes.

Readers might like to try to construct examples of the other eighteen
strong valid forms.

Weak Forms

The five valid weak or subaltern forms are not mentioned by Aristotle,
but they were discovered quite early, in the first century BC.

Briefly, a subaltern form draws a weaker conclusion than it needs
to. All have 'weak' (I or O) conclusions instead of 'strong' (A or E)
ones.

The weak forms are AAI in the first figure (corresponding to AAA),
EAO in the first figure (corresponding to EAE), EAO in the second
figure (corresponding to EAE), AEO in the second figure (corresponding to AEE) and AEO in the fourth figure (corresponding to
AEE).

Example
EAO in the first figure.

No Manicheans are prigs
All slaves are Manicheans.
So some slaves are not prigs.

It can be seen that the validity of the subaltern forms relies on the assumed validity of direct inference. Thus AAI depends on the assumed validity of the inference: if *all* S are P then *some* S are P (e.g. if all slaves are prigs then some slaves are prigs), and EAO and AEO depend on the validity of the inference: if *no* S are P then *some* S are *not* P (e.g. if no slaves are prigs then some slaves are not prigs).

To recapitulate: the quickest ways by which to find out if a syllogism is valid are: to inspect it; or to try an Euler diagram; or to memorize the valid forms and then see if the particular example fits one of those.

Medieval logicians, however, wanted to find general rules which would encapsulate the differences between sound and unsound syllogisms. There is some dispute as to whether all the medieval rules are satisfactory, for instance, the rule known as the 'rule of distribution' has been described as meaningless by some logicians.

Syllogism is the main element in traditional logic but not the only element. Direct inference (see above) is an important subject, and so is the question as to the usefulness or otherwise of the rules for syllogism, such as the rule of distribution. Discussions of these and other related topics can be found in the books listed in the relevant portion of the bibliography.

* In the eight examples *re* sows, mobsters, Poles, etc., the moods were:

In the first figure: AII (valid) and AEE (invalid).
In the second figure: EII (invalid) and EIO (valid).
In the third figure: EIO (valid) and AEI (invalid).
In the fourth figure: IAI (valid) and EAE (invalid).

22
Modern Logic

The value of Aristotle's logic was not seriously questioned for over two thousand years. Books expounding the system continued to appear well into the nineteenth century – John Neville Keynes' big work *Formal Logic with Exercises* was published in 1887.

Aristotelian logic was eventually challenged mainly because it is incomplete, that is, it covers only a few of the possible varieties of deductive argument. It is also at some points ambiguous.

As we have seen, traditional syllogistic logic treats all propositions as stating a relation between a subject and predicate. The subject is quantified by ordinary words, namely 'all', 'no' and 'some'. Only three items or classes can be dealt with in one syllogism, those described by the subject term, the predicate term and the middle term.

It is assumed that every argument, every piece of deductive reasoning, can be expressed either as a direct inference, or as a syllogism, or as a set of syllogisms.

The kind of logic that developed during the nineteenth and twentieth centuries can systematize a much wider range of types of deductive inference. It is, however, more difficult to master than Aristotelian logic.

Modern logic consists of two main bits: the propositional calculus, which is concerned with relations between propositions, and the predicate calculus, which is concerned with the internal structures of propositions. From these standard calculi others have been developed, for instance, modal logic, which deals with necessity, possibility and impossibility, and tense logic, which deals with formal relations involving time (past, present, future). However, these developments lie beyond the scope of this book.

The need for a new logic can be seen from the following considerations:

1 Logic should be able to express arguments which have any number of premises (not just two), and any number of terms (not just three).

Modern logic fulfils these two requirements because the symbolism of the propositional calculus allows any number of propositions to be stacked into an argument, and the symbolism of the predicate calculus allows any number of terms (names and predicates) to be stacked into a proposition. Predicate calculus also allows its two quantifiers to be stacked up over and over (the meaning of this will be explained in the following chapters).

2 Traditional logic crams a big variety of types of proposition into an over-simple mould. It says that all propositions can be turned into one of the four types, A, E, I or O.

Predicate logic, on the other hand, can distinguish between many more types of proposition than that. Predicate logic can not only distinguish between A, E, I and O propositions, it can also differentiate between statements about the properties of things (all cats are carnivores), statements which assert or deny existence (horses exist, centaurs do not exist), statements of identity ('fool's gold' is the very same stuff as iron pyrites) and statements involving number (the solar system has nine planets).

3 The terms of syllogistic logic do not allow a distinction to be made between classes of things (e.g. swans) and individuals (e.g. Socrates). Its terms are generally taken to refer to classes of things while names of individuals are treated as if they mean 'part of a class', so that 'Socrates' is treated as if it meant 'some things' or 'some men' or 'some Greeks' or whatever. Hence the syllogism:

All men are mortal.
Socrates is a man.
So Socrates is mortal.

is treated as being formally similar to the following:

All men are mortal.
Some things are men.
So some things are mortal.

The symbolism of modern logic, on the other hand, can distinguish between classes and individuals.

4   Syllogistic logic cannot refer to things in a non-specific way. Each term refers to a specific class of items; there are no terms corresponding to 'something or other', 'someone or other'.

Predicate logic, on the other hand, contains variables, which are used to refer to things, as it were, in a non-specific way. Thus predicate logic retains some of the complexity and variety of ordinary language. The variables (x, y) of the calculus enable us to translate arguments in ordinary language which contain words like 'thing', or 'thingy', 'whatsit', 'something'.

The concept of a variable will already be familiar to readers who have studied elementary algebra. In algebra the symbols x, y, z can stand either for 'some number', or for 'any number'. For example x stands for a particular number in the equation $x = 13 \times (5 - 8.25)$, to wit, the answer to the equation; on the other hand, in the formula $(x + y)^2 = x^2 + 2xy + y^2$ the symbols x and y stand for any numbers. A variable in logic is roughly similar, but not completely similar, to a variable in algebra. The way variables operate in logic will be explained in chapter 24.

5   The traditional quantifiers of syllogistic logic ('all', 'some', etc.) are not adequate to cover every possibility. Furthermore two of them ('some' and 'some . . . are not') are imprecise. Logic should give us ways of referring to any quantity we want to, for instance 'at least one', 'only two', 'more than ten', and so on. Predicate logic can do this.

6   Although ordinary natural languages have their own, usually quite adequate, ways of disambiguating ambiguous sentences, it is useful to have a symbolism or shorthand in which disambiguation can be performed economically. Modern logic provides such a symbolism.

Although modern logic can cope with many more varieties of argument than syllogistic logic caters for, it should be noted that there remain types of inference which neither the propositional calculus nor the predicate calculus can deal with.

Generally speaking, when the soundness of an inference depends on the specific meanings of ordinary nouns, verbs and adjectives, then it cannot be captured by the symbolism of modern formal logic. One such inference is:

The animal before us is a vixen; therefore it is a female fox.

We will say a little more about this example at the end of chapter 24.

23

The Propositional Calculus

Let us repeat our general definition of validity:

An inference or argument is valid if it is impossible for its premises to be true and its conclusion to be false.

Logic deals with propositions, which we have defined as *sentences of the kind that can be true or false.*

Whereas Aristotelian logic used mainly ordinary language. supplemented with some simple shorthand, the operations of modern logic are conducted almost entirely in symbols. For this reason modern logic is sometimes called symbolic logic, or formal logic, or mathematical logic, or a calculus, or calculi.

Unfortunately modern logicians have not agreed on a standard set of symbols, which can be confusing for students especially as the sets of symbols used overlap a great deal. We will use some of the commoner symbols, occasionally noting the alternatives.

As we have seen, the fundamental concepts of Aristotelian logic are: the three terms (S, M and P), the four quantifiers (all, no, some, some are not), the propositions constructed out of the terms and quantifiers, and the syllogism and its moods and figures.

The fundamental concepts of modern logic are: basic (or atomic) propositions, two 'truth values' (true and false), five operators used to alter basic propositions or to combine them into complex (or molecular) propositions, the concept of inference ('therefore'), two quantifiers roughly equivalent to 'every' and 'some', and the concept of a variable, which we mentioned in chapter 22.

Quantifiers and variables belong to the predicate calculus and will be explained in the next chapter.

Propositions and Truth Values

Propositions are symbolized by P, Q, R, S, i.e. letters taken from towards the end of the alphabet. Some logicians use capital letters, some use small letters.

Since all propositions are by definition either true or false, propositional logic attributes one of two 'values' or 'truth values' to every proposition. The shorthand for 'true' is 't' or 'T' and the shorthand for 'false' is 'f' or 'F'. Some logicians use the symbols 1 and 0 instead.

The truth value of P just means: P's truth or falsity as the case may be.

The two possible truth values of a proposition can be represented on a truth table, as follows:

P
—
t
f

Basic Propositions, Complex Propositions and Operators

Propositions are by definition basic if they contain no operators.

Operators, which are sometimes called connectives, are words or phrases that can be used to change or to join up simple propositions, thus making different, usually longer propositions. It is assumed that all complex, i.e. non-basic, propositions are built up of basic propositions and operators. A proposition is assumed to be basic whenever it is treated as basic for a particular operation. To treat a proposition as basic is merely to assume, for a particular operation, that it will not be broken down into shorter propositions for that operation.

Let us now invent some examples of basic propositions:
'Patrick is wise', 'Peter is silly', 'Mary is fat' and 'Leo is thin'.
Call these P, Q, R and S.
Each might be either true or false.
They can be operated on in a number of ways.

Negation: Patrick is not wise, Peter is not silly, and so on. We call these negations not-P, not-Q, etc.

Double negation is allowed, but cancels out: thus 'Mary is not-not-fat' means the same as 'Mary is fat'.

Conjunction: P, Q, R and S, and their negations, can be joined by 'and'.

Patrick is wise and Peter is silly: P and Q.

Mary is fat and Leo is not thin: R and not-S.

Disjunction: P, Q, R, S and their negations can be joined by 'or'.

'Or' in logic always means 'either or both'. Some logicians read 'or' as 'and/or', which is certainly clearer.

Mary is fat and Leo is thin or both: R and/or Q.

Patrick is not wise and/or Peter is not silly: not-P and/or not-Q.

Conditional: P, Q, R, S and their negations can be connected by the phrase 'if . . . then'. Complex propositions created in this way are called conditionals.

If Mary is not fat then Leo is not thin: if not-R then not-S.

If Peter is silly then Patrick is wise: if Q then P.

An operator (or connective) is defined as a word or phrase which when applied to a sentence creates a new sentence. This definition allows us to say that 'not' is a connective – it is, as it were, a one-place connective. 'Not' is the same kind of thing as 'and', 'or', 'if . . . then', since by adding it to a basic proposition you get a new, different proposition. But the term 'operator' is clearer than 'connective'.

The complex propositions formed by using operaters can be stacked up endlessly, producing longer and longer sentences. So we now see how modern logic allows for any number of premises, and for any degree of complexity of premises.

Take for example the following inference: If you were born in Gorbally Street you were born in Glasgow, if you were born in Glasgow then you are a Scot, if you are a Scot you are British, and if you are British you can get a European passport. So if you were born in Gorbally Street you can get a European passport.

This argument could in fact be turned into a set of several syllogisms, but it is possible, and simpler, to treat it as one single argument. We can begin to do this as follows:

Let P mean 'you were born in Gorbally Street'.
Let Q mean 'you were born in Glasgow'.

Let R mean 'you are a Scot'.
Let S mean 'you are British'.
Let U mean 'you can get a European passport'.

Our argument can be represented as:
If P then Q, and if Q then R, and if R then S, and if S then U:
so if P then U.

Brackets and Ambiguity of Scope

Stacking-up, or iteration, has certain problems; it creates ambiguity of *scope*. The scope of an operation is what it applies to. Ambiguity of scope is not the same thing as ambiguity of the meanings of words.

Consider the sum $2 \times 9 + 3$. This is ambiguous because it can mean either $(2 \times 9) + 3$ which equals 21, or $2 \times (9 + 3)$ which equals 24. Using brackets shows which sum is intended; brackets disambiguate the sum.

In order to disambiguate complex propositions in the logical calculus we use the same device as it used in mathematics, namely brackets. For instance, without brackets 'P and Q or R' is ambiguous because it could mean either 'P and (Q or R)', or '(P and Q) or R'.

The Symbols for and Definitions of the Operators

In the propositional calculus there are five operators. These are: *not, and, or, if . . . then, if-and-only-if.*
Each has a symbol:

Symbol	Description	Meaning
¬	Negation	= not, it is not the case that
&	Conjunction	= and
v	Disjunction	= and/or
→	Conditional	= if . . . then
≡	Biconditional	= if and only if (often written iff).

The Propositional Calculus

The operators are defined in terms of the truth and falsity of the complex propositions they are used to create. The definitions can be stated verbally or demonstrated in truth tables.

Verbal definitions

Negation (¬): ¬P is true when P is false and false when P is true.
Conjunction (&): P & Q is true if and only if P is true and Q is true.
Disjunction (v): P v Q is true if and only if P is true or Q is true or both are true.
Conditional (→): P → Q is true if and only if Q is true or P is false or both.
Biconditional (≡): P ≡ Q is true if and only if P and Q are both true or P and Q are both false.

Truth table definitions

Truth tables for compound sentences place the symbols for true and false first under the basic components, then under the connective or operator. The value under the operator signifies the value of the compound or molecular proposition.

In the following tables the symbols 't' and 'f' are used for the truth values of the basic propositions, and the symbols 'T' and 'F' for the truth values of the compounds which define the operators. This is done simply so that the reader can easily see which truth values belong to the parts and which to the whole, and has no other significance.

Negation: ¬P is true when P is false and false when P is true.

P	¬P
t	F t
f	T f

Conjunction: P & Q is true if and only if both P and Q are true.

P	&	Q
t	T	t
t	F	f
f	F	t
f	F	f

Disjunction: P v Q is true if and only if P is true or Q is true or both are true.

P	v	Q
t	T	t
t	T	f
f	T	t
f	F	f

Conditional: P → Q is true iff P is false or Q is true.

P	→	Q
t	T	t
t	F	f
f	T	t
f	T	f

Biconditional: P ≡ Q iff both are true or both are false.

P	≡	Q
t	T	t
t	F	f
f	F	t
f	T	f

Let us express the inference about Gorbally Street in this symbolism. (The inference was: if you were born in Gorbally Street then you were born in Glasgow, if you were born in Glasgow then you are a Scot, if you are a Scot you are British and if you are British you can get a European passport. So if you were born in Gorbally Street you can get a European passport.) Here it is:

[(P → Q) & (Q → R) & (R → S) & (S → U)], so (P → U).

WFFs and Jumbles

A WFF is a well-formed formula. Obviously not all strings of symbols make sense, and only those which make sense are WFFs.

In written English 'Peter is silly' is a WFF but 'pfff!green(((until/' is not.

In the language of the propositional calculus

$(\neg P \rightarrow Q) \equiv (Q \vee P)$, is a WFF but QP((v &R, is not.

In sum: we have so far given the symbols for basic propositions, namely P, Q, R and S, and the symbols for the five operators, namely $\neg$, &, v, $\rightarrow$, $\equiv$.

We have also given the shorthand (WFF) which stands for 'well-formed formula'.

We need a symbol for 'therefore'. This symbol is $\models$, called turnstile.

Turnstile, $\models$, is not strictly speaking an operator. It does not operate upon propositions to make new propositions, any more than the word 'therefore' does. Rather it enables us to frame arguments, to express inferences.

These together with brackets are the chief symbols of the propositional calculus.

Testing Arguments for Soundness

Arguments or inferences can be represented, as it were, by complex propositions involving $\rightarrow$ (i.e. the conditional if . . . then). By constructing truth tables for these complex propositions we can test our arguments for soundness.

To construct a complex truth table you can't just write in Ts and Fs in any order, since the truth value of the whole is determined by the values of its smaller complexes, which in turn are determined by the basics.

1   Start by inserting the truth values of the basic propositions wherever they appear. Remember consistency: if P is t at the beginning of a line it must be t for the whole line!

2   Insert the values of the negations (if any) of the basics.

3   Insert the truth value of the operator inside the innermost bracket, which in our first example below is the first $\rightarrow$. This value is determined by the values of the basics P and Q – see the truth table for $\rightarrow$.

4   Insert the truth value of the operator inside the next outermost bracket, which in the example is also the most outermost bracket. In the first example below, this operator is &, and its value is determined by the two propositions in the outer bracket, namely, the complex (P → Q) and the basic P.

5   Insert the truth value of the main condition, the → outside the bracket, which in our case is the second →.

Remembering that *an argument is sound if and only if its premises cannot be true and its conclusion false*, we examine the truth table to see if there are any conditions under which the premises are true and the conclusion false. In other words, if there is any row in which the premise is true and the conclusion is false, then the argument is not valid.

First example
If Richard Nixon was President of the United States then he was born in the United States; well, Nixon *was* President of the United States; so he must have been born in the United States.
    Let P represent 'Nixon was President of the United States'.
    Let Q represent 'Nixon was born in the United States'.
We can set out the inference as follows:

If [(If P then Q) and P], then Q.

Or in the symbols of the calculus:

[(P → Q) & P] → Q.

The truth table for this complex proposition is as follows:

P	Q	[(P → Q)	&	P] → Q
t	t	t T t	T	t T t
t	f	t F f	F	t T f
f	t	f T t	F	f T t
f	f	f T f	F	f T f

If the vertical row under the main → contains no Fs then the complex proposition is said to be a *tautology*. A tautology is a proposition which is true whatever the circumstances. For instance, when the component basic propositions are all false (as in the last line of the table), the compound proposition is true.

In such case, an inference made from the left-hand side to the right-hand side of the compound proposition will be a valid inference in the calculus.

In our first example the vertical row under the main connective (the second →) consists all of Ts, so the compound proposition is a tautology, and the corresponding inference, from [(P → Q) & P] to Q, is valid.

At this point we can bring in turnstile ⊨, the symbol for 'therefore'. By substituting ⊨ for the final → in the formula we convert the sequence from a formula representing a compound (if . . . then) proposition into a formula representing an inference, and in this case a sound inference:

$$[(P \to Q) \& P] \models Q$$

The soundness of the above inference form was recognized by the medieval logicians who named it *modus ponendo ponens* (MPP) or *modus ponens* for short. MPP is treated is an axiom, or as a rule of inference, in modern propositional logic.

Second example
If Henry Kissinger is President of the United States, then he was born in the United States (P → Q); but Kissinger was *not* born in the United States (¬ Q): so Kissinger is not the President of the United States (¬ P).

We will rewrite this as a compound proposition in the symbols of the calculus (note that 'but' can be translated as '&'):

$$[(P \to Q) \& \neg Q] \to \neg P.$$

Truth table:

P	Q	[(P → Q)		&	¬Q]	→	¬P
t	t	t T t		F	Ft	T	Ft
t	f	t F f		F	Tf	T	Ft
f	t	f T t		F	Ft	T	Tf
f	f	f T f		T	Tf	T	Tf

211

This also is a tautology (see the vertical row under the second →).
So we can set out a sound inference pattern here too. It is:

$$[(P \rightarrow Q) \& \neg Q] \models \neg P.$$

The medieval name for this inference form was *modus tollendo tollens*
(MTT), or *modus tollens* for short. MTT is treated as an axiom, or as
a rule of inference, in the propositional calculus.

A fallacy
Let us now consider a well-known fallacy, which has been nicknamed
modus morons by contemporary logicians. Its form is:

$$[(P \rightarrow Q) \& Q] \models P.$$

Example
If we are in Toronto then we are a long way north of Sydney (P →
Q), and we *are* a long way north of Sydney (Q), so we must be in
Toronto (P).
    This can be re-written as a compound proposition, namely:

$$[(P \rightarrow Q) \& Q] \rightarrow P.$$

Truth table:

P	Q	[(P → Q)	&	Q] → P
t	t	t T t	T	t T t
t	f	t F f	F	f T t
f	t	f T t	T	t F f
f	f	f T f	F	f T f

The line under the second → contains one F, at row 3, hence there
is one possibility according to which the premises are true while the
conclusion is false. So the *modus morons* argument is unsound.
    Truth tables give a method for testing the soundness of arguments,
so that roughly speaking they serve the same function as the mnemonic
for syllogisms. However, the mnemonic does not *show* that these or
those syllogistic forms are valid or invalid; whereas truth tables actually *show* that an argument form is valid (or invalid, as the case may
be).

24

The Predicate Calculus

Predicate Calculus and Ordinary Language

Ordinary natural languages like English contain various different kinds of words. These include proper names such as 'Emma', common nouns such as 'cat', verbs such as 'run', 'think', 'lambast', and so on, and adjectives and adjectival phrases, some of which, like 'red', signify properties, while others, like 'taller than', signify relations.

Ordinary languages also contain expressions that quantify, for instance, 'all', 'one', 'at least two', 'some' and so on.

Finally, natural languages have ways of referring to things in an indefinite way. In English when we wish to refer to things in an indefinite way we say 'something', 'whatever', 'someone', 'any number' and so on.

The predicate calculus caters for these different elements in a precise manner. It consists of a kind of artificial language which is designed to make plain those internal structural features of ordinary propositions which are held to be important in reasoning.

The Elements of the Predicate Calculus

The elements of the language of the predicate calculus are:

1   The operators of the propositional calculus: symbols ¬, &, v, →, and ≡.

2   Bits of 'machinery', i.e., brackets and full–stops, which are taken from ordinary language.

3   Names: by convention the usual symbols for names are small letters from the beginning of the alphabet a, b, c.

4   Predicates: the usual symbols are capital letters, taken from the middle of the alphabet for properties (F, G, H), and from the end of the alphabet for relations (R, S, T). (We will make a change in the conventional symbolism so that the alphabet can serve as a mnemonic; for instance we'll use p for 'Patrick', L for 'loves' and so on.)

5   Variables: usual symbols as in algebra x, y, z.

6   Two quantifiers: the *universal quantifier*, which is symbolized by ∀ followed by a variable, thus: (∀x), (∀y), (∀z); and the *existential quantifier*, which is symoblized by ∃ followed by a variable, thus: (∃x), (∃y), (∃z).The universal quantifier is read as 'for all x . . .' and the existential quantifier is read as 'there exists at least one x . . .'.

The order of the elements in a sentence in the predicate calculus differs in various ways from the usual order in English. The differences will emerge as we go along.

Stacking: it is possible to have any number of names in a sentence of the predicate calculus, and any number of predicates, and any number of variables, and the two quantifiers can be used any number of times in just one sentence.

The operators

The operators are used in the same way as in the propositional calculus.

Names, common nouns and descriptions

Names can be of people, planets, animals, places, days, and so on. It is assumed that each proper name applies without ambiguity to whatever it names.

Common nouns are expressed with the help of predicates and variables. Common nouns, such as 'cat', are treated like descriptions, so that

'Tibbles is black' and 'Tibbles is a cat' are translated in the same kind of way. 'Tibbles is a cat' is taken to mean 'Tibbles is catlike'.

Predicates

In the predicate calculus 'predicate' means all the sentence except for the names, variables and quantifiers. Contrast English, where the grammatical predicate (1) does not include the verb, and (2) can contain names as grammatical objects. In the predicate calculus the verb counts as all or part of the predicate. The idea of grammatical object is not used.

Some predicates, for instance 'is fat', need one name only to turn them into sentences. These one-place predicates signify properties.

Example: 'Peter is fat.'

Other predicates need two or more names to turn them into sentences. These two (three, four, etc.)-place predicates express relations.

Example: 'Peter hates Majorca.' The predicate 'hates' is two-place, so it needs two names to make a sentence.

Three-place predicates need three names. An example is the predicate 'lies between . . . and . . .'.

Example: 'Chengdu lies between Peking and Lhasa.'

In principle there can be four-place, five-place predicates, up to any number.

In symbolizing predicates the predicate–symbol is placed in front of the name or variable.

Let p mean 'Peter', let m mean 'Mary', let F mean 'is fat'. Then 'Peter is fat' would be Fp, 'Mary is fatter than Peter' would be Fmp and 'Peter is fatter than Mary' would be Fpm.

Stacking: predicates can be stacked.

Basic and compound predicates

Compound predicates are constructed by stacking up simple or basic predicates.

Basic predicates are property terms like 'is red', 'is fat', and relational terms like 'hits', 'loves', 'is taller than'.

Let a, b, etc. mean various names such as 'Betty', 'Ambrose', etc. and let R mean 'relies on'. Then 'Ambrose relies on Betty' can be expressed as Rab, and 'Betty does not rely on Ambrose' is expressed as ¬(Rba), which is understood as negating a proposition; that is, it means 'it is not the case that Betty relies on Ambrose'.

'Loves' is a basic predicate. What about self-love? Logicians differ about this, but some of them say that 'loves himself' is also a basic predicate. That is, they hold that 'Basil loves himself' just means 'Basil loves Basil', which is expressed as Lbb, where L means 'loves'.

Compare these cases with reciprocal relations such as mutual admiration. Mutual admiration is a compound predicate which can be expressed by stacking up two simple predicates. In the example below, one predicate ('admires Philo') belongs to Hume, and the other ('admires Hume') belongs to Philo.

'Philo and Hume admire one another' clearly means 'Philo admires Hume, and Hume admires Philo'.

Let A stand for 'admires', let h stand for 'Hume', let p stand for 'Philo'.

Stacking the two predicates gives a compound: Aph & Ahp.

Unrequited love is another compound predicate.

'Andy unrequitedly loves Bella' means:

'Andy loves Bella and Bella does not love Andy', which can be translated as Lab & ¬(Lba).

The two quantifiers

The symbol (∀x) can be read as 'for every x' or 'for all x' and is called the universal quantifier.

The symbol (∃x) means 'there exists at least one x', and is called the existential quantifier.

Neither ∀ nor ∃ ever appears alone; ∀ always appears as part of the expressions (∀x), (∀y), etc., and ∃ always appears as part of the expressions (∃x), (∃y), etc. Since (∀x), (∀y), (∃x), etc. are units which cannot be further broken down it is better to call these the quantifiers, rather than ∀ and ∃.

Quantifiers generally stand at the beginning of the sentence, except when the sentence starts with the negation operator.

Each quantifier 'binds', i.e. applies to, the variables which follow in the rest of the sentence. Thus (∀x) binds the variable x, and (∀y) applies to the variable y.

Let F mean 'has four legs' and let H mean 'is a horse'.
Then $(\forall x) (Hx \to Fx)$ means 'for all x, if x is a horse then x has four legs'. The 'x' in $(\forall x)$ binds, or applies to, the 'x's in $(Hx \to Fx)$.

When a sentence is constructed around proper names only, then quantifiers are not needed, because it is assumed that each name names just one item. So in a sense names carry their own quantification with them. But when a sentence contains variables then these must be quantified.

Stacking quantifiers: quantifiers can be stacked up; see the section below, 'Examples of translation', subsections 4, 7 and 8.

Variables

The symbols x, y, z stand for objects in an indefinite way. They appear in translations of the expressions 'something', 'anything', 'someone'.

The same variable is used to indicate that the same object is being talked about. Thus 'x is fat and x is grumpy' would usually be taken to refer to the same someone. Using different variables generally indicates that different things are being referred to, though it could also mean that the question of how many things are being referred to has purposely been left open.

Stacking: variables always have to be quantified. When quantified they can be stacked up, as many as you like in one sentence; see the section below, 'Examples of translation', subsections 4, 7 and 8.

Bracketing

With simple predicates no brackets are needed. But sometimes there is ambiguity of scope, and brackets are used to cope with this.

Examples of Translation

1 Names and properties

Let $\to\to$ mean 'translates to'.
Let F mean 'is fat'.

Let G mean 'is greedy'.
Let p mean 'Peter'.
Translating in stages:

'Peter is fat and greedy' means exactly the same as 'Peter is fat and Peter is also greedy'. No quantifier is needed here because 'Peter' is a proper name.
'Peter is fat and greedy'

→→ Fp & Gp.

2   Existence

Let H mean 'horse' and let C mean 'centaur'.
'Horses exist' is taken to mean 'there is at least one thing which is a horse (or horse-like)'

→→ $(\exists x)(Hx)$.

'Centaurs do not exist' is taken to mean 'it is not the case that there is at least one thing which is a centaur (centaur-like)'

→→ $\neg(\exists y)(Cy)$.

3   'Something' and 'someone'

Suppose you want to allege in the language of the predicate calculus that someone, you do not know who, is fat and greedy. The translation will need quantifiers because 'someone' refers to things in an indefinite way. Only one variable is needed, because there is only one someone.
Translating in stages:
'Someone is fat and greedy'

→→ 'There is someone such that s/he is fat and such that s/he is greedy'

→→ 'There exists at least one x such that x is fat and x is greedy'

→→ $(\exists x)(Fx \ \& \ Gx)$.

218

4 Stacking quantifiers and variables

Let 'x = y' mean 'x is the same thing/person as y'.

Consider the sentence 'someone is fat and someone is greedy'. This is ambiguous, it could mean either 'there is one person who is both fat and greedy', or 'there are two people, one fat, the other greedy'. The first version of course means the same as 'someone is fat and greedy' which has already been translated above.

The second version can be analysed as 'there is someone who is such that he is fat, and there is someone who is such that he is greedy, and the first-mentioned someone is not the same person as the second-mentioned someone'.

Two variables are needed here since our sentence is about two different someones.

Translating in stages:

'Someone is fat and someone (else) is greedy'

→→ 'There is someone such that he is fat, and there is someone such that he is greedy, and the first-mentioned someone is not the same person as the second-mentioned someone'

→→ 'There exists an x, and there exists a y, such that x is fat, and y is greedy, and it is not the case that x = y'

→→ $(\exists x)(\exists y)[Fx \ \& \ Gy \ \& \ \neg(x = y)]$.

Here we have stacked up $(\exists x)$ and $(\exists y)$.

5 Removing ambiguity

In ordinary contexts the sentence 'someone is fat and someone is greedy' may well be ambiguous. The sections above show how the two possible meanings of this sentence can be separated and distinguished in the symbolism of the predicate calculus. However it is also possible, of course, to disambiguate ordinary language via ordinary language itself.

Here is a well-known example of scope-ambiguity: 'everyone likes someone'.

This could mean either 'everyone likes someone or other (for instance, his/her own mother)', or it could mean 'there is some one person whom everyone likes'.

Let L mean 'likes'. Assume that xs and ys are persons.

The first interpretation means 'for every x there is a y such that x likes y'

$$\rightarrow\rightarrow (\forall x)(\exists y)Lxy.$$

The second interpretation means 'there is some (one) y such that for every x, x likes y'

$$\rightarrow\rightarrow (\exists y)(\forall x)Lxy.$$

The two translations look rather similar, with only a difference in order. But one can see the difference in meaning by reading back into English.

6 Negation

'No' is an ordinary language quantifier and it is also one of Aristotle's quantifiers. The predicate calculus can do without a special negative quantifier because it takes over the negation operator from the propositional calculus. Using this plus $(\forall x)$ and $(\exists x)$ we can construct the various senses of 'no' found in (standard) English.

Let us look at two examples: 'not everyone is bad', and 'no one is bad'.

Let B mean 'is bad'.

'Not everyone is bad' means 'not all people are bad'

$$\rightarrow\rightarrow \neg(\forall x)Bx.$$

'No one is bad' means 'it is not the case that there is someone who is bad'

$$\rightarrow\rightarrow \neg(\exists x)Bx.$$

7 Plurality and number

Plurality and singularity are translated by using the idea of identity. The symbol '=' can be used to mean 'identical with'. Thus $x = y$ means 'x is identical with y', and $\neg(x = y)$ means 'it is not the case that x is identical with y'.

In English 'some things are ghastly' usually means 'at least two things are ghastly'. Suppose we needed to express the English phrase 'some things are ghastly', i.e. 'at least two things are ghastly' in the language of the predicate calculus.

Let G mean 'is ghastly'.

In the calculus the symbol $(\exists x)$ means 'there is at least one x'. This will have to be used to express the phrase 'at least two things are ghastly'.

What we need to say boils down to 'there is at least one x and at least one y such that x is ghastly and y is ghastly and x is not y'.

We stack up quantifiers and introduce negation and get

$$(\exists x)(\exists y)(Gx \ \& \ Gy \ \& \ \neg[x = y])$$

which means 'there is at least one x and at least one y such that x is G and y is G and x is not y', which is what was needed.

The same principle can be used to express phrases such as 'at least three things are ghoulish', 'at least four things are grumpy', and so on. Just as two variables are needed to express 'at least two things', so three variables are needed for 'at least three things', and so on. (Readers might like to try translating 'at least four things are green'.)

8 'Only one'

How do we say 'only one thing is ghastly'?

This proposition is equivalent to 'at least one thing is ghastly and at most one thing is ghastly', which is equivalent to 'at least one thing is ghastly and it is not the case that at least two things are ghastly'.

This proposition translates as

$$(\exists x)Gx \ \& \ \neg[(\exists x)(\exists y)(Gx \ \& \ Gy \ \& \ \neg\{x = y\})].$$

Or it can also be expressed as:

$$(\exists x)\ Gx\ \&\ [(\forall y)(Gy \rightarrow y = x)].$$

Logic and Ordinary Language

There is an important similarity between inferences expressed in the languages of logic and inferences expressed in ordinary natural languages. This is that the general standard for the validity of deductive inferences is the same in each case. Any deductive argument can be asked to pass the test for validity, which is: *An inference or argument is valid if it is impossible for its premise(s) to be true and its conclusion to be false.*

This similarity is important for more than one reason.

First, since valid inferences expressed in an ordinary natural language do not have an inferior kind of validity, or a worse kind of invalidity, than those expressed in the languages of formal logic, it is possible to reason logically without having studied formal logic.

Second, although modern logic can cope with many more kinds of argument than can Aristotelian logic, there are some types of valid inference which it cannot cope with. Although the precise definitions of special words, such as the logical constants and the quantifiers, are essential for the arguments of formal logic, the meanings of individual ordinary nouns, adjectives, adverbs, etc. play no part therein. Hence when the validity of an argument depends on the meanings of particular ordinary words it cannot be captured by the symbolism of modern formal logic. Formal logic is concerned with the structures of propositions, or with relationships between propositions, and it only defines those linguistic entities which impart structure or connect sentences. Thus it defines e.g. 'bracket', 'name', 'predicate', 'variable', 'operator', but it does not define e.g. 'vixen' or 'horse' or 'centaur'.

Consider again the inference about the vixen, mentioned in chapter 22:

The animal before us is a vixen; therefore it is a female fox.

The validity of this (admittedly trivial) deduction depends on the meanings of the English words 'vixen', 'fox' and 'female', hence its validity cannot be demonstrated by means of formal logic. For instance, truth tables could not be used to demonstrate its validity. Yet it is of course valid for all that. It is valid because it is impossible for 'this animal is a female fox' to be false if 'this animal is a vixen' is true.

Part VI
Philosophy and Life

25

The Meaning of Life

There are three different philosophical questions we can ask about the meaning of life:

Has human life a meaning, a purpose?

Is human life happy on the whole? Should we be pessimists or optimists?

Does human life have value as such, in itself?

Time, Eternity and Purpose

In Dostoievsky's novel *The Brothers Karamazov* the character Ivan Kara-mazov, an atheist, says that unless there is a prospect of immortality human life can have no meaning. For without the possibility of eternal life, and divine reward and punishment, everything is permitted. In Ivan's mind, meaning, purpose, significance are connected with morality and value, and morality and value are connected with eternal life. This is why he believes that the finitude of life is proof that it has no purpose.

Yet some have argued that an eternal life would be purposeless too. In the *Tractatus Logico-Philosophicus* Wittgenstein asks: 'Is not the riddle of eternal life itself as much of a riddle as our present life?'

What have time and eternity got to do with purpose? Are not time and eternity and purpose completely different things? For what reason should it be supposed that eternal things have more purpose than finite things? For all we know the universe may be eternal, matter may be eternal, energy may be eternal, but we cannot tell whether they have a purpose, nor what such a purpose might be. Asking about the purpose of life, meaning God's reason for creating life, is much the same as asking about the reason for the existence of matter and energy. Although some people have claimed to be able to answer these questions we will put them to one side as too difficult altogether.

There is a difference between the possible purposes of a creator and the known purposes of mankind. Even if we knew for certain that life was not brought into being by a creator for his own purposes, humanity could and would still have its own purposes and goals.

Can a single human life, taken as a whole, have one purpose, one meaning? At the human level it is quite possible for an adult individual to have just one large overriding purpose in life. No doubt a life dedicated to religion can be like that. And Schubert's life, dedicated wholly to music, was also probably like that. Most people, though, have a number of different goals appropriate to different times in their lives.

Can the human race as a totality have an aim in life? It is hard to think of any such aim. Of course human beings have aims in common with one another, for example, staying alive, trying to be happy, and so on. They also have communal aims, for example, building cities.

More needs now to be said about individual human purposes, because there is a difference between purposes and meaningful purposes. Having a goal is not necessarily the same thing as having a meaningful goal. Some human goals are quite trivial, in which case they might well be described as meaningless. Goals and purposes must themselves be non-trivial, significant, if they are to give meaning to life, but it is as well if an individual has some serious goals as well as playful ones.

What is a non-trivial goal? What is a meaningful purpose? When the term 'meaningful' is applied to goals and purposes it signifies value, worthwhileness.

(Are examples needed? Well, most people no doubt will agree that helping the poor and oppressed is a worthwhile purpose and that helping cruel oppressors is a despicable one. Cooking for a family is meaningful, whereas collecting train numbers is mere play, and play suitable only for children. Learning to read and write is meaningful, learning to play card games is less so. And so on.)

Dostoievsky's character Ivan Karamazov thinks that all morality, all value, comes from God; thus no goal can be really worthwhile unless God exists to make it so. Without God there is no difference between helping the poor and oppressed and helping their cruel oppressors.

Dostoievsky describes how moral nihilism leads Ivan to mental breakdown and Ivan's half-brother Smerdyakov to murder and suicide. So that it might seem that the character Ivan expresses the author's own conviction that only a belief in God can give meaning to life.

Yet there are two ways of interpreting this novel. The first interpretation is to see it as showing that 'the death of God' leads inexorably to 'the death of value'. The second interpretation is to see it as showing that even the ultimate catastrophe, 'the death of God', does not destroy value. Value survives at least as long as the human race survives whether or not human beings believe in a god. This second interpretation is supported by the skilful way in which Dostoievsky induces his readers (believers and unbelievers alike) to evaluate the consequences of Ivan's nihilism. The reader judges Ivan, and Ivan's pride, while feeling sympathy with his predicament. And it is surely impossible not to feel awe and sorrow at the fate of Smerdyakov. Dostoievsky's description of Smerdyakov's last interview with Ivan, and of the subsequent suicide, has almost biblical power, partly no doubt because of its ambiguous similarity to the story of Judas. The Judas of this story is not Smerdyakov, but Ivan, who betrays humanity when he betrays his despised, weak, epileptic brother.

For non-believers the second interpretation of Dostoievsky's novel makes sense because unlike Ivan most of them are not in a state of despair at 'the death of God'. *Contra* Ivan Karamazov, it is possible, and even quite common, for non-believers as well as believers to love justice, to hate cruelty, to respect humanity and to believe in the sanctity of life. Few Buddhists believe in a god, but they all believe in the sanctity of life. Not all the members of the modern medical profession believe in a god, but most of them, one hopes, respect the human person and the autonomy of the human person, and most of them, one hopes, do not feel that kindness and cruelty are morally indistinguishable.

Life and Happiness: Pessimism

To deny in a general way that life can be happy is to be a philosophical pessimist. The best-known pessimist in philosophy is Arthur Schopenhauer. In his big work *The World as Will and Representation* he seems to say that it would have been better if the world had never existed. He has two kinds of reason, metaphysical and empirical.

The chief metaphysical reason, which is developed in volume I of his book, has to do with the idea that existence is based on the Will. The manifold wants and desires which every animal and every human being experiences are manifestations of Will, and these desires and wants are a perpetual source of misery. For if a desire is not satisfied then that state of affairs is inherently miserable; on the other hand when desires *are* satisfied they are inevitably and immediately replaced by other desires, which probably will not be satisfied. Life itself is a kind of long-term itch, a state of perpetual frustration.

The empirical reason for pessimism, which Schopenhauer develops in volume II, lies in the fact that wherever we look we see much pain and unhappiness. Schopenhauer lists at length all the many terrible things that afflict human beings and the other animals. The wise man, he concludes, will recognize that life is dreadfully miserable. The wise man will try to give up all desires, for desires are the source of frustration and other evils. The wise man must not even desire death, though he will know that death is better than life. The wise man resigns himself to being alive and accepts death calmly.

Empirical pessimism of the kind defended in the second volume of Schopenhauer's book seems to presuppose that comparisons can be made, not only between the possible and the actual, but also between the existence and non-existence of some or all human beings, both in an abstract way, and also from various points of view. Are these assumptions correct?

Here we need to answer five questions:

1   Can we imagine merely possible worlds?
2   Can one imagine one's own non-existence?
3   Is it possible to *compare* the actual with the merely possible?
4   Is it possible to compare an individual's existence with his possible non-existence *from his own point of view*? For instance, can one compare one's own existence with one's own non-existence *from one's own point of view*?
5   Is it possible to compare the actual with the possible in a purely abstract way, as it were from *no* point of view?

1   It is easy to *imagine* merely possible situations. Thus it is easy to imagine a possible world in which some person, the present President of Peru, say, has never existed.

2   It is also possible to imagine a state of affairs in which one does not exist oneself. Whenever I imagine the earth's distant past or distant future I imagine a state of affairs without myself.

3   We are also able to *compare* the actual with the possible, in the imagination. For instance, one might imaginatively compare the real world with a possible world not containing the AIDS virus, and decide that the actual world is less good than the merely possible one would be.

One can compare anyone's existence and possible non-existence, including one's own, from the point of view of other people. For example, people sometimes say that if some evil dictator like Stalin had never been born the world would have been a comparatively better place. This does not mean that it would have been better for Stalin himself, but better for other people.

4   But it is sometimes said of very unfortunate people that it would be better for *them*, the people themselves, if they had never existed. Does this make sense?

The statement cannot be a comparison between two states of a person, for non-existence is not a state of the person. In this context, the use of the comparative 'better for the individual himself' must be a *façon de parler*.

Yet is it not possible all the same to wish that one had never been born? For whom, then, would it be better?

As we have seen it is possible to compare, in imagination, a world with oneself in it and a world without oneself in it, from some other person's point of view. However, someone who laments 'I wish I had never been born!' is not usually thinking of the good of others.

Must we conclude that the lamentation is irrational, or that its meaning is a mystery? Its meaning is not really a mystery because it is possible to make wishes without making comparisons. The wish is real, the comparison is not. If the wish is supposed to express a *comparison between two states of myself* then it will incorporate a muddle.

5   The wish that Stalin (for instance) had never been born is based on a comparison, made in the imagination, between an actual state of affairs (a world containing Stalin) and a different possible state of affairs (a world without Stalin). The comparison is not purely abstract but is made from the point of view of Stalin's victims.

231

Can the real world be compared with a merely possible world from no point of view, purely as it were in the abstract? For instance, does it make sense to affirm that a world without life would be *better*, in the abstract, than a world with life? It seems that if a comparison is abstracted from all possible points of view then it must be *inherently reasonless*. Life is good for those living it. If life has intrinsic value it has intrinsic value for the living.

Life and Happiness: Optimism

Not many philosophers bother to defend optimism as a creed, though that certainly does not mean that they are all pessimists.

Bertrand Russell, however, does defend optimism, in his book *The Conquest of Happiness*. He agrees that human life often is unhappy, but argues that it can be happy, there being no metaphysical reason against this possibility. Much unhappiness is quite unnecessary, he says, caused either by foolishly greedy economic arrangements, or simply by people not knowing how to be happy. Huge numbers of ordinary people are miserable purely and simply because they do not know how to be happy. Russell writes:

> In the work-hour crowd you will see anxiety, excessive concentration, dyspepsia, lack of interest in anything but the struggle, incapacity for play, unconsciousness of their fellow creatures.

As to the rich, he says this:

> It is held that drink and petting are the gateways to joy, so people get drunk quickly, and try not to notice how much their partners disgust them.

Even great kings are not happy. Russell quotes King Solomon:

> The rivers run into the sea; yet the sea is not full
> There is no new thing under the sun.
> There is no remembrance of former things.
> I hated all my labour which I had taken under the sun; because
> I should leave it unto the man that shall be after me.

Russell remarks that the facts as stated are insufficient grounds for general pessimism. Take for instance Solomon's son; from his point of view the fruit trees left 'unto the man that shall be after me' are no reason at all for feeling unhappy.

Russell gives advice on how to be happy. There are many sources of happiness, he says, including 'zest', affection, the family, work, impersonal interests (such as archaeology or the theatre or books), and the ability to find for oneself a golden mean between effort and resignation. To avoid unhappiness one should try to free oneself from envy, from too much competition, from persecution mania and from fear of public opinion.

Russell's advice might perhaps seem trite, but much of it is fairly sensible, and with this little book he probably helped some unhappy people to feel happier.

The Intrinsic Value of Life

Optimists and pessimists alike seem to adopt the utilitarian theory that happiness is the ultimate value and is what gives human life its value. Some contemporary philosophers have actually argued that when a human being has no hope of happiness, and cannot contribute to the happiness of others, then he or she should be 'helped to die'.

Classical utilitarianism (see chapter 10) is founded on the thesis that everyone desires happiness above all else. Yet the ordinary behaviour of ordinary people contradicts this thesis. Ordinary people wish to go on living even when they are very unhappy. In reality people behave as if they believe that just being alive is intrinsically good. In reality ordinary people behave as if life itself is the ultimate value.

Such behaviour may well be instinctive, but that does not show it is unreasonable. The desire for well-being, for health and happiness, is also instinctive. In attributing ultimate value to happiness utilitarianism puts the cart before the horse. We do not instinctively desire to stay alive in order to be happy and healthy, rather we instinctively want to be healthy and happy because that helps us to stay alive.

Philippa Foot is one of the few philosophers who has discussed the question of the intrinsic value of life, arguing, against utilitarianism, that it makes perfect sense to believe that life without happiness is worth living. It is only in extreme cases that dying is the better option, and even then it is not an option that a third party has any right to choose for another. In her paper 'Euthanasia' she explains how and why it is possible to regard even an unhappy life as having value.

She begins by making the important point that a life worth living must mean a *life worth living for the person who is living it*. Whether or not your life is worth anything to anyone else (to the state, for example) must not be allowed to count against the worth it has for you, the person who is living the life. (We might note too that the idea that the value of each individual life lies only in its usefulness to someone else leads to an infinite regress and is ultimately absurd.)

What makes life worth living? Philippa Foot rightly says that people generally wish to go on living even when unhappiness greatly out-weighs happiness; and she discusses some such possible lives.

Life in captivity can be good, that is, better than premature death; life with a prolonged illness can be good, that is, better than prema-ture death; and a life of perpetual shortages (of food, of housing, of health care) is generally regarded as better than premature death by those who live it. She writes:

> What about severely handicapped people? Can life be a good to them? Clearly it can be, for even if someone . . . is living in an iron lung . . . we do not rule him out of order if he says that some *benefactor* saved his life [our italics].

She goes on:

> Nor is it different with mental handicap. There are many fairly severely handicapped people – such as those with Down's Syndrome – for whom a simple affectionate life is possible.

She concludes that human life itself is good. Nevertheless there are some kinds of life which are so awful that it would be reasonable to want to die. So though we can say that human life is good in itself it is necessary to add that it must be in some sense *a genuinely human life*. It must be an 'ordinary' human life in some minimum sense. She describes her idea of 'ordinary human life' as follows:

> The idea we need seems to be that of life which is ordinary human life in the following respect – that it contains a minimum of basic human goods. What is ordinary in human life – even in very hard lives – is that a man is not driven to work far beyond his capacity; that he has the support of a family or community; that he can more or less hope to satisfy his hunger; that he has hopes for the future; that he can lie down to rest at night.

Foot argues that this account of the 'ordinary' human life shows up a connection between the concept of *life* and the concept of *the good*. 'Ordinary' human life as described above is good in itself and does not have to be happy to be worth living. It should perhaps be noted in passing that her sense of the word 'ordinary' is a bit unusual. Her 'ordinary lives' will include many which from another point of view are very extraordinary. For instance, Beethoven's life was extraordinary in many ways, yet it was also 'ordinary' in Foot's sense of the word 'ordinary'. Similarly the life of a man in an iron lung is unusual in several ways, but it can be 'ordinary', it would seem, in Foot's sense of the word 'ordinary'.

Philippa Foot's conclusion about the intrinsic value of life fits the feelings which most people have about their own lives. Thus as well as explicating a conceptual connection between *life* and *good* it also follows common sense – which is no bad thing in philosophy.

To sum up:

The concept of purpose has no special connection with the concept of eternity.

If God exists his purposes are different from ours, and it is not true that without God there can be no human purpose, no morality. 'The death of God' is not the death of value.

Pessimism seems to rest partly on the supposition that we can compare better and worse from no point of view; partly on the idea that it is possible to compare an individual's existence and non-existence from his own point of view; and partly on the assumption that happiness is the only ultimate value. The third of these three pre-suppositions is at best unproven, the first two are just plain false.

Russell's optimism is not so much philosophical as commonsensical, but some of the advice he gives to unhappy people is good advice.

Finally, it makes sense to regard life itself, whether it be happy or unhappy, as having value; and this indeed is the way in which most people usually regard their own lives.

26
The Influence of Philosophy on Life

Is philosophy relevant to the problems of real life?

Yes, and in several ways.

Philosophy disambiguates questions, and disambiguation is useful when one is facing real-life choices.

Philosophy analyses complex ideas, and getting clear about complex ideas is often a necessary prelude to making informed and rational decisions.

Philosophy concerns itself with considering possible explanations of a variety of abstract things – like sound and unsound reasoning, justice and injustice, meaning and value. By coming to a better understanding of abstract notions such as these one can increase one's understanding of life and the possibilities in life.

Philosophy also raises old questions which have been forgotten and new ones which have not been raised before. The relevance, or irrelevance, to life of forgotten questions, and of new questions, cannot be decided in advance of looking at those questions.

Wide and Narrow Views of Philosophy

In some eras of history philosophers have taken a wide view of their subject, in others a narrow view. During the first half of the twentieth century philosophers on the whole took a rather narrow view of their subject. As it happens the theories of Viennese positivism, and the methods of linguistic analysis, or 'Oxford philosophy' so-called, both seem to have encouraged a narrow view. Perhaps this came about partly as a result of the rise of science in the nineteenth century, which might have produced unacknowledged feelings of intellectual intimidation in the secret hearts of some professional philosophers.

Dissatisfaction with narrow views of philosophy is bound to occur from time to time. In 1959 considerable dissatisfaction with the narrow view was expressed in a negative, destructive but rather amusing book by Ernest Gellner called *Words and Things*. Gellner claimed that professional philosophers in Oxford and elsewhere no longer perceived their subject as having any bearing either on the big questions of metaphysics or on real-life decisions about morals and politics. According to Gellner these academics, these so-called philosophers, were wasting all their efforts on endlessly analysing essentially uninteresting 'ordinary language' propositions.

Applied Philosophy

At the time it seemed that Gellner's strictures fell on deaf ears. More recently, however, analytic philosophers have been turning back to the traditional 'big' questions of metaphysics, and not a few have been thinking and writing about 'real-life' problems.

In the 1970s the Australian Peter Singer published a defence of the rights of non-human animals, in a work entitled *Animal Liberation*. This is perhaps the first philosophy book in the history of the universe to contain photographs of abattoirs, not to mention a batch of (meatless) recipes; it converted a number of readers to (temporary) vegetarianism. Other philosophers writing on applied philosophy include G. E. M. Anscombe (on contraception), Sisela Bok (on lying and secrecy in public and private life), Stephen Clark (on animal rights), Philippa Foot (on euthanasia), Judith Jarvis Thompson (on abortion), Mary Midgeley (on animals, on wickedness, on feminism, and on the theory of evolution), Roger Scruton (on conservative politics and on sexuality), Amartya Sen (on philosophy and economics) and Bernard Williams (on obscenity). New philosophy journals have been founded, devoted to discussion of real-life problems; for example, the American journal *Philosophy and Public Affairs*. In the 1980s the British Society for Applied

Philosophy was set up, together with its associated publication, *The Journal of Applied Philosophy*.

Philosophy in Public Life

From time to time philosophers are invited to serve on bodies concerned with drawing up guidelines for legislators in areas involving moral issues. It cannot be claimed that the philosophical input has invariably been top class, for philosophers are not always free of unclarity and obfuscation, and occasionally they have social prejudices and psychological attitudes, particularly attitudes of philosophical scepticism, which can get in the way of common sense. Much twentieth-century thinking was still influenced by Hume, and not a few contemporary philosophers consciously or unconsciously accept Hume's scepticism about causation (see chapter 18). When faced with social issues these philosophers are liable to sit on their hands, claiming that no one knows whether racist or sexist propaganda (say) causes any bad effects: for (they silently assume) no one really knows whether anything really causes anything.

More importantly, it has too often been the case that the bodies set up by government to investigate moral issues are faced with impossible tasks and impossible questions. For instance, they might be invited to calculate the consequences of redrawing bits of legislation which embody ancient ethical principles. Or they might be expected to think up arguments in favour of breaking profoundly important taboos. Philosophers are not necessarily much good at estimating practical consequences (for example, the practical consequences of unbanning hard pornography), nor are they necessarily any better than anyone else at deciding what should be our fundamental taboos.

In spite of these occasional drawbacks, philosophers can do good work in public life. 'Public' applied philosophy is best when it can start from some central principle which is accepted by more or less every civilized society – for example, the principles of the UN Charter relating to human rights. If some such basic principle is accepted to start with, a philosophically-minded committee or commission can proceed to clarify whichever concepts are important and relevant to the question under investigation, and possibly too can begin to develop practical ways of implementing its decisions.

A good example is the 1989 *Draft Paper on Informed Consent*, published by the New Zealand Health Council's Working Party. This paper is a real-life example of how philosophy can be usefully applied to public decisions affecting many people; we describe it below.

The Working Party was made up of doctors, nurses and lawyers, and a number of lay people who between them representd patients, and the Maori community, and the rest of the general public. One lay member was a retired professional philosopher of no special fame outside New Zealand but with a head screwed on in the correct position.

The draft paper moves easily and unselfconsciously from philosophical analysis and disambiguation, to practical ways and means, and back again. It covers four main areas of discussion:

1   The paper first explains why the topic is important. It says:

> Informed consent is a basic legal and ethical issue. It concerns the autonomy of the individual, the individual's right to make decisions about actions which affect them, in ways which are in line with their own aims and values, and their right to freedom and protection from interference by another.
>
> Modern emphases on informed consent grew out of the 1947 Nuremberg Code (which itself arose from the Nazi trials after World War II), and the 1964 Helsinki Agreement. These clearly identified an obligation to obtain a person's consent to participation in therapeutic and non-therapeutic research . . . The underlying principle is that a person's bodily integrity should be protected from unauthorised touching or invasion.

2   Having set out fundamental principles the paper goes on to list and classify the different ways in which informed consent increases the control people have over their own lives. Informed consent promotes trust between the medical profession and its clients; it promotes rational decision-making by doctors and patients; it protects people from unnecessary treatment and unnecessary medical procedures; it contributes to the successful outcome of treatment by increasing the probability that patients will willingly and fully participate in the treatment; and it ensures that patients are not coerced and manipulated into participating in commercially profitable experimental projects.

Informed consent also ensures that the values of health professionals remain humane and stay in line with the wishes of the patients and with the values of the wider community, including the values of minority groups; lastly, it protects the medical professional if things go wrong.

3   The draft paper next analyses a lot of relevant subsidiary ideas. In doing this it uses philosophy to increase understanding of important practical matters. The ideas it looks into here might seem humdrum, perhaps, but unless they are brought to the forefront of consciousness, and clarified, the high principles adopted could not be put into practice. These significant and relevant notions include: explicit consent, implied consent, general consent, specific consent, written consent, spoken consent; emergency and non-emergency; risk, high risk, low risk, side-effect; competence (i.e. competence to decide), responsibility, information; language difference, cultural difference.

4   Finally the paper considers the ways and means needed to put its findings into effect. It answers questions about how to make really sure *in practice* that patients (who are themselves various in respect of language, age, understanding, etc.) are always properly informed about treatments, including their possible side-effects and risks. It is clear from this portion of the paper that the Working Party was of a practical and unpompous turn of mind, as well as being philosophically astute.

The Effects of Philosophy

This chapter began by asking whether philosophy can have any relevance to real life. Some answers have been given, first in general terms, and then in the form of examples of the ways in which philosophy is being applied to real-life problems today. But the influence of philosophy on life is not a new thing. Philosophical ideas have often had profound long-term effects on human societies – whether the societies realize it or not. Sometimes the influence of philosophy is good, and sometimes no doubt it is bad; but that is another question.

The societies of today have been deeply affected by philosophical ideas trickling down from many different sources. A few historical examples will quickly show how this is so.

Examples from ancient times: Hebrews and Greeks

It has often been said, but it bears repeating, that the whole of Western civilization is based on the ethics of the ancient Hebrews and the science and metaphysics of the ancient Greeks.

Neither the scribes and sages of Jerusalem, who recorded the Ten Commandments and the wisdom literature of the Hebrew people, nor Jesus of Nazareth, were mere philosophers. These great teachers taught more than philosophy. (For one thing, in those times no one distinguished theology from philosophy, or ethics from metaphysics. This is a comparatively small point, however.)

There can be no doubt at all of the widespread influence of the fundamental moral laws set out in the Old Testament, and there can be no doubt, either, about the enormous influence of the personality and teaching of Jesus, who reinterpreted and explained, often by means of parables, those ethical laws. Judaic and Christian teaching, broadly philosophical in character, forms the bedrock of the national and international laws, and the moral thinking generally, of Western civilization. That people and their governments too often lapse from these standards does not mean that the standards themselves are not accepted as theoretically correct.

Turning to the Greeks, it is generally acknowledged that Greek philosophy and science created a bedrock of 'intellectual methodology', which is applicable not only to philosophy and science but to many other enquiries as well. The Greeks gave us our first, and in some ways our most fundamental ideas on how to do philosophy, how to investigate nature and society, how to do science, in short, how to think.

Here we can best concentrate on Aristotle, for he is unquestionably the most influential professional philosophy teacher in history. He is also one of the most influential thinkers of any kind who has ever lived. It is not possible to give anything like a short overview of Aristotle's thinking, because of the vastness and the variety of the topic, but we can perhaps give some idea of that very vastness and variety. Not only did Aristotle invent logic (as we have seen); he also wrote major works on metaphysics, and on ethics, and on many branches of what is nowadays called science, including mechanics and biology and psychology. And he wrote important treatises on politics, on religion, and on literature.

In the thirteenth century Thomas Aquinas set out to reconcile the rediscovered lost works of Aristotle with the theology of the Christian church. He managed to do this to the satisfaction of the Church authorities of the time, so that Aristotelianism became the official philosophy of Christianity. Because of this it has continued to influence the ideas and ideologies of Europe right down to the present day.

John Stuart Mill

Those who in English-speaking countries defend the principles of freedom of the press and freedom of speech quite often refer sooner or later to the ideas of John Stuart Mill. Feminists too owe some of their best arguments to Mill, and to his wife, Harriet.

Logical positivism

In the 1920s the Vienna Circle, or logical positivists, boosted science as superior to all other human endeavours. Contemporary governments too accept that science has an exceedingly important role to pay in modern life, not least because it is perceived as a creator of wealth. Positivism provides professional and governmental proponents of 'the scientific ideal' with a degree of theoretical justification for their stance, so that garbled or ungarbled versions of positivistic principles can sometimes be heard in public discussions about science and science funding.

Logic and the computer industry

Readers who know things about computers possibly found chapter 23 of this book strangely familiar. That is because some of the inventors of the computer were mathematicians who had studied modern formal logic. The binary system embodied in the computer is basically the same binary ('true/false') system we saw operating in the truth tables of the propositional calculus. The huge computer industry has been made possible by the ideas of mathematicians and engineers – and philosophers.

Does philosophy influence real life? It certainly does. That is one of the reasons why it is worth studying.

Appendix I
The Great Philosophers

Socrates and Plato   Socrates was born in Athens 469 years before the birth of Christ and was executed in 399 BC. He wrote no books and virtually everything that is known about his life, teachings and personality comes to us from the writings of his pupil Plato.

Plato (427–347 BC), wrote thirty-five or so philosophical works of varying length, all in dialogue form. In most of these he makes Socrates the main protagonist. He represents Socrates as a physically ugly man who was nevertheless admirable and lovable, being brave, modest, wise, witty, optimistic and intellectually honest.

Plato's earlier dialogues are generally supposed to be quite close in manner and content to Socrates' own philosophizing. They are chiefly concerned with the nature and possibility of knowledge, especially knowledge about virtue, and with questions about the soul.

Plato's later dialogues are believed to represent his own philosophy. The topics include knowledge, perception, grammar, paradoxes, immortality and the teachings of other philosophers. Plato constructs a theory, the theory of Forms, which he uses to explain many things, including the possibility of knowledge, the importance of the good, and the difference between particularity and generality. Two of his longer dialogues – the *Republic* and the *Laws* – are concerned with political philosophy and describe ideal states. In the first of these Plato argues that there will never be good government until kings become philosophers or philosophers become kings.

At the age of seventy Socrates stood trial in Athens on charges of having 'corrupted the youth of Athens'. He was convicted and condemned to death, and refused to co-operate with his friends' attempts to spring him from prison. The death sentence was carried out by poisoning (hemlock). Plato, then aged twenty-eight, seems not to have been present at the execution; but he wrote a moving account of the scene. After the death of Socrates Plato set up a school in Athens called the Academy where Aristotle was one of his students.

Plato died at the age of eighty, at a party.

Zeno the Eleatic   This Zeno lived in the fifth century before Christ. He invented a number of paradoxes which are still sometimes referred to in teaching mathematics. The best-known paradoxes of Zeno are 'Achilles and the Tortoise' and 'The Flying Arrow'.

Zeno the Stoic   This later Zeno (342–270 BC) taught that the objects of earthly desire are only relatively good, if at all, and that one should reduce one's desires as much as possible. He committed suicide at the age of seventy-two.

Aristotle   Aristotle was born in 384 BC at Stagira in Macedonia. His father was court physician to the King of Macedonia. At the age of seventeen Aristotle went to Athens where he remained for twenty years as a pupil and colleague of Plato. He was one of the three candidates for Head of the Academy when Plato died in 347 BC; however, he did not get the job, the successful candidate being Plato's nephew Speusippus. Aristotle then left Athens, taking a few of his students with him, and spent some years living in various parts of Asia Minor and Macedonia. For a short time he was tutor to Alexander the Great, then aged fourteen. He returned to Athens in 335 BC and set up a school called the Lyceum. In 323 BC there were anti-Macedonian riots in Athens, and a charge was trumped up against Aristotle. Unlike Socrates he did not wait for trial but left the city as soon as he could. He died in Euboa aged sixty-two.

Aristotle more or less invented logic, he lectured on subjects which later became metaphysics, ethics and psychology, and he carried out research in subjects which later became mechanics, biology and political science. He encouraged his students at the Lyceum to collect material for him, and therefore can be said to have invented the idea of a research programme.

Hundreds of commentaries have been written on Aristotle, including extensive works by Averroes, Maimonides and Aquinas (see below). Many centuries after his death the Christian church adopted his teaching as the basis of its own philosophy. Later still, at the time of the Reformation, there was a philosophical backlash against Aristotle because of this connection. The anti-Aristotle attitude persisted for quite some time but the late twentieth century saw a backlash against the backlash.

Euclid   Euclid was a Greek mathematician who lived in Alexandria in about 300 BC. His geometry had an important influence on philosophical thinking about method.

Cicero   Marcus Tullius Cicero (106–43 BC) was a Roman statesman and man of letters. He wrote several philosophical treatises, including essays on the nature of the gods, on duty and on friendship.

Andronicus   Andronicus of Rhodes was a Greek philosopher who lived in Rome in about 60 BC. He collected and edited the works of Aristotle.

Augustine   The African philosopher and theologian Augustine was born in what is now Algeria 354 years after the birth of Christ and died in Hippo (North Africa) in AD 430. His mother brought him up as a Christian.

St Augustine left home at about the age of seventeen, and lived first in Carthage, then in Rome and Milan, where he studied the Bible and the works of Plato. After several years in Italy he returned to Africa and set up a monastic community; he was subsequently made Bishop of Hippo.

Augustine lived during times when the Roman Empire was being overrun by Goths, Huns and Vandals. When Rome itself was invaded by Goths he predicted that a new, Christian empire ('The City of God') would one day replace the paganism and heresy of the barbarian invaders. His own writings helped to form the ideology of the Christian polity that did in fact eventually come into being.

For about 800 years Augustine was regarded as the chief authority on Christian teaching, with the result that when the works of Aristotle were rediscovered in the twelfth century they were banned in the University of Paris. However, Aquinas managed to forge a kind of synthesis between the philosophy of Aristotle and the theology of Augustine, and Aristotle was eventually unbanned.

In AD 430 the Vandals surrounded the town of Hippo and Augustine died during the siege.

Boethius (475–524)   Boethius was a Roman philosopher who lived at a time when the Roman Empire was ruled by the Goths. He fell out with the Gothic king, who imprisoned him and then had him executed. In prison Boethius wrote his best-known work, *The Consolation of Philosophy*. He knew Greek and translated some of Aristotle's works into Latin.

Anselm (1033–1109)   St Anselm was born in Piedmont and became Archbishop of Canterbury during the reigns of William Rufus and Henry I. He is known to historians because of his disputes with these kings, and to philosophers on account of his ontological argument for the existence of God (see chapter 2).

Abelard (1079–1142)   Peter Abelard, who was born into a family of Breton nobles, is probably remembered today chiefly because of his catastrophic love affair with his pupil Eloise.

Abelard wrote on theology, logic, ethics and metaphysics, and during his lifetime was regarded as one of the greatest thinkers of the age. His theology, however, was condemned by various opponents, including St Bernard of Clairvaux, a founder of monasteries and a supporter of the Crusades. In 1142 Abelard started off for Rome in order to defend himself against a charge of heresy. He died on the journey.

Averroes (1126–1198)   Averroes was born in Cordova, the son of the Cadi (Muslim judge) and became a Cadi himself, in Cordova, Seville and Morocco.

Averroes wrote commentaries on Aristotle and expounded the Koran in Aristotelian terms; this earned him the nickname 'the Expositor'. His philosophy influenced the development of medieval Christian theology, and also became the basis of some Muslim heresies.

Maimonides (1135–1204)   Maimonides was born in Spain and died in Egypt. His biographer A. J. Heschel says this of him: 'Maimonides had a lofty political position [as head of the Jewish community]; he was considered the premier physician of his age, the most important Talmudist of the millennium, an epoch-making philosopher, an outstanding mathematician, scientist and jurist; he was admired by the masses, honoured by princes and celebrated by scholars.'

Maimonides wrote commentaries on Aristotle which together with those by Averroes were ultimately responsible for the integration of Aristotle's teaching into Christian philosophy and Western philosophy generally. His popular book *A Guide for the Perplexed* is still read after 850 years.

Aquinas (1225–1274)   St Thomas Aquinas was born in Italy into a noble family. His father refused to give him permission to join the Dominican Order, but he did so all the same, and was then captured by his brothers and imprisoned in the family castle for two years. Eventually he escaped and travelled to France where he became a teacher of philosophy. His numerous works include the *Summa Theologiae*, which was intended to be a complete system of theology. It is still the standard authority on theology in the Roman Catholic Church.

Duns Scotus (1265–1308)   Johannes Duns Scotus, or John Dun of Scotland, was a Franciscan monk. He studied in Oxford where he subsequently taught philosophy. Scotus wrote commentaries on Aristotle and on the Bible, and also on Aquinas, with whom he disagreed.

Ockham (1300–1349)   William of Ockham or Occam was born in Surrey. He entered the Franciscan Order and studied in Oxford and in Paris. He fell out with the Pope, who had him imprisoned at Avignon, but he escaped from there and fled to Bavaria, where he became a favourite of the King. He argued that temporal rulers have a divine authority independent of any authority bestowed on them by the Pope. He also wrote treatises on logic, and commentaries on Aristotle. His famous dictum, called 'Ockham's Razor', states 'do not multiply entities beyond necessity'.

Grotius (1583–1645)   Hugo Grotius was a Dutch jurist and theologian and author of a great book on the philosophy of law: *De Jure Belli et Pacis* (*On the Law of War and Peace*). The 'law' in the title refers to natural law or moral law, not man-made law. Hobbes and Locke were both influenced by Grotius' work.

Hobbes (1588–1679)   The English philosopher Thomas Hobbes, who was born in the year of the Spanish Armada, lived through the English Civil War – an experience which strongly influenced his political philosophy.

Hobbes' theory of government includes the thesis that the king or other head of state must be allowed absolute power, for divided power can lead to civil war. Hobbes' ideas naturally came into conflict with the views of the men who eventually ordered the decapitation of Charles I. He fled to Paris in the early stages of the conflict between King and Parliament (1640), and stayed in France for twelve years, taking the opportunity to engage in discussion and controversy with Descartes. For a time he was tutor to the young Charles II, also an exile. At the Restoration of the Monarchy he was given a pension by Charles II.

Hobbes' most important book, *Leviathan*, was published in 1651.

Descartes (1596–1650)   René Descartes' 'method of doubt', or 'methodological scepticism', which he outlines in his *Meditations on First Philosophy*, has had a profound influence on modern thought. In the same book he constructs several arguments for the existence of God, including his own version of the ontological argument (see chapter 2). Descartes is also the inventor of Cartesian geometry.

Locke (1632–1704)   The English philosopher John Locke spent a considerable part of his life in Oxford. He is the founder of British Empiricism, a philosophy which bases all theory on experience. Locke holds that the human mind is a *tabula rasa* or blank sheet of paper upon which experience writes information, as it were.

His *Two Treatises On Civil Government* influenced the authors of the American Constitution, but there is disagreement among scholars about whether or not he himself was a supporter of democratic ideas. His major work is his *Essay Concerning Human Understanding*.

Spinoza (1632–1677)   Baruch Spinoza was born in Amsterdam, the son of a family of emigré Spanish Jews. He was excommunicated from the synagogue when he was twenty-four, supposedly because he was too interested in non-Talmudic studies like astronomy and optics.

He was an unworldly man who made a living grinding lenses. Spinoza's *Ethics* is modelled on Euclid's *Elements*. It begins, like the *Elements*, with 'axioms' and develops 'theorems' from those. His other writings include commentaries on Descartes' geometry, and the *Treatise on God and Man*.

Leibniz (1646–1716)   Gottfried Wilhelm Leibniz, whose father was a professor of philosophy at Leipzig, was one of the great polymaths. His productions include a calculating machine, a plan for a French invasion of Egypt (consulted 100 years later by Napoleon), a plan for the reconciliation of the Catholic and Protestant churches, and many philosophical treatises. Leibniz was a mathematician as well as philosopher, and discovered the differential calculus independently (it is thought) of Newton. His dictum 'this is the best of all possible worlds' was satirized by Voltaire in *Candide*.

Berkeley (1685–1753)   George Berkeley (Bishop Berkeley), born in Kilkenny, was the Irish member of the British Empiricists, the other two being John Locke (see above) and the Scotsman David Hume (see below).

Berkeley holds that the world is made of spirits (people and God), and ideas. Human ideas are fleeting and impermanent, those

251

of God permanent and ordered. Berkeley expresses his doctrine in the slogan *esse est percipi*, that is, *to exist is to be perceived*. His principal philosophical works are *A New Theory of Vision*, *Principles of Human Nature* and *Three Dialogues between Hylas and Philonous*.

Hume (1711–1776)   David Hume published books on British history in which he sided with the Stuart kings. However, he is chiefly remembered as a philosopher.

In his young days Hume worked for his living, first as a junior diplomat, then as the tutor of an insane young nobleman, and later still as a librarian. He saved and invested his money and was able to devote most of the later part of his life to writing.

Hume expounds his sceptical account of the nature of causation (see chapter 18) in his *Treatise on Human Nature*, and again in the first of his three *Enquiries*. In the *Dialogues on Natural Religion* he discusses and criticizes the well-known 'argument from design' for the existence of God (see chapter 2). His *Essays* cover a wide range of topics, philosophical, historical and general.

Kant (1724–1804)   Immanuel Kant was born in Konigsberg in Germany, and it is said that he never travelled more than ten miles from that town in his whole life.

Kant relates that on reading Hume he was 'awakened from dogmatic slumbers'. From that time on he attempted to find ways of supporting conceptions which seemed to be threatened by the scepticism of Hume. Thus he tries to prove that causal necessity rules the empirical world, and that freedom and morality rule the world of the human will. He discusses all the traditional proofs of the existence of God, deciding in the end that human reason cannot cope with God, or Eternity, or Infinity. His major books are *The Critique of Pure Reason* (on metaphysics) and *The Critique of Practical Reason* (on ethics).

Wollstonecraft (1759–1797)   Mary Wollstonecraft, a political philosopher and a feminist, was described by one of her contemporaries as 'a hyena in petticoats'. She still arouses wrath today, and has even been criticized (by the historian Richard Cobb) for having a peculiar surname.

Wollstonecraft began her career as an author in 1790 with the publication of *Vindication of the Rights of Man*. This is essentially a radical's reply to Edmund Burke's anti-radical *Reflections on the French Revolution*. In 1792 she published *Vindication of the Rights of Woman*, her most important work, which made her both famous and infamous. She begins it by demolishing Rousseau, whose proposed system of education (described in his *Emile*, and *Emile and Sophie*) expressly aimed at subordinating the female to the male from earliest childhood. Wollstonecraft's other works include *View of the French Revolution*, an eye-witness account, and a volume of short stories based on real life.

She died in childbirth.

Hegel (1770–1831)   Georg Wilhelm Friedrich Hegel is probably the most notable system builder in the history of philosophy. He claims that all knowledge can be systematically organized under the three headings of Logic, Philosophy of Nature and Philosophy of Mind. Hegel also introduces a new conception of 'dialectic'. He says that history is a progression brought about by a dialectical clash of 'thesis' and 'antithesis' followed by 'synthesis'. The elements of this progression are spiritual or intellectual, not material.

Hegel when young was a supporter of the French Revolution and of Napoleon, but quite soon developed a hatred of all democratic institutions and a great admiration for the authoritarian Prussian state. According to him 'the state is the march of God upon earth'. His chief works are his *Logic* (so-called), the *Encyclopaedia of the Philosophical Sciences* and *Philosophy of Right*.

Ricardo (1772–1823)   David Ricardo was an English economist. The son of a London stockbroker, he himself had made a large personal fortune by the time he was forty-two. Five years later, in 1819, he was elected to Parliament as a Radical.

His major work, on which his reputation rests, and which had a considerable influence on Marx, is the *Principles of Political Economy and Taxation*. This book contains important analyses of various economic concepts including value, wages and rent.

Schopenhauer (1788–1860)   Arthur Schopenhauer regarded Hegel as nothing better than a fraud and Hegelianism as completely fatuous and senseless: he says as much in volume 2 of his book *The World as Will and Representation*. As a young man he gave lectures at the same time of day as Hegel but did not succeed in weaning students away from the philosophical dictator. Schopenhauer gave up teaching in 1821 and devoted the rest of his life to writing.

Schopenhauer was one of the first in Europe to study the religions of India and his ideas show the influence of Indian thought. For Schopenhauer the mind and the will are real, in contrast to the material universe, which is in some sense a phantasmagoria. Reality is not good, but bad, because desires and the will cause only misery. Pessimism is the only rational philosophy of life.

James Mill and John Stuart Mill   James Mill (1773–1836), the father of John Stuart Mill, was a man of letters who worked as a journalist and later for the East India Company. His chief writings are on jurisprudence and political philosophy; politically he was a Radical. He took charge entirely of the education of his son, who states in his *Autobiography* that he began his studies, including the study of Greek, at the age of three.

John Stuart Mill (1806–1873) earned his living as a civil servant in the India Office. His best-known works of philosophy are *Utilitarianism*, his *System of Logic*, *The Subjection of Women* and the essay *On Liberty*.

As well as being a philosopher and a civil servant, John Stuart Mill was an active political reformer. He was arrested in 1824 for distributing birth control literature to the poor. He supported universal education and the extension of the suffrage (including votes for women). He helped to found Newnham College, Cambridge, one of the earliest colleges for women in England. In 1865 he successfully stood for Parliament, for the constituency of Westminster, as 'the working man's candidate'. He spent most of his term in Parliament campaigning for women's suffrage, and since this was not a popular cause with the voters he lost the seat at the next election.

Marx (1818–1883)   Karl Marx, the son of a lawyer, was a founder of modern international communism. He studied at Bonn and Berlin and became interested in Hegelianism. He saw that it might be possible to apply a type of Hegelianism to economic history and to radical politics.

On becoming a political refugee Marx moved to London where he and his family were supported by Friedrich Engels, a wealthy manufacturer.

Marx's philosophy is a kind of Hegelianism turned inside out. Thus while Hegel says that the state is the march of God on earth, Marx claims that states and rulers are merely instruments of oppression. And while Hegel says that 'the dialectical forces of history' consist of a clash of ideas, Marx claims that these dialectical forces are material.

Marx's philosophy is not important as philosophy but rather on account of its tremendous influence on the political history of the twentieth century. This would have pleased him, for he wrote 'the point is not to understand the world but to change it'.

James (1842–1910)   William James, the American psychologist and philosopher, and brother of the novelist Henry James, was educated first in New York, and later at Harvard, where he studied medicine.

James was a psychological behaviourist, arguing that emotions are the perception of physiological changes, and a philosophical pragmatist, claiming that beliefs do not work because they are true but are true because they work.

Nietzsche (1844–1900)   Friedrich Nietzsche, the son of a Lutheran pastor, studied in Bonn and in Leipzig, and was cosidered so brilliant that he was offered, and accepted, the chair of Classical Philology in the University of Basel before he had completed his studies. He was then twenty-four. In his youth he greatly admired Schopenhauer (whom he never met) and Richard Wagner (whom he did), but eventually he became disillusioned with both of them.

Nietzsche gave up academic work in order to serve as a hospital orderly in the Franco-Prussian war, and quite soon after that gave it up altogether in order to live a wandering life, supported by a sickness pension from the university. He is thought to have contracted syphillis during his time in the Prussian army. Twelve years before his death he became insane.

Nietzsche sets out to undermine traditional moral values, and to substitute for those a kind of aristocratic egoism (see chapters 8 and 9). But his overall project is to undermine metaphysics, logic and, it seems, rationality itself, as well as morality. He often writes as if he believes that religion, philosophy, science and in fact all systems of thought are nothing but fraudulent attempts by various professions to seize power.

Nietzsche's doctrines were taken up with enthusiasm by the Nazis, who were encouraged in this by his sister Elisabeth, a friend of Hitler.

Frege (1848–1925)　　Gottlob Frege was a German mathematician and logician who taught in Jena. He is thought by several scholars to be the most important logician since Aristotle. In 1879 he outlined a complete system of symbolic logic, which, however, contained a contradiction or paradox about classes, noticed by Russell, who tried to resolve it.

In the theory of meaning Frege draws a distinction between sense and reference, a distinction which has played a significant role in modern philosophy.

The sense-reference distinction can be best explained by means of examples. For instance, the two expressions, 'The Morning Star' and 'The Evening Star' have the same reference (since they both refer to the same planet, namely Venus), but they have different senses (or meanings).

Appendix II
Philosophy in the
Twentieth Century

Husserl (1859–1938)   Edmund Husserl was made professor at the University of Freiburg in 1916. He is the founder of *phenomenology*, a theory or school of thought now adopted in many of the academies of Continental Europe, India and Japan. Husserl reintroduced the term EPOCHĒ to philosophy, thereby naming a process which forms an important part of the phenomenological method. EPOCHĒ, borrowed from the philosophical sceptics of ancient Greece, means *suspending judgement*. The first principle of phenomenology is encapsulated in the dictum that in order to discover the truth about some things it is necessary to suspend judgement on others.

Dewey (1859–1952)   John Dewey became a professor at Columbia University (New York) in 1904. He had a considerable influence on the ideology of education in the United States, arguing that the prime aims of education should be to ensure that the child develops socially and psychologically, and becomes a well-adjusted member of its community.

Russell (1872–1970)   Bertrand Russell competes with Frege for the title of most important logician since Aristotle. He studied mathematics and philosophy at Cambridge and economics in Berlin, and corresponded with Frege. In 1910 he published (with A. N. Whitehead) the big book *Principia Mathematica*, regarded as a milestone in logic. His Theory of Descriptions is also regarded as a milestone.

During the second half of his life Russell wrote many popular books and essays, including *The Conquest of Happiness, Marriage and Morals, Why I am not a Christian*, and *On Education*.

Russell was a political controversialist of some note. In 1907 he stood for Parliament (unsuccessfully) as a supporter of votes for women. During the First World War he took up the cause of pacifism, and was gaoled for distributing anti-conscription pamphlets. After the Second World War he wrote a number of letters to world leaders about the dangers of nuclear war. As an old man he was gaoled again for obstructing the highway in London in front of the Ministry of Defence.

Wittgenstein (1889–1951)

Ludwig Wittgenstein, who was born in Vienna, studied engineering at Berlin and Manchester, then became interested in mathematical logic. He visited Frege who recommended that he contact Russell. In 1912 Wittgenstein went to Cambridge and became Russell's pupil. Russell was impressed with the young Wittgenstein and did a great deal to further his reputation as a philosopher.

Wittgenstein served as an artillery officer in the Austrian army in the First World War. He was captured by the Italian forces, and wrote his first book, the *Tractatus Logico-Philosophicus*, while a prisoner of war. The book was published in 1921 and propounds a theory which Russell labelled 'logical atomism'.

Wittgenstein's ideas changed radically in the 1930s. He came to believe that philosophical questions and problems arise out of misunderstandings concerned with or derived from language. However, as he records in a preface, he found himself unable to construct a coherent book out of these new notions. After his death his manuscripts were edited and translated by G. E. M. Anscombe, G. H. von Wright and Rush Rhees. They include *The Blue and Brown Books, Philosophical Investigations, Remarks on the Foundations of Mathematics* and *On Certainty*.

The Logical Positivists, or Vienna Circle

The Vienna Circle, which came into existence in the early 1920s, was a group of scientists, mathematicians and philosophers who met regularly to discuss logical and philosophical questions. Its members included Morris Schlick (the founder), Kurt Gödel, Rudolf Carnap,

Otto Neurath, Herbert Feigl, Friedrich Waismann and Philip Frank.

In 1929 the Vienna Circle published a sort of manifesto listing a number of earlier and contemporary thinkers who were perceived as exemplifying the positivist position. The list included Hume, Mill, Einstein, Russell and Wittgenstein. The positivists believed themselves to be doing philosophy in a 'scientific' way, and on the whole seemed to think that the point of philosophy as such is to provide science with sound foundations.

The group broke up in the 1930s after the assassination of Schlick (1936) and the advent of Nazism.

Marcuse (1898–1979)   Herbert Marcuse was born in Berlin, studied at the Universities of Berlin and Freiburg, and helped to found the Frankfurt Institute of Social Research. After the Institute was closed down by the Nazis Marcuse fled to the USA and became a professor of philosophy, first in Massachusetts, then in California. His work consists, in the main, of extended critiques of modern society and contemporary culture.

Heidegger (1899–1976)   The German philosopher Martin Heidegger, a supporter of Nazism, succeeded Edmund Husserl as professor of philosophy at Freiburg. He was removed from his academic post in 1945 because of his connection with the Hitler regime.

Heidegger's work is mainly concerned with the study of existence or being, which he thinks is a sort of super-property. His philosophy is thus in direct conflict with Russell's analysis of existence according to which existence is not a property at all (see chapter 1).

Heidegger's writings are abstruse and seem to be hard to translate from the German. In English translation some of his propositions, for example, the statement 'the Nothing Noths', look to be incomprehensible.

Adorno (1903–1965)   Theodor Adorno was a prominent member of the Frankfurt Institute of Social Research. When the Institute was closed down after Hitler came to power Adorno fled first to Oxford, then to the USA.

He was a notable teacher whose post-war pupils include several of the big names of German philosophy. Adorno's main interests lay in culture criticism and aesthetics, especially the aesthetics of music; he studied composition with Arnold Schoenberg and wrote a considerable quantity of music himself.

Popper (1902–1994)   Karl Popper, formerly professor at the London School of Economics, was best known as a philosopher of science. He was the author of *The Logic of Scientific Discovery*, which is in part a critique of logical positivism. He also wrote a major work of political philosophy, *The Open Society and its Enemies*.

Sartre (1905–1980) and de Beauvoir (1908–1986)   Jean-Paul Sartre and Simone de Beauvoir, who lived together, were prominent members of the French existentialist school, and leading lights of the left-wing intelligentsia of Paris during the years following the Second World War.

Sartre, originally a disciple of Heidegger, holds that man is nothing over and above the sum of his choices, which are both fallible and free. He insisted that it is important not to be guilty of 'bad faith', which is a kind of double thinking. For many years Sartre was close to, but not a member of, the French Communist Party.

De Beauvoir studied philosophy at the Sorbonne where for a short time she was a professor. In 1949 she published an important work of feminist philosophy, translated in 1956 as *The Second Sex*. Her other writings include novels and memoirs.

Until very recently Sartre was assumed to be by far the better philosopher of the two. However, current discussions, by feminist philosophers and others, have cast some doubt on this assumption. On the other hand it may be that Sartre's work is not strictly comparable with de Beauvoir's. His is grounded in Heideggerian metaphysics whereas hers strikes out in a new direction, her most important book being a foundational work of modern philosophical feminism.

Ryle (1900–1976)   Gilbert Ryle's adult life, apart from some years in the Army during the Second World War, was spent in Oxford, teaching and writing philosophy. His book *The Concept of Mind*, published in 1949, is a best-seller which has never been out of print. Ryle taught a number of well-known philosophers, including A. J. Ayer.

Rand (1905–1982)   Ayn Rand was born in Russia. She emigrated to America, where she studied philosophy. She was not a professional philosophy teacher but a popular writer who produced a regular journal in which she expressed her philosophical and political ideas (*Ayn Rand's Newsletter*).

Ayn Rand was a strong supporter of capitalism and seems to have had some influence on the political climate of the United States. Being a trained philosopher, and possessed moreover of a lucid and sometimes witty literary style, she was able to provide right-wing American businessmen with theoretical justifications for their activities.

Rand's metaphysical writings embody a robust common sense, based partly on Aristotle. She is a sort of commonsensical dualist, describing idealists (such as Berkeley) as 'the Mystics of the Spirit', and modern materialists as 'the Mystics of Muscle'. Her moral philosophy emphasizes her profound faith in the ethical superiority of capitalism.

Ayer (1910–1989)   Alfred Jules Ayer studied philosophy in Oxford with Gilbert Ryle, who advised him in 1932 to visit Vienna to talk to the logical positivists. The result was Ayer's best-known book *Language, Truth and Logic*, an introduction in English to the ideas of the Vienna Circle. The philosophy of logical positivism has now given way to some extent to other developments, but *Language, Truth and Logic* remains one of the most famous philosophical works of the century.

The book takes the concept of scientific verification as its key: the central idea is the 'verification principle', which asserts that no proposition has meaning unless it either (1) belongs to mathematics or logic, or (2) can be verified by the methods of science, which are taken to be based on direct sense experience.

Ayer, who became professor of philosophy, first at London University, and later at Oxford, subsequently wrote many other books, remaining always within the broad tradition of British empiricism, and regarding himself as the heir of David Hume and Bertrand Russell.

Murdoch (1919–1999)   The novelist Dame Iris Murdoch was trained as a philosopher and taught the subject for some years at St Anne's College, Oxford. Her philosophical books include *The Sovereignty of the Good* and *Metaphysics as a Guide to Morals*.

Appendix III
Philosophy Today

This is a brief list of contemporary philosophers, most of them working in the analytic tradition, who seem to us to be influential, either as teachers, or as authors, or as both. In the nature of the case such a list cannot pretend to be complete. It is a selection only.

The list is in alphabetical order.

Anscombe   G. E. M. Anscombe (Elizabeth Anscombe), formerly professor of philosophy at Cambridge, studied in Oxford and then with Wittgenstein in Cambridge. She is the chief translator of Wittgenstein's later (post-*Tractatus*) writings. Anscombe has also published many original works of her own on a wide range of philosophical topics.

Davidson   The American philosopher Donald Davidson, who has taught at Princeton and elsewhere in the United States, is best known for his contributions to analytic metaphysics. These include essays on the nature of events and on the nature of the mind.

Dummett   Sir Michael Dummett, formerly professor at Oxford, is a world authority on Frege. He was knighted in 1999 'for services to logic and race relations'.

Foot   Philippa Foot studied and taught at Oxford and later worked in California. Interested mainly in ethics, she is critical of utilitarianism and of semi-subjectivist theories such as prescriptivism. Many of her papers are published in her book *Virtues and Vices*.

Gettier   Edmund Gettier invented 'the Gettier problem' or 'Gettier salt mine'. The Gettier problem consists of ingenious counter-examples destructive to the classical three-part definition of knowledge.

Goodman   Nelson Goodman invented 'the new problem of induction'. He imagines a new concept, 'grue' ('green now but blue in the future'), and argues that it is impossible to know now whether current emeralds are green or grue. He concludes that any prediction based on induction must be problematic.

Kripke   Saul Kripke is the author of seminal papers on philosophical logic and on interpreting Wittgenstein.

Kuhn   Thomas Kuhn's work on philosophy of science is widely regarded as a big breakthrough in this subject.

Lewis   The American philosopher David Lewis invented 'possible worlds theory'.

MacIntyre   Alasdair MacIntyre has written widely-read books on ethics and on medieval philosophy. Educated at Oxford and in France, he is now a professor at Notre Dame University.

Midgeley   The British philosopher Mary Midgeley is a full-time author who writes books on applied philosophy for the lay reader.

Nagel   Thomas Nagel teaches philosophy in New York. His book, *The View from Nowhere* (1986), argues that a materialistic philosophy necessarily fails to account for subjective experience and therefore cannot provide a complete description of the world.

Nozick   Robert Nozick, a disciple of the right-wing philosopher Ayn Rand, wrote an influential book, *Anarchy, State and Utopia*, in which he attacks American liberalism and 'New Deal' ideas.

Place   The British philosopher and psychologist U. T. Place taught for a time in Australia, where he formulated what has since become known as 'the mind brain identity theory', also called physicalism. He is acclaimed by colleagues (e.g. J. J. C. Smart – see below) as the originator of the Australian materialist school of philosophy.

Quine   Willard van Orman Quine is a Grand Old Man of American philosophy. He works mainly on logic, and on the nature of existence. He has also written an autobiography.

Sainsbury   Mark Sainsbury, of London University, works on metaphysics, logic and the nature of paradox, and is also editor of the journal *Mind*. He commissioned a spoof edition of *Mind* to celebrate the year 2000.

Sen   The Indian scholar Amartya Sen, formerly of Harvard, now Master of Trinity College, Cambridge, is a philosopher and an economist. The topics he discusses in his writings include the nature and causes of poverty, the definition of well-being and the significance of the concept of human rights. In 1998 Professor Sen was awarded the Nobel Prize for economics.

Singer   The Australian Peter Singer introduced vegetarianism into philosophic debate. A hard-line utilitarian, he advocates euthanasia and infanticide.

Smart   The English-Australian philosopher J. J. C. Smart has been professor in Adelaide, Latrobe and Canberra. He is a former colleague of U. T. Place and an expounder of the physicalist theory of the mind. His philosophy is materialist and scientistic.

Strawson   Sir Peter Strawson, formerly professor at Oxford, is best known for his writings on philosophical logic and metaphysics, and for his attack on Russell's Theory of Descriptions. He has also written an important paper on free will, and he is an authority on Kant.

Bibliography and Further Reading

This section gives the titles of most of the books and essays directly or indirectly referred to in the text, together with a small number of related works. Each section can be taken as a guide to further reading on the topics of the corresponding chapters.

An asterisk signifies that the book so marked is easy to read and non-technical. A double asterisk signifies that the work was originally written for beginners and students.

Chapter 1   Some Puzzles about Existence

Aristotle, *Categories* (trans. J. L. Ackrill), Oxford, Clarendon Press, 1962.
G. R. Lloyd, *Aristotle: The Growth and Strength of his Thought*, Cambridge, CUP, 1968.
B. Russell, 'Lectures on logical atomism'★★, in his *Logic and Knowledge* (ed. R. C. Marsh), London, Unwin Hyman, 1988.

Chapter 2   The Existence of God

R. Descartes, *Meditations*, in his *Selected Writings* (trans. J. Cottingham, R. Stoothof and D. Murdoch), Cambridge, CUP, 1988.
J. Hick, *Philosophy of Religion*★★, London, Prentice-Hall International, 1990.
J. Hick and A. McGill (eds), *The Many-Faced Argument*, London, Macmillan, 1968.
D. Hume, *Dialogues on Natural Religion*, Harmondsworth, Penguin.

Chapter 3   The Existence and Identity of Persons

J. Locke, *An Essay Concerning Human Understanding* (ed. Alexander Campbell Fraser), New York, Dover Publications; esp. Book II, ch. 27.

Bibliography and Further Reading

P. F. Strawson, *Individuals*, London, Methuen, 1959; ch. 3.

Jenny Teichman, *Polemical Papers*, Aldershot, Ashgate, 1997.

M. Tooley, 'A defense of abortion and infanticide', in *The Problem of Abortion* (ed. J. Feinberg), California, Belmont, 1973.

Chapter 4   The Problem of Free Will

M. Hollis, *Invitation to Philosophy*★★, Oxford, Blackwell, 1986.

D. Hume, 'On liberty and necessity', in his *A Treatise of Human Nature*, Harmondsworth, Penguin.

I. Kant, *Grounding for the Metaphysic of Morals* (trans. J. W. Ellington), Indianapolis, Hackett, 1983; Part III.

B. F. Skinner, *Beyond Freedom and Dignity*, Harmondsworth, Penguin.

Chapter 5   The Existence of Evil

A. J. Heschel, *Maimonides*★ (trans. J. Neugroschel), New York, Farrar, Straus and Giroux, 1982.

D. Hume, *Dialogues Concerning Natural Religion*, Harmondsworth, Penguin.

Maimonides, *A Guide for the Perplexed*★, (trans. M. Friedlander), London, Routledge and Kegan Paul, 1942.

Voltaire, *Candide*★ (trans. J. Butt), Harmondsworth, Penguin.

Chapter 6   The Problem of Knowledge

D. M. Armstrong, *Belief, Truth and Knowledge*, Cambridge, CUP, 1973; part III.

E. Gettier, 'Is justified true belief knowledge?', in *Knowledge and Belief* (ed. A. Phillips Griffiths), Oxford, OUP, 1967.

Plato, *Protagoras* (with *Meno*) (trans. W. C. K. Guthrie), Harmondsworth, Penguin.

F. Ramsey, *Foundations of Mathematics* (ed. D. H. Mellor), Cambridge, CUP, 1990.

Chapter 7   Scepticism Old and New

G. Berkeley, *A New Theory of Vision and other Writings*, London, J. M. Dent and Sons [Everyman's Library no. 483].

OR:

G. Berkeley, *Philosophical Writings* (ed. D. M. Armstrong), New York, Collier Books.

Susan Haack, *Manifesto of a Passionate Moderate*, Chicago, Chicago University Press, 1998.

D. Hume, *A Treatise of Human Nature*, Oxford, Clarendon Press; esp. Book 1, Part 4, chs 1 and 2.

R. Kimball, *Tenured Radicals*, New York, Harper and Row, 1991.

J. Locke, *An Essay Concerning Human Understanding*, New York, Dover Publications: esp. Book II, chs 8 and 13.

Plato, *Protagoras* (with *Meno*) (trans. W. C. K. Guthrie), Harmondsworth, Penguin.

Chapter 8   Morality and Illusion

A. J. Ayer, *Language, Truth and Logic*, Harmondsworth, Penguin.

J. L. Mackie, *Ethics: Inventing Right and Wrong*, Harmondsworth, Penguin.

F. Nietzsche, *The Genealogy of Morals*★ (trans. W. Kaufmann), New York, Random House, 1969.

Jenny Teichman, *Social Ethics, a Student's Guide*★★, Oxford and Cambridge MA, Blackwell, 1996.

Chapter 9   Egoism and Altruism

R. Dawkin, *The Selfish Gene*★, Oxford, OUP, 1989.

F. Nietzsche, *Beyond Good and Evil*★ (trans, R. J. Hollingdale), Harmondsworth, Penguin.

Chapter 10   Utility and Principles

I. Kant, *Grounding for the Metaphysic of Morals* (trans. J. W. Ellington), Indianapolis, Hackett, 1983; Part I.

J. S. Mill, *Utilitarianism*★ (with other works), London, Dent, 1993.
OR:
J. S. Mill, *Utilitarianism*★ (with other works), London, Collins, 1979.

J. J. C. Smart and B. A. O. Williams *Utilitarianism For and Against*, Cambridge, CUP, 1973.

Chapter 11   Life and Death

G. E. M. Anscombe, 'War and murder', in her *Collected Papers III*, Oxford, Blackwell, 1981.

T. Hobbes, *Leviathan*, Harmondsworth, Penguin; chs 12–16.

R. Holland, 'Suicide', in *Moral Problems* (ed. J. Rachels), New York, Harper and Row, 1979.

A. J. P. Kenny, *A Path from Rome*★, Oxford, OUP, 1985; ch. 13.

T. Nagel, *Mortal Questions*★★, Cambridge, CUP, 1991.

Bibliography and Further Reading

Chapter 12   Authority and Anarchy

G. E. M. Anscombe, 'On the source of the authority of the state', in her *Collected Pagers III*, Oxford, Blackwell, 1981.

J. Aubrey, *Brief Lives★*, London, Mandarin Books, 1992; the 'Life' of Hobbes.

T. Hobbes, *Leviathan*, Harmondsworth, Penguin; chs 12–16.

J. Locke, *Two Treatises on Civil Government* (ed. P. Laslett), London, Dent, 1963.

P. J. Proudhon, *The General Idea of Revolution in the Nineteenth Century* (trans. J. B. Robinson), London, Zwan Publications, 1988, and New York, Free Press, 1988.

Chapter 13   Liberty

T. Jefferson, *Selections from the Writings of Thomas Jefferson* (ed. M. Peterson), Cambridge, CUP, 1984.

J. Locke, *Two Treatises on Civil Government* (ed. P. Laslett), London, Dent, 1963.

J. S. Mill, *On Liberty★* (with *Utilitarianism*), London, Collins, 1979.

J. Milton, *Prose Selections* (ed. C. A. Patrides), Harmondsworth, Penguin.

T. Paine, *Common Sense* (ed. I. Kramnik), Harmondsworth, Penguin.

Chapter 14   Equality

K. Dixon, *Freedom and Equality*, London, Routledge, 1986.

R. Nozick, *Anarchy, State and Utopia★*, Oxford, Blackwell, 1990.

Ayn Rand, *The Ayn Rand Lexicon★* (ed. Howard Binswanger), New York, Meridian, 1986.

M. Walzer, *Spheres of Justice*, New York, Basic Books, 1983.

Chapter 15   Marx and Marxism

T. W. Adorno, *Problems of Modernity* (ed. A. Benjamin), London, Routledge, 1989.

V. I. Lenin, *What is to be Done?* (trans. J. Fineberg and G. Hanna), Harmondsworth, Penguin.

H. Marcuse, *One-dimensional Man: Studies in the Ideology of Advanced Industrial Society*, London, Routledge, 1991.

K. Marx and F. Engels, *The Communist Manifesto★*, Oxford, OUP, 1992.

Chapter 16   Politics and Sex

Simone de Beauvoir, *The Second Sex* (trans. H. M. Parshley), London, Pan Books, 1983.

Margaret Mead, *Male and Female*, London, Gollancz, 1949.

Kate Millett, *Sexual Politics★*, London, Virago, 1977.

Claire Tomalin, *Mary Wollstonecraft*★, Harmondsworth, Penguin.
Mary Wollstonecraft, *Vindication of the Rights of Woman*, London, Dent, 1992.

Chapter 17   The Methods of Science

P. Feyerabend, *Against Method*, London, Verso, 1993.
C. Hempel, *Aspects of Scientific Explanation*, New York, Free Press, 1970.
K. Popper, *The Logic of Scientific Discovery*, London, Routledge, 1992.

Chapter 18   Causation

D. A. T. Gasking, 'Causes and recipes', *Mind*, vol. 64, 1955.
D. Hume, *A Treatise of Human Nature*, Harmondsworth, Penguin; Book I, Part 3.
J. S. Mill, *A System of Logic*, London, Longmans Green, 1961; Vol. I, Book 3, chs 4–6, and Vol. II, Book 3, ch. 21.
B. Russell, 'On the notion of cause', in his *Mysticism and Logic*, London, Unwin, 1986.

Chapter 19   Induction

B. Russell, *The Problems of Philosophy*, Oxford, OUP, 1991.

Chapter 21   Syllogistic Logic

Aristotle, *Prior Analytics* (trans. A. J. Jenkinson), in J. Barnes (ed.), *The Complete Works of Aristotle (Vol. I)*, New Jersey, Princeton UP, 1985.
OR:
Aristotle, *Prior and Posterior Analytics* (trans. W. D. Ross), Oxford, Clarendon Press, 1949.
J. N. Keynes, *Formal Logic with Exercises*★★, London, Macmillan, 1894.

Chapter 23   The Propositional Calculus and
Chapter 24   The Predicate Calculus

S. Guttenplan, *The Languages of Logic*★★, Oxford, Blackwell, 1986.
E. J. Lemmon, *Beginning Logic*★★, London, Nelson, 1972.
W. H. Newton-Smith, *Logic*★★, London, Routledge, 1990.

Chapter 25   The Meaning of Life

F. Copleston, *Arthur Schopenhauer, Philosopher of Pessimism*, London, Burns, Oates and Washbourne, 1975.
F. Dostoievsky, *The Brothers Karamazov*★ (trans. Constance Garnett), London, Heron Books, 1964.

Bibliography and Further Reading

Philippa Foot, 'Euthanasia', in her *Virtues and Vices*, Oxford, Blackwell, 1977.

B. Russell, *The Conquest of Happiness*★, London, Allen and Unwin, 1930.

A. Schopenhauer, *The World as Will and Representation* (trans. E. F. J. Payne), New York, Dover, 1966.

Chapter 26   The Influence of Philosophy on Life

Sisela Bok, *Lying*★, Sussex, Harvester, 1978.

Mary Midgeley, *Evolution as a Religion*★, London, Methuen, 1985.

The New Zealand Health Council Working Party, *Informed Consent*, Wellington, New Zealand Government Printer, 1989.

Rosemary Rodd, *Biology, Ethics and Animals*, Oxford, OUP, 1990.

R. Scruton, *Sexual Desire*, London, Weidenfeld and Nicolson, 1986.

Index

Index

Index